OKLAHOMA
City

"Partners in Progress" by

Kenny A. Franks and Paul F. Lambert

Produced in cooperation with the

Centennial Committee of the

Oklahoma City Economic

Development Foundation and the

Oklahoma City Chamber of Commerce

Windsor Publications, Inc.

Northridge, California

OKLAHOMA
City

A CENTENNIAL PORTRAIT

ODIE B. FAULK, LAURA E. FAULK, AND BOB L. BLACKBURN

Windsor Publications wishes to acknowledge two
community leaders who lent valuable guidance
in the preparation of this volume—
Clayton Anderson, Director of the Public Relations
Division of the Oklahoma City Chamber of Commerce,
and Paul Strasbaugh, President of the Centennial
Committee, Oklahoma City Economic
Development Foundation.

Windsor Publications, Inc.—History Books Division
Managing Editor: Karen Story
Design Director: Alexander D'Anca

Staff for *Oklahoma City: A Centennial Portrait*
Manuscript Editor: Karl Stull
Photo Editor: Loren Prostano
Text Production Editor: Doreen Nakakihara
Editor, Corporate Profiles: Brenda Berryhill
Production Editor, Corporate Profiles: Una FitzSimons
Senior Proofreader: Susan J. Muhler
Editorial Assistants: Didier Beauvoir, Thelma Fleischer, Kim Kievman,
    Rebecca Kropp, Michael Nugwynne, Kathy B. Peyser, Pat Pittman, Theresa
    J. Solis
Sales Representative, Corporate Profiles: John Compton
Layout Artist: Ellen Ifrah
Layout Artist, Corporate Profiles: Mari Catherine Preimesberger
Designer: Thomas McTighe

Library of Congress Cataloging-in-Publication Data
Faulk, Odie B.
    Oklahoma City : a centennial portrait. Odie B. Faulk, Laura E. Faulk, and
Bob L. Blackburn. Partners in progress / Kenny A. Franks and Paul F.
Lambert.—1st ed.
    p. 256 cm. 23 x 31
    "Produced in cooperation with the Centennial Committee of the Okla-
homa City Economic Development Foundation and the Oklahoma City
Chamber of Commerce."
    Bibliography: p. 252 Includes index.
    ISBN 0-89781-284-0
    1. Oklahoma City (Okla.)—History. 2. Oklahoma City (Okla.)—Industries.
3. Industrial promotion—Oklahoma —Oklahoma City. I. Faulk, Laura E. II.
Blackburn, Bob L., 1951- . III. Franks, Kenny Arthur, 1945- Partners in
progress. 1988. IV. Lambert, Paul F. V. Oklahoma City Economic Development Foundation. Centennial Committee. VI. Oklahoma City Junior Chamber
of Commerce. VII. Title.
F704.041F38 1988   88-20594   976.6'38—dc19 CIP

Windsor Publications, Inc.
Elliot Martin, Chairman of the Board
James L. Fish III, Chief Operating Officer

*Another day draws to
a close for Oklahoma
City residents.
Photo by Jim Argo*

The authors wish to
dedicate this book to
Ida B. Blackburn,
a television personality
and businesswoman
who personifies the
entrepreneurial spirit
and civic consciousness
that has made
Oklahoma City such
a dynamic, forceful
community.

Contents

Chapter Eleven

Professions 205

Greater Oklahoma City's professional community brings a wealth of service, ability, and insight to the area.

Quality of Life 229

Chapter Twelve

Medical and educational institutions contribute to the quality of life of Oklahoma City area residents.

The sun shines brilliantly on this crisp winter day.
Photo by Jim Argo

Lights of the holiday season dazzle downtown Oklahoma City. Photo by Jim Argo

Part One

A Century of Progress

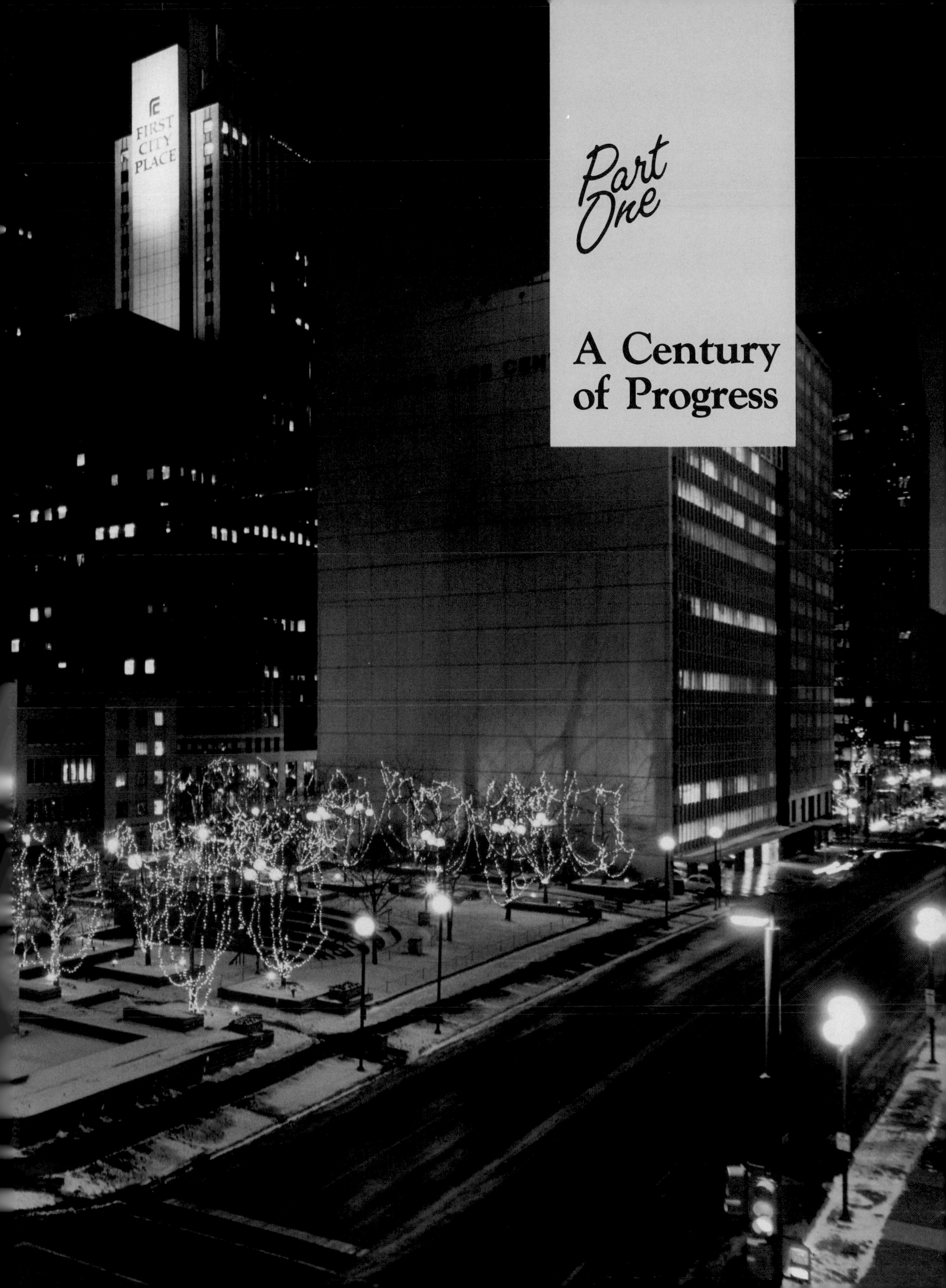
FIRST CITY PLACE

Charles M. Russell painted
Red Man's Wireless
in 1916, as part of a
series, depicting life in
the Oklahoma Territory
prior to settlement.
Photo by Matt Bradley.
Courtesy, National
Cowboy Hall of Fame and
Western Heritage Center

Chapter One

"Born Grown" and Growing

Just a century ago the site of Oklahoma City was a grass-and-timbered land of gently rolling hills flattening into prairie in the west. Today Oklahoma City's homes, skyscrapers, asphalt, and concrete sprawl across more than 620 square miles. Its metro population numbers almost a million—30 percent of Oklahoma's total population.

Geography offered no compelling reason for a great city to grow in the center of what would come to be the State of Oklahoma. No mighty rivers brought steamboats to its vicinity, there was no mountain pass, nor yet, some great valley or fertile farmland. No deposits of iron or coal or other minerals had been discovered to attract industry. No great harbor offered safe anchorage for ships coming from foreign ports.

Rather, this land, before it was settled, was an area of rolling hills covered with scrub timber interspersed with fields of open grassland flattening out to the west into red rolling prairies. Through it passes the North Canadian River, a

ABOVE, BELOW AND FACING PAGE: *The National Cowboy Hall of Fame and Western Heritage Center houses extraordinary works of western art and artifacts. These oil paintings by Charles M. Russell exemplify life in the Oklahoma Territory prior to settlement:* When Mules Wore Diamonds, *1921,* Smoke Talk, *1924, and* Whiskey Smugglers, *1913. Photos by Matt Bradley. Courtesy, National Cowboy Hall of Fame and Western Heritage Center*

stream which can flow heavily during spring rains and then dry up to a trickle during dry spells. Oklahoma City receives slightly more than 30 inches of rainfall a year, and its weather is subject to most of the extremes of the North American continent, making it hot in summer, cold in winter, and windy year-round.

No, it was not geography or topography or climate or rainfall nor fertility of soil that caused a great city to rise in this place and then grow to become a major Midwestern city. It was, rather, the remarkable people who settled Oklahoma City and who have continued to lead its destiny in the century since its founding.

In the 1880s many frontier Americans wanted to move into the center of Indian territory where the so-called Unassigned Lands lay vacant—1,877,640 acres that had never been given over as homeland to any tribe of Indians. Landless pioneers began slipping into this area without authorization, "Boomers" who were trying to force the government to open the area to homesteaders. However, such colonists were removed by the army under orders from Washington.

On March 2, 1889, President Benjamin Harrison signed legislation to open this land to homesteading, and proclaimed it would be opened by means of a run, which would commence at noon on April 22, 1889. The rules were simple. Any head of a household over age 21, male or female, could claim a so-called quarter section (160 acres) or a town lot in one of the townsites being planned. A townsite consisted of 320 acres that were platted into lots. Anyone who wanted to claim a quarter section or a town lot had to start the run from outside the Unassigned Lands at 12 noon on April 22. Of course, there were those, known as Sooners, who slipped inside the Unassigned Lands and hid from army patrols in order to stake the choicest farmlands and town lots, but an estimated 50,000 non-Sooners seeking homesites and farms were in place at the appointed hour and date to make the dash for land.

They came on horseback, in wagons or buckboards, and on foot. There even were a few making the great race on bicycles and many made the run sit-

ting on the train. As authorized by Congress in 1884, the Southern Kansas Railway Company, a subsidiary of the Santa Fe, had built tracks through the Unassigned Lands. One of its depots, erected in February 1887, was on the north bank of the North Canadian River. This watering point was named Oklahoma Station.

To Oklahoma Station on that fateful April 22, 1889, came two rival groups determined to plat a city. The Seminole Townsite and Development Company surveyed to the north of Grand Avenue (today Sheridan Avenue), and the Oklahoma Town Company surveyed to the south. A year later, after endless disputes and quarrels, the two would combine into one city registered with the post office as Oklahoma. Not until July 1, 1923, would the post office change the official name of the community to Oklahoma City—although it was called this from the days of the opening of the Unassigned Lands.

On the morning of April 22 there had been only a railroad depot and a scattering of crude buildings at Oklahoma Station. By nightfall there were an estimated 4,000 to 6,000 people in the vicinity, each trying to defend as big a lot as he could. Claim jumping was common, as were boundary quarrels that led to

One of four murals which decorate the Oklahoma State Capitol rotunda, this mural, painted by Charles Banks Wilson, depicts state historical events from 1870 to 1906. Photo by David Fitzgerald

fights. Tents were thrown up in haphazard fashion on streets that led off at odd angles, and mass confusion seemed to reign.

Congress had made no provision for city government in Oklahoma Territory, so leaders had to be chosen to restore order and bring organization to the community. At a mass meeting the day after the run, a provisional government was chosen, and elections were held on May 1 to select permanent officials. Next came ordinances for restoring and maintaining public order.

A provisional police force was soon organized, consisting of men not afraid to use their fists and guns to enforce municipal ordinances. Fire-fighting was handled by a volunteer department that used a hand-drawn converted beer wagon until the city in 1891 bought a hook and ladder wagon for $570. In 1892 a central fire station was built at Main and Robinson; it had a 65-foot tower from which "watchmen" could see the entire town. When the watchman spotted smoke, he would ring an

alarm bell that brought volunteer firemen to fight the blaze.

At the time of its founding, Oklahoma City was a boomtown without an economic base. It had no industry or factories and no agricultural marketing facilities. It had only unbounded optimism and the investment funds brought by pioneer businessmen. Just a month after the April 22 run the merchants and professional people of the city banded together to form a Board of Trade. This was the forerunner of the Commercial Club, later renamed the Oklahoma City Chamber of Commerce, and was organized to promote the city and its business.

The best way to give their city a sound economic base, in the opinion of the leaders who emerged, was to make Oklahoma City a rail center for the region. By attracting railroads, Oklahoma City would become the wholesale merchandising center of the state. This effort was successful, and soon freight and passenger trains were arriving with astonishing frequency.

Another area of concentrated effort by the board of trade was agriculture, for city leaders wanted their community to become the center of marketing for state farmers and the place where farmers came to make their major purchases. Thus Oklahoma City sponsored an annual territorial (later

TOP: This camp of Boomers in Kansas awaited the opening of the Unassigned Lands in April 1889. Courtesy, Archives and Manuscripts Division, Oklahoma Historical Society

ABOVE: On April 22, 1889, these pioneers ran for town lots in Guthrie. Courtesy, Archives and Manuscripts Division, Oklahoma Historical Society

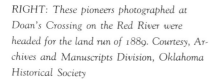

RIGHT: These pioneers photographed at Doan's Crossing on the Red River were headed for the land run of 1889. Courtesy, Archives and Manuscripts Division, Oklahoma Historical Society

state) fair and annual livestock shows. Members of 4-H clubs and the Future Farmers of America were encouraged to show their work and market it in Oklahoma City, thus making the city a center of ranching and agriculture along with transportation, business, and industry.

Hard times followed the Panic of 1893, but still there was optimism for the future. Bond issues financed a municipal water system, while a franchised Oklahoma City Light and Power Company provided electricity and the Missouri-Kansas Telephone Company provided their service to those desiring it. A public school system was organized, as were civic clubs, a Public Library Association, and numerous women's charities. By 1900 the population of the city had almost doubled from its 4,000 inhabitants in 1890, and it was, without question, the fastest growing town in Oklahoma.

By the time statehood came for Oklahoma on November 16, 1907, Oklahoma City had grown still larger, its population rising to 14,369 in 1901—and exploding upward. By 1907 Main Street and Grand Avenue (now Sheridan) were citified with brick buildings and were lined with shops, stores, and restaurants that would have been an asset to any city in America. Fashionably dressed men and women strolled broad avenues along which were parked buggies and a few gasoline-powered automobiles. Farmers in large numbers came to town in wagons piled high with cotton, and bales of it were spread on the platforms of the compress at Reno and Eastern.

Telephone and electric lines adorned both major thoroughfares and streets in residential areas, making the city look as if it were covered with one huge spiderweb, while the tracks of the electric trolley system snaked through most parts of the

ABOVE: An average Oklahoma homestead in 1897 was constructed with a combination of sod and planks, with a dugout in back. Courtesy, Archives and Manuscripts Division, Oklahoma Historical Society

LEFT: Thomas B. Ferguson was the territorial governor of Oklahoma from 1901-1906. Courtesy, Archives and Manuscripts Division, Oklahoma Historical Society

TOP: Elias C. Boudinot attempted but failed to lobby through Congress an Oklahoma Territory Bill, which would have opened the Unassigned Lands to white settlement in 1878. Courtesy, Archives and Manuscripts Division, Oklahoma Historical Society

ABOVE: In 1921, Alice M. Robertson was elected as United States representative from Oklahoma. Courtesy, Archives and Manuscripts Division, Oklahoma Historical Society

RIGHT: Kate Barnard convinced members of the constitutional convention to pass provisions for a department of charities and corrections. She was later the first commissioner of that department. Courtesy, Archives and Manuscripts Division, Oklahoma Historical Society

city and soon to outlying towns. Packing plants were brought to Oklahoma City by the Oklahoma City Chamber of Commerce, and by 1910 they were employing more than 4,000 people. The downtown skyline changed dramatically as the Colcord building, the Baum building, the Skirvin and Huckins hotels, the Hales building, and numerous other multistory structures were erected. By 1910 the city was approaching 64,000 residents, many of whom thought their community should be the state capital.

TOP: *The first governor of Oklahoma, Charles N. Haskell, was inaugurated in Guthrie in 1907. Courtesy, Archives and Manuscripts Division, Oklahoma Historical Society*

ABOVE: *The Oklahoma Constitutional Convention was held in Guthrie City Hall in 1906. Courtesy, Archives and Manuscripts Division, Oklahoma Historical Society*

Since the creation of Oklahoma Territory, the capital had been at Guthrie, some 30 miles to the north of Oklahoma City. In 1910 a petition was circulated which received sufficient signatures for Governor Charles N. Haskell to call a special election on June 11 that year. Oklahoma City received 96,261 votes, a majority of 56,573 over Guthrie and Shawnee, the two rival aspirants. That night Governor Haskell sent his secretary of state to Guthrie to get the state seal, and the next morning the governor declared the Lee-Huckins Hotel to be the temporary capitol. Lengthy court battles followed, and there was another statewide vote on the issue in 1912. Despite Guthrie's efforts, however, Oklahoma City stayed the capital. Governor Haskell later said that he removed the capital in 1910 to save the state from years of arguing over a removal that was inevitable.

The capitol building was erected to the northeast of downtown Oklahoma City at 23rd Street and Lincoln Boulevard.

The structure was dedicated in 1917. Originally the plans called for a dome atop this neoclassical structure, but excessive costs and a wartime shortage of materials ended that idea. In later years additional buildings would be constructed in the immediate area, leading to a government complex of substantial proportions in that vicinity.

By the time World War I ended, Oklahoma City boasted residential sections located along oak- and elm-lined streets. In more affluent sections of town were brick mansions of two and three stories, while in modest areas there were attractive brick or frame one-story residences. Nine railroads served the city with dozens of freight and passenger trains daily, while electric trolleys plied 68 miles of track. There were more than 100 churches, a dozen or more movie theaters, two vaudeville houses, a school system of excellent reputation, and Belle Isle Park with its dance floor and amusement rides.

The ebullient, optimistic 1920s saw a short-lived depression in 1921-1922 that soon turned to yet more growth and prosperity, more majestic skyscrapers, and expanding residential districts. Retail sales grew from $85 million to $146 million between 1922 and 1928, while bank deposits soared from $40 million to more than $100 million. Then on December 4, 1928, came the discovery of oil at a test well at the corner of Southeast 59th and Bryant. In the 27 days before the well could be capped, 110,496 barrels of oil gushed out—creating a stampede to the fabulous Oklahoma City field. In those days of scant regulation, oil men drilled where they wished and as close to other wells as they wished, and the city soon looked like a forest of derricks. Wells were even drilled on the grounds of the state capitol.

The Oklahoma City field did more than spray the surrounding countryside with oil from wells gushing high into the air. It created dozens of millionaires, men such as Frank Buttram who would endow various civic projects. The local economy benefited from the payroll of the various oil firms, and landowners getting royalty checks poured their money back into the community with their purchases. Additional oil capital provided investment funds, while cheap petroleum energy brought yet more industry to the city.

Downtown changed as the Petroleum building took its place beside the 31-story Ramsey tower and the banks that built tall and dignified skyscraper homes for themselves. In the suburbs G.A. Nichols began a 2,780-acre addition called Nichols Hills. In this area of large lots and professional landscaping would be built many new mansions along with a new country club featuring a $300,000 clubhouse. Nichols also made large profits by building middle-income housing, for he was one of the first to realize that people wanted to move out of cramped downtown apartments and into individual homes. The streetcar made it possible to build large tracts of homes in the distant suburbs.

There were some Oklahomans who found opportunity in the late 1920s and the 1930s. C.R. Anthony founded his chain of dry-goods stores and moved its headquarters to Oklahoma City; from there it would spread across the United States with more than 300 stores. Another Oklahoman, R.A. Young, moved the headquarters of TG&Y Stores to Oklahoma City. Eventually this chain, whose main offices were in the Santa Fe industrial area, would number more than 900 stores before its

A Civilian Conservation Corps crew planted Bermuda grass on this gully to prevent erosion in 1935. Courtesy, Archives and Manuscripts Division, Oklahoma Historical Society

sale to an out-of-state firm.

Income oil somewhat mitigated the rigors of the Great Depression, but did not ease the suffering when oil fell to 10 cents a barrel and cotton to less than 5 cents a pound. In Oklahoma City there were soup lines, and transients gathered in cardboard shanties on the edge of town. At one point during the 1930s more than 6,000 people were classified as "destitute" in Oklahoma City.

To provide employment for some of these people, City Manager Orval "Red" Mosier in 1935 proposed a bold plan of construction. Since 1930 the city had owned a broad strip of land through the heart of downtown where railroad tracks once had run. Mosier proposed the construction of a complex of municipal buildings on this land using some local money and some Public Works Administration (PWA) relief funds from the federal government. A bond issue of $1,787,500 passed, and an additional $1,462,500 came from Washington. With this the city built a new city hall, city police headquarters, and a municipal auditorium (while Oklahoma County constructed a new county courthouse in the area).

The hard times of the Great Depression prevailed until the world began moving toward another global conflict. When preparedness and national defense became the policy of the Roosevelt administration in 1939, the Oklahoma City Chamber of Commerce and its legendary executive director, Stanley Draper, worked diligently to secure defense plants and defense contracts. Joined by numerous civic leaders, Draper pointed out Oklahoma City's many advantages, including mild climate and hardworking people. Also, the Industries Foundation of Oklahoma was organized as a trust to purchase land that could be used for federal facilities.

The major contract landed by the Industries Foundation was an air depot known as Tinker Field. This was located on Southeast 29th Street and eventually would become the largest employer in the Sooner State. Douglas Aircraft Company opened a plant adjacent to Tinker Field, which by 1943 was employing 34,000 people to produce C-47 cargo planes. These defense plants brought a renewed prosperity to Oklahoma City, but rationing and wartime shortages left few places for those remaining at home to spend their newfound wealth.

World War II brought hardship and rationing to residents of Oklahoma City, as it did elsewhere in the nation. But it also brought a determination to see the war through to successful conclusion. Oklahoma Cityans raised more than $40 million for construction of a light cruiser, the U.S.S. *Oklahoma City*.

The Oklahoma City that emerged from World War II seethed with restless energy and excitement. The population stood at an estimated 220,000 in 1945, and the slogan of the Chamber of Commerce became "300,000 by 1950."

Downtown was alive day and night as both an economic and social center. Along every sidewalk were busy stores, banks, and shops, while soaring above were office buildings and plush hotels. The Criterion, the Orpheum, the Liberty, the Home Theatre, and the Midwest were movie theaters that rivaled Turkish palaces in their use of lavish colors and neon opulence, and within easy walking distance of downtown was the Municipal Auditorium where the Oklahoma City Symphony and visiting fine arts groups regularly played. An increasing number of buses, along with taxis and private automobiles, brought people in from the residential sections of town to crowd the sidewalks from early morning until late at night.

Every store faced monumental shortages of almost everything as residents sought to buy the goods denied them during World War II. Automobile and appliance dealers were getting more than suggested retail prices from people who did not want to place their names on waiting lists.

Oklahoma City became home to the University of Oklahoma's Medical Center, which was increasingly important for its research. Near it the Veterans Administration of the federal government was building a $15-million, 500-bed hospital. Oklahoma City University, on Northwest 23rd Street, teemed with veterans seeking an education, as did Oklahoma Christian College, which moved from Bartlesville in 1957 to a new home on the north side of town.

In 1890, the Territorial University was founded in Norman. This building was later to be the first administration building of the University of Oklahoma. Courtesy, Archives and Manuscripts Division, Oklahoma Historical Society

To supply water for both human consumption and industrial use, Oklahoma City's leaders in the 1930s had begun a program of building reservoirs at Lake Overholser and Lake Hefner. In the postwar era would come Stanley Draper Lake, Lake Thunderbird, Lake Atoka, and Arcadia Lake. These lakes not only provided water for industrial and human consumption but also became prime recreational areas.

In the midst of postwar boom and prosperity, there were major changes underway which eventually would threaten the downtown area and change the face of the city. In the years immediately following the end of World War II, there was a house-building boom as real estate developers sought to keep

up with demand for new homes. The population surged past 300,000 and kept growing. Every family, it seemed, dreamed of owning its own home.

As the suburbs expanded and the population spread over a larger, less concentrated area, trolley tracks were torn up or paved over as buses became the primary means of public transportation. Gradually, however, the number of riders on city buses declined, for it seemed that every worker wanted to drive to his place of employment in his own car. Eventually families wanted two cars so that wives would be freed from having to shop along a bus route.

To accommodate the increasing number of automobiles owned by residents of Oklahoma City and the commuter communities growing all around it, civic leaders planned four-lane arteries to speed traffic through all parts of town. Between 1950 and 1956 roads were built along what had been the right-of-way for trolley lines: Grand Boulevard, Shields Boulevard, 39th Street Expressway, and Classen Boulevard. After 1956 came

Residents of Oklahoma City are of diverse cultural and religious backgrounds. Four significant houses of worship are: Facing page, the First Baptist Church; Left, the First Unitarian Church; Above, the First Lutheran Church; Below, the First Christian Church. Photos by Matt Bradley

the beginnings of the federal interstate highway system. Three of these—I-35, I-40, and I-44—now pass through Oklahoma City. Eventually an interstate bypass—I-240—was constructed along the southern part of Oklahoma City, while the Broadway Extension and the new Central Expressway allow fast passage through downtown and to the north.

These highways enabled ever more of those who worked in downtown Oklahoma City to live in surrounding towns such as Del City, Midwest City, Spencer, Nicoma Park, Jones, Choctaw, Harrah, Luther, Arcadia, Edmond, The Village, Bethany, Piedmont, Yukon, Mustang, Tuttle, Moore, and Norman, along with several other incorporated areas.

Eventually Oklahoma City's suburbs sprawled to the point where strip shopping centers sprang up to supply the needs of people not wishing to make the long trip downtown. In 1959 came the development of Penn Square on Northwest Expressway at Pennsylvania Avenue; a restaurant and 46 retail stores, including the largest Montgomery Ward retail store in the nation, were housed in seven buildings (that would be enclosed into a

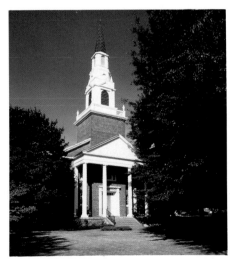

Crown Heights is a lovely residential section of Oklahoma City. Photo by Jim Argo

mall in the 1980s). Then in 1963 came the start of construction of Oklahoma City's first enclosed mall, Shepherd Plaza, a $15-million, 70-store complex at Northwest 23rd Street and Pennsylvania. Still other giant shopping malls would be built in the years ahead in all sections of the city. Suburbanites found they had no problems finding parking space at these shopping centers, nor did they have to drive downtown and fight traffic congestion.

Retail merchants were quick to join the growing trend toward shopping centers located away from downtown. By ones and twos, merchants shut their doors downtown to open new stores in the suburbs. This left shoppers ever fewer places at which to shop in the city's central core, and thus still larger numbers turned to strip shopping centers and the malls to make their purchases. Soon the movement of storekeepers from downtown to the suburbs snowballed. The owners of restaurants and movie theaters likewise began building in the suburbs, leaving no social reason to come downtown at night. Increasingly the central core of the city became a place to which office workers and civic employees went in the morning and then deserted at the end of the day. With the coming of dark, the downtown streets became a ghost town.

Civic leaders became so concerned with the gradual decay of the central core of the city that in 1961 they formed the

Oklahoma City Urban Action Foundation. It in turn helped organize the Oklahoma City Urban Renewal Authority, which planned and worked for development of a great medical center to the south of the state capitol complex, as well as the Central Business District. The urban renewal authority hired the architectural firm of I.M. Pei and Associates to draw up a far-reaching plan for the redevelopment of the central core of the city. The Pei plan called for clearing most of 528 acres downtown and construction of a new central core. This would consist of five elements: a business/financial office area; a garden area based on Copenhagen's famed Tivoli Gardens, which eventually was named the Myriad Gardens; a convention center; a residential area; and a downtown shopping area, known as the Galleria.

Heritage Hills, one of the first affluent neighborhoods of Oklahoma City, which includes over 300 homes, is a National Historic District. Each year a select number of homes are opened for tours. Photo by Jim Argo

The first step in the downtown urban renewal project, a convention center, was financed by general obligation bonds. Known as the Myriad and extending over four city blocks, it consists of a 950,000-square-foot building that was dedicated in 1972. Other parts of the Pei plan have been completed. The American First Tower, a 14-story retail building, stands at Main and Robinson, and next to it is the First Oklahoma Tower, an office building that soars 31 stories into the sky.

After adjacent land was secured, construction on the Myriad Gardens began in 1977. The gardens boast a lake and a botanical garden called the Crystal Bridge that is more than 300 feet long and 7 stories high. New apartments, a 200-unit building for the elderly, and more than 1,000 new homes have been constructed within the urban renewal area—in all, a total of more than 2,000 living units. With completion of the proposed Galleria, with its shops and hotel, the Pei plan will have transformed downtown Oklahoma City. Some historic buildings have been demolished to make way for this progress, but in the process there has been dramatic change.

Another feature of the reborn downtown Oklahoma City is the Metro Conncourse, a series of underground walkways that connect most major buildings. More than 30,000 pedestrians pass through this concourse each day, totally protected from the outside weather. Remarkably, the concourse was built without one cent of government money.

Oklahoma City is the chief market for livestock in the state and is a major processing center for both livestock and agricultural products. To warehouses in Oklahoma City comes the merchandise that is wholesaled to businesses across the state, and from factories in the vicinity emerge a variety of goods. There are more than 900 manufacturing firms employing almost 60,000 workers in the greater Oklahoma City area.

In the years after World War II, the railroad ceased to be a prime mover of people to and from Oklahoma City. Eventually all passenger trains halted. However, rail service has not ended, for many freight trains still arrive and depart daily from Oklahoma City although a growing percentage of freight, like people, is moved in airplanes.

Oklahoma City has long been a center of aviation, both military and civil. Will Rogers World Airport, on the southwest side of town, has been expanded several times to accommodate

the largest commercial airplanes. Beside this airport is the Mike Monroney Aeronautical Center; here the Federal Aviation Administration trains the air traffic controllers for the country, keeps federal aviation records, and conducts advanced aviation research. On the southeast side of town is Tinker Air Force Base with its logistics service for the United States Air Force and its large civilian work force. And on the northwest side of town is Wiley Post Airport, Oklahoma City's secondary airport and the center of much of the region's civil aviation activity.

Oklahoma City was the birthplace of Braniff and Central airlines, and it serves as the headquarters of the Ninety-Nines, an organization of women civil pilots. A facility near Wiley Post Airport was used to manufacture the Aero-Commander; first in a piston version, then as a prop-jet. One indication of Oklahoma City's great role in aviation is the Air Space Museum, which operates in the Kirkpatrick Center.

At the end of its first century of existence, Oklahoma City and its suburbs contain almost 30 percent of the population of the state—almost a million people. The city serves as the hub of Oklahoma's economic, governmental, cultural, and social life. It has a mayor-city council form of government, with a city manager functioning as chief administrative officer. He answers to the eight members of the city council who are elected from the city's eight wards.

Residents of Oklahoma's capital city have been tested by the downturn in oil prices that began in 1982 along with a fall in agricultural prices. These combined to cause failed banks, real estate foreclosures, and bankruptcies. But the Oklahoma Cityans of the 1980s are descendants of hardy pioneers. They found the promise of a better future and of opportunity in the dark and difficult days and emerged with their faith in themselves and their city intact.

Oklahoma City offers golden opportunities for all. Photo by Matt Bradley

The sun sets, silhouetting the West Edmond Oil Field. Photo by Jim Argo

Chapter Two

Foundations for the Future

Oklahoma City was caught in the grip of a depression in 1897. Population was down, bankruptcies were up, and the entire community seemed to accept the inevitability of economic stagnation and failure.

Then came the Frisco Railroad. Choosing Oklahoma City instead of Guthrie for its western terminus, the railroad tipped the balance of urban rivalry, opened new markets for the city's businessmen, and provided essential ties to the financial centers of Kansas City and St. Louis.

Angelo Scott, an '89er journalist and historian, recognized the great impact of the arrival of the Frisco Railroad: "Most of all there was a new psychology, or shall I say the returning of the old psychology. The old hope, the old expectation, and the old spirit came back, and with redoubled strength." Fired by this rekindled boom mentality, Oklahoma City entered a period of economic expansion that propelled the population from 4,000 to 64,000 in only 13 years.

Scott recognized that the

economic prosperity of his community was affected in large part by the spirit of its people. But important as it was, that spirit was not enough; businessmen could do little without the over-arching superstructure of capital formation, market expansion, and industrial diversity. As the arrival of the Frisco Railroad proved in 1897, a common factor that made all of that possible was efficient transportation.

The very location of Oklahoma City was determined by the Santa Fe Railroad, which had laid tracks through the Unassigned Lands in 1887 and established a water stop near the North Canadian River. Known as Oklahoma Station, it became the second most coveted urban destination when the territory was opened to homesteaders on April 22, 1889.

Two years later the city gained its second major railroad when the Choctaw, Oklahoma, and Coal Railway (later the

ABOVE: The MK&T Railway depot on Reno Avenue was constructed in 1902. Courtesy, Archives and Manuscripts Division, Oklahoma Historical Society

LEFT: Santa Fe Railroad engine No. 1313 pulls into the Flynn Switching Yard in Oklahoma City. Photo by Jim Argo

Rock Island) laid track east and west through Oklahoma City, eventually opening trade territory from McAlester to the Texas border. Then came the Frisco in 1897, bridging the obstacles of distance to the northeast and southwest. The network of 21 economic lifelines was completed in 1902 and 1904 when the Missouri-Kansas-Texas Railway (Katy) built two more trunk lines through Oklahoma City to the northeast, southeast, and southwest.

Efficient transportation was essential for urban development on the frontier, but as in all free-market economies, the foundations of free enterprise in Oklahoma City depended on capital for investments and the creation of jobs. For the first few decades after 1889, most of the capital needed for development came into Oklahoma from outside the state. Men like Henry Overholser, George Sohlberg, and Richard Vose brought money into the city with them and invested in the future. Only gradually did the banks of Oklahoma City build enough capital to finance internal development.

Within a couple of years of the land run, Oklahoma City was home to four banks, but two of them were liquidated during the financial crisis of 1893. The two survivors, First National and State National, eventually merged in 1897. Following numerous openings and mergers, there were seven major banks

ABOVE: Liberty Bank was founded in Oklahoma City prior to the Great Depression. Photo by Matt Bradley

RIGHT: Good rail service and solid leadership resulted in prosperous growth for Oklahoma City, seen here in 1933. Courtesy, Archives and Manuscripts Division, Oklahoma Historical Society

BELOW: Numerous Art-Deco reliefs are found on the First National Bank Building. Photo by Jim Argo

in Oklahoma City by the Great Depression. Chief among them were First National, Liberty, Fidelity, and City National. Combined deposits exceeded $107 million in 1936, forming a substantial capital base that could finance a myriad of enterprises, from oil exploration to major construction projects.

Another source of capital accumulation was the insurance industry, and early on Oklahoma City became headquarters for several firms. One of the most prominent was the Mid-Continent Life Insurance Company, founded in 1909 by Robert T. Stuart. By the mid-1930s the company had more than $5.5 million in reserves. Other native-born insurance companies included Standard Life and Globe Life, aggressive firms led by executives such as Thomas Braniff, who later gained fame as co-founder of Braniff Airlines.

Armed with the advantages of transportation and capital, the pioneer businessmen of Oklahoma City found countless opportunities for investments and production, especially in the field of agricultural processing and marketing. After an extended period of drought and low commodity prices from 1893 to 1897, the farmers of Oklahoma entered the "golden age of American agriculture." The bounty of the land, from cotton and wheat to

cattle and hogs, provided the raw material for production and jobs.

One of the city's most important "founding fathers" was C.G. "Gristmill" Jones, who came to Oklahoma City to establish a corn gristmill. From his economic base of agricultural processing, Jones sponsored the ill-fated grand canal project during the crucial winter of 1889-1890, used his influence as mayor to lure the Frisco Railroad to Oklahoma City in 1897, and organized the first Oklahoma City State Fair in 1907.

Another industrialist attracted to Oklahoma City by the profits in agricultural processing was George Sohlberg, a native of Minnesota, who built the Acme Milling Company in 1894. Within five years, running day and night, the mill was producing more than 500 barrels of flour and 100 barrels of meal each day. Sohlberg used this base of operation to become president of the Pine Tree Lumber Company, vice president and a charter stockholder in the First National Bank, and an investor in the Cleveland Brick Company, the Oklahoma Export Company, and the Oklahoma City Packing Company.

Other industrialists who depended on agriculture to launch their fortunes were Richard Vose, who came to Oklahoma City to start a cotton oil mill; William T. Hales, Oklahoma City's richest man, who started with a mule- and horse-trading business; and William Clayton, who started as a cotton broker in

ABOVE: *The sophistication of farm equipment now enables one person to do the work of several. Photo by Jim Argo*

FACING PAGE: *At the Farmers Market in downtown Oklahoma City, this farmer stands behind his pumpkins. Photo by Jim Argo*

Oklahoma City and went on to create one of the largest corporations in the nation, Anderson Clayton. These individual achievements were essential for early industrial growth, but the most dramatic turning points in the economic history of the city were the packing plants.

In 1908 officials of Nelson Morris and Company of Chicago approached the Oklahoma City Chamber of Commerce with a proposal. If the Chamber would raise a $300,000 bonus and make other concessions, the company would build a $3-million packing plant. Led by men such as Sidney Brock, Anton Classen, John Shartel, E.K. Gaylord, and Charles Colcord, the Chamber of Commerce met all terms of the agreement, and the plant was built.

Within a year the Chamber struck a similar deal with a second packing house that built another plant in Stockyards City. By 1910 the two packing houses and nearby holding yards were employing more than 4,000 people in a town of 64,000 total population. As proven by the packing plants, the economic prosperity of early Oklahoma City was dependent on a combination of leadership and the bounty of the land.

Whereas agricultural processing reaped the benefits of abundant raw materials and efficient transportation, general manufacturing responded to population growth and the expanding trade territory along the railroad tracks. As early as 1898 promotional literature was touting Oklahoma City as an industrial center of the territory with "two iron foundries, two sash, door and blind factories, two machine shops, four cigar factories, one shirt factory, one large harness and saddle factory, one marble works, one candy factory, two carriage and wagon factories, and four brick factories."

A good example of heavy industry in the young town was the Klein Iron and Foundry Company, founded in 1909 to "manufacture ornamental iron, wire and brass work." The firm also advertised "foundry work of every description, structural iron work, fire escapes, and elevator enclosures." After Klein's death in 1925, Richard W. Robberson purchased the company, renamed it Robberson Steel, and specialized in steel works for buildings, bridges, and roads.

Henry Ford recognized the urban achievements of Oklahoma City and built a major assembly plant in 1915 to produce his Model T Car. Not only did the plant employ hundreds of workers at the unheard of wage of $5 a day but it also added greatly to the industrial output of the town. Eventually, the

Shortly after achieving statehood, Oklahoma's cotton crop emerged as its major cash crop. Courtesy, Archives and Manuscripts Division, Oklahoma Historical Society

building was converted to a regional parts distribution center and then to an engine and parts remanufacturing plant that was a subsidiary of Fred Jones Industries.

Another important industry in the early decades was brick manufacturing. The American Brick Company was established in 1897 on the present site of McKinley Park. The firm was later purchased by the Acme Brick and Tile Company and moved to a new pit at 2700 Northwest 10th Street. In 1937 the brick plant employed more than 60 men who produced 60,000 bricks each day.

Despite the spreading Great Depression, one count listed 550 manufacturing firms in Oklahoma City in 1935, ranging from casket companies to ice plants and employing thousands of men and women. Together, they accounted for production of goods valued in excess of $67 million.

All of this early activity attracted a company that was destined to become one of the largest employers in the state, Pioneer Telephone and Telegraph. Organized in 1898 in Perry, the communication firm started with a long-distance line between Pawnee and Perry. Within six years the young company was operating almost half of all lines in the territory.

In 1904 Pioneer moved into the Oklahoma City market and negotiated a working partnership with an AT&T subsidiary. John Noble, who had installed the first long-distance lines out of Perry, became general manager of the communication giant and oversaw its rapid expansion from his headquarters in Oklahoma City. In 1916, nine years after the company had built the city's first true skyscraper at the corner of Northwest 3rd Street and Broadway, the company was completely absorbed by AT&T. Its name was changed to Southwestern Bell.

Oklahoma Gas and Electric had roots in the territorial period. It predecessor, the Oklahoma Ditch and Water Power Company, had sponsored the Grand Canal, a six-mile channel cut into the North Canadian River to bring water power to downtown Oklahoma City. The soil was too porous, however, and the project failed.

In 1902 city pioneers George Wheeler, E.H. Cooke, Henry Rule, and W.W. Storm reorganized the electric utility under the name of Oklahoma Gas and Electric (OG&E). Although it later was sold to other interests, the firm retained its headquarters in Oklahoma City. By 1922 OG&E maintained more than 315 miles of cable and wire in Oklahoma City alone, provided service to another 30 towns, and employed more than 600 persons statewide. Six years later, spurred by an expanding economy, service was extended to 148 towns.

RIGHT AND FAR RIGHT: *Bricktown, once an active commercial district, is currently being renovated, creating commercial space and residential housing with old-fashioned charm. Photos by Matt Bradley*

Manufacturing, whether it was generating electrical current or fabricating steel rails, was essential for economic vitality and creation of jobs in Oklahoma City. Alone, however, manufacturing could not provide the diversity needed for long term, sustained growth. Another sector of the local economy that added to this diversity was wholesaling.

The emergence of Oklahoma City as a wholesale distribution center was a natural consequence of its central location in the territory and state and its unequaled railroad connections. After the run of 1889, Oklahoma City was located in the heart of an economic island surrounded by undeveloped Indian lands. As each reservation was opened to non-Indian settlement, Oklahoma City served as the logical source of trade goods, equipment, and essential supplies.

One of the most lucrative fields of wholesale enterprise was in groceries and produce, and one of the most aggressive leaders in the industry was Thomas D. Turner, who moved to Oklahoma City in 1892 and started the Turner Wholesale Produce Company at 1 West Main. Recognized for his success, he was elected president of the Oklahoma City Chamber of Commerce in 1904 and 1905. Another wholesale grocery firm was the Williamson-Halsell-Frasier Company, incorporated in 1898 with seven traveling salesmen and a "small army" of office and

warehouse employees.

Other pioneer wholesale firms included the Oklahoma Sash and Door Company, founded in 1897 with "the largest stock of any house of the kind west of Kansas City and east of Denver;" the Oklahoma City Hardware Company, established in 1901 as the largest source of hardware in the territory; and the Patterson and Hoffman Company, also founded in 1901 to distribute P&H cigars throughout eight states. By 1935 the wholesale houses of Oklahoma City were doing a $250 million business each year.

Much of that business remained close to home through the retail stores of Oklahoma City. Until the 1920s virtually all retail businesses were located downtown, especially along Grand, California, and Main between the tracks and Walker. Although this concentration remained intact until after World

War II, several small strip malls were built for retailers near residential developments during the 1920s.

One of the first pioneers to open a retail store in Oklahoma City was William J. Pettee, a young merchant from Kansas who made the run of 1889 and claimed a lot on Main Street. Before the dust of the run had settled, he was selling hardware from a boxcar on a railroad siding. By the 1920s, Pettee's Hardware Store was famous as a place where you could buy "hardware, vehicles, house furnishings, chinaware, paints, sporting goods, and electrical supplies."

An equally famous, latter-day retailer was Stephen F. Veazey, who came to Oklahoma City in 1900. At first he worked as a night watchman, then as a delivery boy for a small drugstore. In 1906 he formed a partnership with boyhood friend Tom Roach, and together they purchased the Security Drug Store at Grand and Harvey. In 1917 Veazey married Helen Finnerty, whose brothers had recently organized the Fidelity Bank. With this financial backing, Veazey bought out his partner and started expanding. By the 1930s there were 22 Veazey Drug Stores, a large warehouse, and a company payroll of $300,000 with 350 employees.

Territorial Oklahoma City also provided a springboard for several retail furniture empires, none more successful than Harbour-Longmire's. J. Franklin Harbour came to Oklahoma City in 1901 as a partner in the Bass-Harbour Furniture Company. Nine years later that partnership dissolved and Harbour joined forces with William Longmire, a furniture retailer from Shawnee. Their new company grew steadily until the 1920s when they used the financial backing of William T. Hales to build the ornate Harbour-Longmire building on West Main between Hudson and Walker. Completed in 1925, the 11-story building was advertised as a "huge department store for the home," complete with an enclosed two-story model house and

FACING PAGE AND ABOVE: The Oklahoma National Stockyards Company is located in Oklahoma City. Photos by Matt Bradley

ABOVE: *The oil industry created a major impact on the early economic development of Oklahoma City. Photo by Jim Argo*

RIGHT: *Alphia Hart photographed these oil derricks against the Oklahoma City skyline from atop Douglass High School in 1935. Courtesy, Archives and Manuscripts Division, Oklahoma Historical Society*

FACING PAGE: *Work in the oil fields is as significant as it is dirty. Photo by Jim Argo*

departments for custom cabinetry, upholstering, flooring, and drapery. Until the end of World War II, Harbour-Longmire's reigned as the "furniture showcase of the Southwest."

A highly visible sector in the growing retail market of Oklahoma City was in automobile sales. In 1905, only five city dealers offered automobiles; that number increased to 34 by 1910 and to 76 by 1920. In 1916 the people of Oklahoma City registered more than 1,900 cars and trucks, outnumbering horses for the first time.

By the early 1920s the automobile agencies of Oklahoma City were concentrated along North Broadway, a strip from 4th to 13th Street that became known as "automobile alley." In 1921 that one street had 52 of the city's 76 dealerships, offering makes from Reo and Hupmobile to Chalmers and Franklins. Proof of the district's success appeared in 1923, when a study revealed that 95 percent of the 244,883 vehicles registered in the state had been distributed through dealerships or

manufacturers in Oklahoma City.

The success of automobile sales was only part of the general prosperity in retail merchandising from 1889 to the 1930s. During the short period from 1922 to 1928 the number of retail stores increased from 1,516 to 2,110 while sales jumped from $85 million to $146 million. Although that pace slowed substantially during the Great Depression, the people of Oklahoma City were proven consumers.

The Pioneer Building (detail seen here) is listed on the National Register of Historic Places. Photo by Jim Argo

Adding to this joyride of economic development was oil. The search for petroleum in the Oklahoma City vicinity had been a longtime preoccupation of wildcatters and investors. In 1890 the first driller arrived in Oklahoma City, erected a rig at 4th and Santa Fe, and started sinking hole. At a depth of 600 feet he gave up, little knowing that oil was there, only deeper.

From 1890 to 1928 more than 20 test wells were drilled in Oklahoma County, but none went deep enough. Meanwhile, wildcatters and oil companies were opening a string of producing fields from Osage to Carter counties. Although the closest field was 60 miles away, more than 100 oil firms had established offices or headquarters in Oklahoma City by 1928.

Interest in the Oklahoma City area reached new heights as technology made deeper drilling feasible. On December 4, 1928, what so many oilmen had suspected came true—a sea of oil was discovered under Oklahoma City at a depth of 6,300 feet. During its first 27 days of open flow, the discovery well at Southeast 59th and Bryant produced 110,496 barrels of 40-gravity oil, which at the time sold for $1.56 a barrel.

By 1930 the oil boom in Oklahoma City was well under way, with 135 completed wells and 173 drilling rigs piercing the landscape of the city. During the next five years the field expanded from the Cleveland County line through the southeast quadrant of the city, to the Capitol complex between 13th and 23rd. Then the field skipped to the West Edmond Field at the far northwest part of the county, which had been discovered in 1930. By 1935 the 1,713 wells of the county had produced 290,730,062 barrels of oil, a total that increased to 475 million barrels by 1940.

The city hall of Oklahoma City was built at the turn of the century. Photo by Jim Argo

This enormous production had a major impact on Oklahoma City. The Indian Territory Illuminating Oil Company alone pumped more than $69 million into the local economy in less than 8 years, including $11 million in payrolls, $21.5 million to contractors, $11 million in leases and royalties, $23 million in supplies, and $2.6 million in direct taxes. Oil also created or expanded vast fortunes for men such as Frank Buttram, W.R. Ramsey, and Thomas Slick, who in turn invested in banks, buildings, and job-creating companies. From supply houses to roughnecks, the oil industry had a major impact on Oklahoma City's early economic development.

Unlike smaller towns such as Seminole, Cushing, and Ardmore, Oklahoma City absorbed the oil boom with little disruption of the base economy or quality of life. In part that was due to the city's size, but just as important, the oil boom fit neatly into the pattern of Oklahoma City's growth, a boom and bust cycle that had begun with the land run. There is no better gauge for this up and down pattern than the record of commercial construction in Oklahoma City.

Appropriately, Oklahoma City began with a boom. On April 22, 1889, approximately 10,000 people transformed a lonely railroad outpost into a congested city of tents and shacks, starting a four-year building boom that left the city with its first generation of buildings. Typical of those one- and two-story structures were Henry Overholser's six prefabricated wooden buildings at Robinson and Grand and the rusticated sandstone Farmer's State Bank building on Broadway.

Following a down period in the cycle from 1893 to 1897, construction activity rebounded even more strongly. In 1900 Oklahoma City issued building permits valued at more than $1.2 million, an amazing figure considering that most of the buildings were one- and two-story brick structures. By the end of the year the city's streets had more than 7,900 front feet of brick or stone buildings, with 17 structures exceeding 3 stories. This generation of buildings included landmarks such as the sandstone county courthouse at Main and Walker, the Lee Hotel, and the first brick structures in the warehouse district east of the tracks from Reno to Main streets.

The building boom was fairly steady throughout the next decade, but the pace quickened dramatically from 1907 to 1910. This burst of activity began with construction of the Pioneer building at 3rd and Broadway. Designed by William A. Wells, it was the city's first true skyscraper and one of the most ornate ever to grace the skyline. Then came an entire generation of major buildings such as the Huckins Hotel, the Colcord building, the Hales building, the Baum building, the Insurance building, the Terminal building, the stock exchange building, the Skirvin Hotel, the Oklahoman building, the Patterson building, and the Kingkade Hotel. In 1909 developers were issued $6,415,000 in building permits, followed by another $6,937,675 in 1910.

Inevitably, this runaway boom was followed by contraction. In 1913, developers requested just $174,727 in building permits, a mere shadow of the frenzied activity only three years earlier. This sluggish record would persist until the early 1920s, when once again the boom mentality would return.

In 1922 the city's businessmen began shaking off the effects of the postwar recession and started thinking of expansion. Major construction projects included the Tradesmen's National Bank building, the Braniff building, the Indian Temple Shrine building, and the Cotton-Exchange building, all completed by 1923.

The boom gained even more momentum after 1924, and by 1926 the annual total of building permits exceeded $16.8 million. The skyline was pierced by major buildings such as the Elks Lodge (ONG) building, the Harbour-Longmire building, the Perrine building, the Medical Arts building, the OG&E

building, the Hightower building, the Montgomery Wards building, and the telephone building.

Spurred by the oil boom mentality, developers finished the phenomenal decade with an even greater burst of construction. The most ambitious of the projects were the Ramsey Tower, a $3-million skyscraper, and the First National building, a $5-million tower that topped 30 stories. The shadows of these skyscrapers fell across other major projects such as the Petroleum building, the Black Hotel, the Skirvin Tower, the Biltmore Hotel, and to the south, the Spanish-style Union Station. It was the golden age of commercial construction in Oklahoma City, a boom time frenzy of aggressive investment and unbridled optimism reminiscent of '89.

Once again, the boom came to an end, this time brought to a screeching halt by the spreading collapse of the international economy known as the Great Depression. Apart from construction of the civic center complex, completed in 1937 with Public Works Administration assistance, the downtown commercial district would remain relatively unchanged for the next 30 years.

As proven by the record of construction in Oklahoma City, for every downturn of the economy between 1889 and 1931 there was an even more exhilarating acceleration that pushed the economy into a higher gear. Decade by decade, brick by brick, the foundations of free enterprise were rising from the sandy soils of Oklahoma City.

Darkness falls upon this Oklahoma City skyline. Photo by Jim Argo

Engines for Expansion

Every community has certain turning points that mark the trail of history. In early Oklahoma City, historians point to the arrival of the Frisco Railroad in 1897, construction of the packing plants in 1909, and the discovery of oil in 1928. But of all the important stepping stones, all the chapters in the saga of Oklahoma City's development, none has been more important than the establishment of Tinker Air Force Base.

As the country prepared for war in late 1940, rumors spread that the army would build air bases, aircraft plants, and air depots somewhere in the heartland. That was all the Depression-weary leaders in Oklahoma City needed to know. Under the direction of Stanley Draper, Managing Director of the Oklahoma City Chamber of Commerce, 14 men organized the Industries Foundation of Oklahoma with a subscription of almost $300,000 to buy land for defense installations. The first acquisition was a 1,200-acre tract next to Municipal Airport for an air base.

Major General Clarence L. Tinker died during the battle of the Midway in 1942. Both Tinker Air Force Base and Tinker Field were named in his memory. Courtesy, Archives and Manuscripts Division, Oklahoma Historical Society

In February 1941 air corps officials asked the city to bid for a major supply depot. The Chamber secured options on 960 acres 5 miles southeast of town on 29th Street, raised enough subscribed funds to remove pipelines and build roads, and convinced the city government to call a bond election. On April 29, 1941, the people of Oklahoma City cleared the final hurdle when they approved a $982,000 bond issue by a margin of 19 to 1. By 1942 Tinker Air Depot was a vital link in the national defense system.

In the short run, Tinker created thousands of jobs in an area reeling under the decade-long shadow of depression. The construction tab of $21 million and the subsequent assembly-line jobs offered new hope to a generation of workers and accelerated the rural-to-urban shift of the population in Oklahoma. Before, the lament had been unemployment; under the stress of war the catchword became labor shortage.

In the long run, Tinker inaugurated the modern era of large-scale, labor-intensive enterprises that employed thousands of men and women at single sites. By the 1980s Tinker Air Force Base would become the single largest employer in the state, employing more than 26,000 workers with an annual payroll of more than $673 million, and make a $2.39 billion impact on the economy of central Oklahoma.

Perhaps as important, Tinker reinforced Oklahoma City's reputation as a center for aviation, a trend that had started in 1923 when the Chamber of Commerce established the first airport on Southeast 89th Street between stops 10 and 11 on the interurban streetcar line. A year later the Chamber sponsored another airport at Southwest 29th and May Avenue. Finally, in 1932 the citizens of Oklahoma City voted for a bond issue to build Will Rogers World Airport.

Commercial aviation started early in Oklahoma City. The first airmail routes came through the city in 1926, and a year later the first passenger service began with a fare of 10 cents per air mile or $78.80 to Chicago. In 1928 what would become Braniff Airlines began with a short flight from Oklahoma City to Tulsa. By the postwar era, the city was served by most major airlines.

Responding to the rapidly changing world of aviation, Will Rogers World Airport underwent a series of expansions and improvements. In June 1941 the Army Air Corps took complete control of the field, which became the base of a light bombardment group. By the end of the war, the 640-acre field had been expanded to 1,272 acres with 35 buildings and 5 hangars.

After the war, the city continued its evolution. In 1957 a bond issue was passed for improvements, followed by an $11.2-million terminal and runway expansion dedicated in 1966. Thereafter the Airport Trust expanded or replaced runways several times, created a buffer zone of undeveloped land around flight patterns, made three additions to the terminal, and built a new parking facility. By 1987 the airport had expanded to 7,500 acres, making it one of the largest airports in area in the United States.

Recognizing this commitment to aviation, the Civil Aeronautics Administration (CAA) moved its training school for air

This AWACS (Airborne Warning And Control System) aircraft is stationed at Tinker Air Force Base in Midwest City. Photo by Jim Argo

RIGHT: *Will Rogers World Airport occupies 7,500 acres of land. Photo by Matt Bradley*

BELOW: *Commercial carriers await passengers at Will Rogers World Airport. Photo by Jim Argo*

traffic controllers to Oklahoma City in 1946. The Oklahoma City Chamber of Commerce was instrumental in the transfer, providing land and buildings for the facility and equipment and manpower for the move. After the city government established the Airport Trust to build additional facilities, the CAA steadily expanded its operations. By 1987 total employment at Will Rogers World Airport, including the Federal Aviation Administration complex, was estimated at 6,935 men and women.

The aviation industry added to Oklahoma City's edge in transportation, giving the city an important economic advantage that had started with railroads and expanded with trucking. As early as 1948 the Oklahoma City Chamber of Commerce set the goal of developing a system of four-lane, high-speed highways in the city. Within a few years work was completed on the Northeast Highway, Northwest Highway, 39th Street Expressway, 23rd Street, and Classen and Shields boulevards. This pace accelerated even faster when the federal government began funding the interstate highway system.

In 1958, five years after the Turner Turnpike was completed as far as Tulsa, the first section of I-35 opened from the Northeast Highway south to 23rd Street. Work followed on I-40 from Tinker Air Force Base west through the heart of the downtown business district, on I-35 south to Norman and north to the Kansas line, and on the connecting loop of I-240 south and east of town. This urban interstate system continued its expansion for many years, from the Central Expressway to the completion of the outer loop.

When combined with the suburban flight of residential developments and the distant locations of major employers such as Tinker Air Force Base and Will Rogers World Airport, this network of super highways created new opportunities for economic development in Oklahoma City. Always eager to recruit new industry, the Chamber of Commerce created Okla-

homa Industries, Inc., to purchase land on the city's periphery and develop industrial parks suitable for a new generation of manufacturing and wholesaling firms.

The first such project was the Oklahoma Industries Industrial District, a 90-acre development opened in 1946. Another successful venture was the Willow Springs Industrial Park, created in 1951 along the 39th Street Expressway. Willow Springs provided the setting for the Western Electric pilot plant, a building that later was used by General Electric's Military Communications, Honeywell, and eventually Magnetic Peripherals. The park also encouraged the expansion of local industries such as Norick Brothers, Corken Pump, Little Giant, and others.

Other industrial districts that opened soon after World War II included the Santa Fe Industrial Park, a 140-acre site opened in 1947; the Cain Rock Island Industrial District, a 240-acre site established in 1951; and the Oklahoma Industrial Park, a 320-acre district opened about 1955. By the 1980s the Chamber of Commerce and various trusts had established 12 industrial parks. All provided facilities for recruiting new industry or relocating and expanding existing plants.

Responding to improved transportation, industrial planning, and a growing labor market, a host of national and international firms chose Oklahoma City for new capital investments. In 1957 Western Electric, a subsidiary of AT&T, announced that a pilot plant built for them by Oklahoma Industries, Inc., had been so successful that they would build a $35-million manufacturing plant at an Oklahoma City site. The facility eventually employed 5,400 workers and incorporated more than 1.3 million square feet of space. Five years later, General Electric moved into that same pilot plant and eventually built a major industrial complex on a 1,000-acre site.

After 1966 and the creation of the nonprofit Okla-

FACING PAGE, TOP: The Mike Monroney Aeronautical Center is part of the Future Farmers of America complex. Photo by Jim Argo

LEFT: Turner Turnpike tollbooths dispense tickets. Photo by Jim Argo

ABOVE: Dopler Radar, including these color monitors, is used to track storm systems at the National Severe Storms Lab in Norman. Photo by Jim Argo

RIGHT: Switching equipment is manufactured at the AT&T Technology Plant in Oklahoma City. Photo by Jim Argo

homa Industries Authority (OIA), the pace of industrial recruitment quickened in response to low-interest financing and exemption from ad valorem taxes. In 1969 Dayton Tire and Rubber Company, a division of the Firestone Tire and Rubber Company, built a large, labor-intensive plant near Will Rogers World Airport. CMI Corporation, a road construction machinery manufacturer, built a major complex off I-40 near Morgan Road. And Trammel-Crow, a large development firm based in Dallas, announced plans for a 236-acre industrial park near I-40 and Meridian.

After a brief recession in the early 1970s, the pace of industrial development resumed, topped by the construction of the General Motors assembly plant on OIA property. Located in an industrial park near the intersection of I-35 and south I-240, the new plant was designed to assemble front-wheel drive, fuel-efficient automobiles. By the mid-1980s the complex employed more than 5,500 workers.

While these large international companies made headlines, long-established firms in Oklahoma City responded to the same favorable conditions and announced plans for relocation and expansion. Cain's Coffee Company had roasted and processed coffee and tea from the old warehouse district since 1919. In 1962, lured to a new industrial site north of town on the Broadway Extension, the firm moved and expanded its operations.

Macklanburg-Duncan, another native-born firm, expanded its manufacturing operations in the Santa Fe Industrial Park and steadily boosted its payroll to 850 workers. Norick Brothers, Inc., a pioneer printing firm founded in 1910, expanded operations several times and built a new plant at 36th and Portland in 1959. Aero-Commander, later a division of Gulfstream Aerospace Corporation, continued its expansion until it employed almost 750 people at its Wiley Post Airport site. All were joined by high-tech firms such as Magnetic Peripherals and Organon Technika to provide a job-creating, diversified economic base of manufacturing.

The same factors that attracted heavy industry to Oklahoma City—transportation, central location, and community support—guaranteed the city's traditional leadership in wholesale distribution, especially in produce and groceries. One of the most successful in this business was Scrivner's, started by Enoch Scrivner in 1901 from his farm just outside Oklahoma City. To complement the wholesale operations, he expanded into retail outlets, then built a large warehouse in the downtown business district in 1927. By the 1980s, after a series of acquisitions, the company operated a string of warehouses and more than 70 retail stores from Nebraska to Georgia.

Fleming Companies was another wholesale giant that entered the Oklahoma City market in 1941 after purchasing the Carroll-Brough-Robinson Company. Three years later, the warehouse operations were moved to a site on North Santa Fe, and in 1978 to a $15-million, 400,000-square-foot plant on the Broadway Extension. With operations spread from coast to coast, the Fleming Companies moved its corporate headquarters to Oklahoma City.

Transportation advantages and central location attracted several large trucking firms to Oklahoma City, which in turn reinforced the city's reputation as a distribution center. Lee Way Motor Freight, a firm that began in Clinton, 86 miles west of

This General Motors Assembly Plant manufactures both Buicks and Chevrolets. Photo by Jim Argo

Oklahoma City, moved its headquarters to Oklahoma City in 1934 and specialized in hauling freight from Oklahoma City to destinations west. After World War II the firm grew dramatically until it operated 3,653 pieces of equipment over some 23,000 route miles in 19 states. Lee Way eventually built a large terminal at I-40 and May Avenue. Another industry leader was Transcon Trucking Lines, started in Oklahoma City in 1946. In 1957 Transcon opened a $1-million cross-

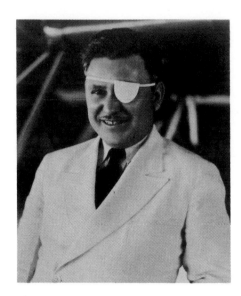

ABOVE: *Wiley Post set numerous flight records before his death in 1935. Courtesy, Archives and Manuscripts Division, Oklahoma Historical Society*

RIGHT: *Famed Oklahoma aviator Wiley Post is commemorated with this statue by Leonard McMurray in Civic Center Park. Photo by Jim Argo*

country terminal on Southeast 15th Street to accommodate its coast-to-coast operations.

Oklahoma City's role as a transportation and distribution center extended even to air freight. Airmail service had started as early as the 1920s, but hauling volumes of freight by air did not become big business until long after World War II. To attract its share of this business, Will Rogers World Airport added an air cargo terminal during its major expansion in 1966. Later, with plans for a larger facility, the Airport Trust built a $5-million air freight apron between the two main runways. In mid-1988, work was to begin on a new 94,000-square-foot air cargo facility that would improve handling capacity and distribution.

Just as manufacturers and wholesalers were attracted to planned industrial districts, retailers were attracted after the war to planned retail districts, or malls. The first large shopping center was Mayfair, which opened on North May Avenue in 1949, followed by Penn Square, the first large suburban shopping mall, built in 1957 near the old Belle Isle generating plant. Using a pattern that would be followed by later malls, Penn Square combined anchor stores such as Montgomery Ward and John A. Brown's with a wide variety of smaller retailers offering everything from clothes and shoes to books and sporting goods. The advantages included free, plentiful parking, modern marketing, and concentrated diversity.

Other malls followed in quick succession. Shepherd Mall at 23rd and Pennsylvania was the first totally enclosed mall. Then came Crossroads Mall, 50 Penn Place, North Park Mall, French Park Mall, Quail Springs Mall, and a host of other retail centers. As merchants moved to these new locations, the downtown retail district slowly contracted. By 1965 only 11 percent of all retail sales in the area originated in the downtown business district.

As usually happens during a period of rapid change, some companies withered when confronted by the changing times, while others adapted and prospered. One company that made the transition was John A. Brown's, which had grown steadily in the downtown business district from 1915 to the 1940s. Unlike some department store competitors, Brown's adapted to the suburban trend and became a leading force in establishing the largest malls.

Hertz operates a Worldwide Reservation Center in Oklahoma City. Photo by Jim Argo

Streets, which Theodore "Ted" Greenberg founded in Oklahoma City in 1930, was another leader in suburban expansion. The original Streets, located downtown on West Main, specialized in ladies' clothing and children's apparel. Soon after World War II, Greenberg opened his first suburban store in the 400 block of Northwest 23rd Street, then followed quickly with stores in Midwest City and in the Mayfair Shopping Center. As new malls opened at Reding, Penn Square, and Shepherd Mall, Streets was there. By the 1980s Streets operated nine stores in Oklahoma City, including one downtown in the First National Bank Arcade.

Another retailer who followed the suburban trends after World War II was C.R. Anthony. Starting with a small clothing store in Cushing in 1919, Anthony expanded steadily until 1927, when he moved his company headquarters to Oklahoma City. By the 1980s, the retail company operated more than 300 clothing stores across the nation, including several stores in strip malls throughout Oklahoma City.

Penn Square Mall, Oklahoma City's first mall, reopened in the spring of 1988 following a multimillion-dollar renovation adding a second level and new buildings. Photo by Jim Argo

The explosive postwar prosperity and suburban drift also influenced new trends in the service industries, especially in banking and hotels. Responding to increased consumer loans and checking accounts, new banks and savings and loans appeared alongside an endless succession of new residential developments. To illustrate the phenomenon, Oklahoma City had 11 banks at statehood in 1907, and only 8 at the end of World War II; by the late 1980s there were still 9 banks downtown, but more than 50 banks, 75 savings and loan branches, and 40 credit unions in the suburbs.

Hotels underwent a similar transformation. In 1946 virtually every hotel in Oklahoma City was located within a radius of 10 blocks from the heart of the Santa Fe Depot at Broadway and Grand. This included a few luxury hotels, such as the Biltmore, the Black, the Huckins, and the Skirvin, but most were small apartment hotels. By the late 1980s, there were 93 hotels and motels in Oklahoma City, but only 13 downtown, and of those, the only luxury hotels were the Skirvin and the Sheraton. Some 80 hotels and motels, including several world-class luxury hotels, had been built outside the downtown area, most along the major highways or near exclusive neighborhoods.

This radical redistribution of manufacturers, wholesalers, retailers, and businesses may have been the sign of a healthy, expanding economy, but it created a problem in the downtown business district. Prior to World War II, the district had renewed itself periodically with new booms and new construction removing old, antiquated buildings as market forces dictated. Booms from 1897 to 1900, 1909 to 1911, and 1924 to 1931 had kept the city modern and alive. Then, with the combined blows of the Great Depression, the war, and the shift of postwar development to the suburbs, some of the older, obsolescent

buildings downtown were not updated or displaced as part of the natural process. For 30 years, the downtown skyline was frozen in time.

Just as they had organized to attract and retain industry, Oklahoma City's political and business leaders organized to replace the natural market forces downtown. Under the influence of Stanley Draper, the Chamber of Commerce created the Urban Action Foundation to attract federal dollars flowing into a national campaign of urban renewal. That led to the hiring of I.M. Pei and Associates to prepare a long-range plan for downtown redevelopment.

The Urban Renewal Authority applied the same philosophy to the older sections of the downtown district that the Chamber of Commerce had for the suburban industrial parks. The plan was to buy large blocks of property, much of it with buildings already sitting vacant, raze them, and prepare the land for sale to developers. To pump-prime the process, the first two construction projects were the Mummers Theatre and the Myriad Convention Center.

Fortunately for the planners, the initial phase of clearing coincided with general prosperity in the greater Oklahoma City economy. From 1960 to 1969 the number of industrial jobs in the city increased more than 85 percent, creating economic activity that lured developers to land available through the urban renewal program.

In 1968 Kerr-McGee announced that it would construct a 30-story tower between Robinson and Broadway just north of 2nd Street. That same year Liberty National Bank announced plans for a 35-story skyscraper east of Broadway. Then Fidelity Bank released plans for an 18-story building and park downtown. By the end of the boom in 1973, the downtown redevelopment plan had attracted $263 million in investments, of which $218 million was private money.

In 1973 the downtown project was expanded when the Urban Renewal Authority received permission to purchase a six-block area bounded by Robinson, Sheridan, Walker, and Park avenues to be used for a retail galleria. In 1974, with $16 million in federal funds and $18.7 million from the city, the authority began purchasing and razing buildings to prepare for a mixed retail/office complex.

After several delays caused by hesitant investors and the economic recession of 1974, an investment firm from Dallas, Texas, was chosen for the development. Flush with oil-boom dollars, the developer began construction in 1979 of the American First Tower, a $200-million, 14-story building at Main and

FACING PAGE: The Skirvin Plaza Hotel, built in the early 1900s, is one of two luxury hotels in downtown Oklahoma City. Photo by Matt Bradley

FOLLOWING PAGE: I.M. Pei and Associates were hired to plan the downtown redevelopment of Oklahoma City including this Crystal Bridge (right). Photo by Matt Bradley

ABOVE: *Numerous varieties of flora are found within the Crystal Bridge. Photo by Matt Bradley*

FACING PAGE: *The Crystal Bridge is a tremendous botanical garden open to the public. Photo by Jim Argo*

Robinson. Then came the second and even larger First Oklahoma Tower, a 31-story office complex, and Leadership Square, a $70-million glass-plated tower. The retail galleria, however, failed to materialize before the recession of 1982 brought most downtown redevelopment to a halt.

The oil boom from 1978 to 1982 encouraged office building projects in other parts of the city as well. On Northwest Highway, from the Classen Circle to Council Road, construction crews raised a seemingly endless row of towers and strip malls. A similar transformation occurred on Memorial Road between the Broadway Extension and Portland. Even after the twin disasters of the oil bust and bank failures, construction continued, although at a slower pace.

A new wrinkle in Oklahoma City's economic development during all of this was historic preservation. In 1978 the federal government offered the first tax credits for rehabilitating historic buildings, ultimately providing for a 25 percent tax credit on certified rehabilitations and lesser credits for simply renovating older structures. The new tax benefits sparked an interest in historic properties, especially downtown.

Among the best of the rehabilitations was the Colcord building, a project that preserved the elegance of the 1909-era skyscraper. Then came the renovation of Central High School, an award-winning rehabilitation that turned an outdated school building into the state corporate headquarters of Southwestern Bell.

Due to a combination of tax credits and a growing appreciation for architectural variety, other historic buildings were saved from the wrecking ball. The long list included the Skirvin

ABOVE: *Construction sites in the downtown area have been countless since the early 1960s. Photo by Jim Argo*

FACING PAGE: *Reflective glass towers of new construction contrast, yet blend, with the older buildings of downtown Oklahoma City. Photo by Matt Bradley*

Hotel, the Harbour-Longmire building, the Hightower building, the old Cravens building, the Tradesman's Bank building, the Medical Arts Tower, the Petroleum building, the Braniff building, the Ramsey tower, the India-Temple Shrine, and others.

Softening the international look of the reflective-glass towers were other distinctive reminders of the past, such as the Sullivanesque Pioneer building, the Art Deco-detailed First National building, and the WPA-era civic center complex. Architecturally, the downtown business district had developed into a mixture of old and new.

Like the skyline downtown, the economic profile of greater Oklahoma City had become a mixture of old and new. The old spirit of boomtown optimism, the old reliance on self-determinism, the old belief in the benefits of growth had survived intact, blended into a new recipe of economic success. From attracting the Frisco Railroad to town in 1897 to the development of industrial districts in the postwar era, Oklahoma City had demonstrated an uncommon capacity for growth and change. The future will reap the benefits of this economic development.

Rare medical problems as well as ordinary childhood illnesses are treated at Children's Memorial Hospital. Photo by Shelly R. Harrison

Chapter Four

Healing and Health

During the nineteenth century Leigh Hunt correctly noted, "The groundwork of all happiness is health." The pioneers who settled Oklahoma wanted the happiness brought by health, yet theirs was an age of agues and bilious fevers, of boils and chills, of pneumonia and tuberculosis, of a dozen or more dreaded childhood diseases. Every family had its own preferred home remedies, while drugstores were filled with salves, powders, pills, and purgatives.

Making the run into Oklahoma with the pioneers were doctors and dentists. Many of them settled in Oklahoma City, and there the doctors were soon busy prescribing for ailments, probing for bullets, dispensing pills, and sewing up wounds, while the dentists pulled teeth and filled cavities. In that era, however, checking the credentials of someone calling himself "doctor" was difficult—and there were those claiming to be physicians who had little or no training. Each doctor developed his own following of those who swore by his medical skills as he made his rounds of patients' houses and treated those who came to his office.

The first organized health-care facility in Oklahoma City was St. Anthony Hospital. Founded by the Sisters of St. Francis, it opened its doors on November 24, 1899, a 3-story, half-basement structure with 24 beds. Water had to be carried four blocks from a nearby school. The structure was wired for electricity in 1902, and two years later came natural gas lines and the institution's own windmill-driven water well. When an outbreak of smallpox and scarlet fever struck Oklahoma City early in the twentieth century, the Sisters converted the hospital's barn into a quarantine facility, which was renamed St. Patrick Isolation Hospital. Thanks to the Sisters' willingness to improvise and because of charitable donations from city leaders, the hospital survived those early lean years. In 1908 the Sisters opened the state's first school of nursing at St. Anthony, and in 1911 it acquired a motor-driven ambulance.

The Oklahoma Territory Medical Association, headquartered in Oklahoma City, wanted to raise the quality of medical service in the region, and in 1906 it joined with the Indian Territory Medical Association to form the new Oklahoma State Medical Association. Almost immediately this organizationbegan working for better training of medical personnel and for the creation of a modern medical school.

The state's first school for the training of doctors was established in 1907 under the auspices of Epworth University, a Methodist institution which had opened its doors in 1904. The Epworth School of Medicine was founded when 21 physicians and surgeons in Oklahoma City each donated $1,000 so that the university could purchase the Angelo Hotel, located at the corner of Northwest 6th Street and Broadway Avenue. After the hotel was remodeled, 23 doctors donated their services as members of the medical faculty, and it began accepting students for training in what at first was a two-year curriculum.

In 1908 the University of Oklahoma began what was called a pre-medical school at its Norman campus. Students aspiring to become doctors attended classes for two years, then transferred to an accredited medical school, such as Epworth, for the training that would get them certified to practice medicine. Dr. C.S. Bobo was dean of the university's pre-medical school, and Dr. L.A. Turly was professor of pathology (at the same time as he was charged with organizing a bacteriological laboratory for the State Board of Health and acting as the state bacteriologist). Others working in this pioneering effort were John Dice McLaren, head of the department of physiology, and Edwin DeBarr, head of the department of chemistry (and also state chemist).

In 1910 the Epworth School of Medicine merged with the university's pre-medical school. This transfer to university ownership saved Oklahoma's only school of medicine, for Epworth University closed its doors in May 1911. Under the terms of the agreement struck in 1910, students at Epworth School of Medicine were allowed to transfer without loss of credit into the university's medical training program. For a time all this work was at the Norman campus, but university officials knew they needed a suitable hospital at which its students could train. Rather than build its own, which would have required a large appropriation from the state, it chose to lease Rolater Hospital, located at the corner of Northeast 4th Street and Stiles Avenue in Oklahoma City.

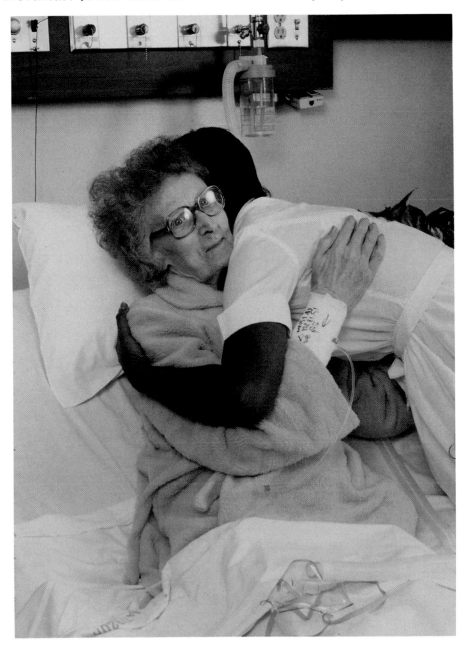

A nurse makes this elderly patient more comfortable. Photo by Shelly R. Harrison

Dr. J.B. Rolater was one of the pioneer doctors who had made the run on April 22, 1889. Coming from Georgia, where he had earned a medical degree, he had become chief surgeon for the Rock Island Railroad and for the telephone company. Years later Harvey Everest, one of Oklahoma City's great bankers, would recall that Dr. Rolater was regarded as one of the city's best early surgeons and had "a tremendous practice," but that "he didn't keep his tools very sharp or very clean."

When the university acquired Rolater Hospital, it was equipped with 60 inpatient beds, a dispensary, and a kitchen that was used as a clinical laboratory under the direction of Annette B. Cowles. Renamed State University Hospital, it was used for the purpose of training physicians. However, the structure was inadequate for the needs of the university medical school. Therefore, in 1917 the state leg-

This doctor and head nurse discuss a patient's program of treatment. Photo by Shelly R. Harrison

islature voted $200,000 for acquiring and constructing a building to be known as University Hospital on the condition that Oklahoma City sell to the state for $100 the Oklahoma City General Hospital (usually known as Emergency or Municipal Hospital) located at the intersection of Stiles Avenue and 3rd Street. This act of the legislature further stated that any resident of the state could be a patient at University Hospital merely by paying for room and board; there was to be no charge for medical attention or medicines. In 1919 an additional $76,000 had to be appropriated by the legislature to complete construction of what became known as "Old Main." Located on Northeast 13th Street, just southeast of the state capitol, this was a 176-bed teaching hospital with wards in which the beds were arranged in nonmilitary fashion. It admitted its first patients on August 1, 1919, with Dr. Raymond L. Murdock as the first resident surgeon.

The creation of the university medical school in 1910 and the opening of University Hospital in 1911 were simultaneous with the construction of several other hospitals in Oklahoma City during that boom period. The institution that would become known as Deaconess Hospital, associated with the Free Methodist Church of North America, was started in Guthrie as a home for unwed mothers. In 1900 William M. and Della Jenkins endowed the Home of Redeeming Love in what was then the territorial capital city. In 1909 the home purchased 80 acres of land at 5501 North Portland in Oklahoma City in order to move the home for unwed mothers there.

The first building, a three-story brick facility, was built with $12,000 of donated cash and $11,000 of donated materials and services. When it opened, the nearest telephone was a mile away, and no electricity was available. Other buildings were added, and in 1944 the institution changed from merely serving unwed mothers to providing hospital care to the general public;

at that time it was renamed Deaconess Hospital.

In 1910, the same year Deaconess moved from Guthrie to Oklahoma City, Dr. Foster K. Camp and his wife, Janet, purchased the 8-bed St. Luke's Sanitarium, renamed it Wesley Hospital, and relocated it from the 9th floor of the Campbell building to the 11th and 12th floors of the Herskowitz building in downtown Oklahoma City. A year later it moved yet again, this time to the corner of Northwest 12th Street and Harvey Avenue. In 1912 the Wesley Training School for Nurses was established as a three-year diploma-granting school. After World War I, six physicians returning from the conflict bought Wesley Hospital from Dr. Camp.

The Wesley Hospital owners chose to affiliate their institu-

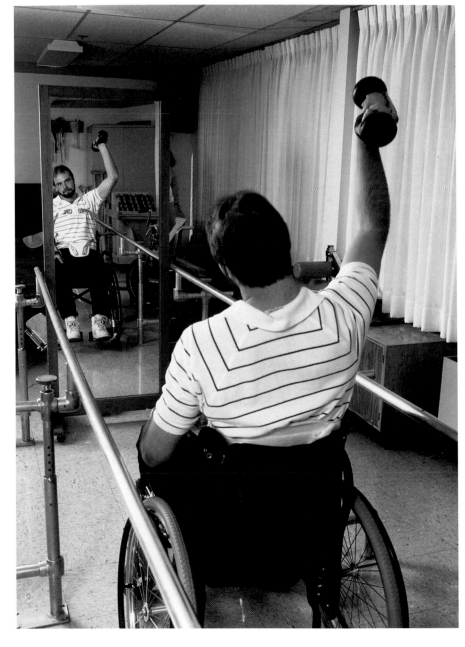

The Don H. Donoghue Rehabilitation Institute provides rehabilitative care to children and adults. Photo by Shelly R. Harrison

tion with the University of Oklahoma School of Medicine in 1911 as a teaching hospital. The agreement stipulated that Wesley Hospital physicians were to be members of the university faculty. Through this relationship Wesley provided intern and residency programs in surgery, internal medicine, gynecology, obstetrics, and radiology, making it the first privately owned hospital in the southwestern United States to receive university medical school accreditation for its affiliated teaching programs. Because of its reputation, Wesley Hospital received patients from across the Sooner State, and numerous expansions of its facilities were necessary: in 1927, 1929, 1930, 1947, 1951, 1960, and 1964.

Also growing in the period prior to World War I was St. Anthony Hospital. In 1916 a new wing was added, bringing to 150 the number of patient beds. Other expansions that year included a new room for surgery, a clinical laboratory, a

Dr. Christiaan Barnard was once affiliated with the Oklahoma Transplantation Institute, a subsidiary of the Baptist Medical Center. Photo by Jim Argo

medical library, interns' quarters, and a classroom. Two years later the hospital's initial class of interns arrived. A further wing would be built onto St. Anthony Hospital in 1932.

The beginning of what would become yet another major hospital in Oklahoma City came in 1917 when the 25-bed, 3-story Baptist State Hospital opened at the corner of 12th and Walker streets. Despite its name, this facility was actually owned by a group of private physicians. However, in 1922 it was purchased by Oklahoma baptists and operated as a denominational hospital named the Baptist Hospital. Operating the facility proved more expensive than the denomination had anticipated, however, and in 1924 it was sold to two physicians, Drs. J.E. Harbison and Paul E. Haskett, who then operated it as a private venture. In 1927, when Dr. Charles E. Barker became a partner, the institution was incorporated as the Oklahoma City General Hospital. That year a fourth floor was added to the building, bringing its bed count to 85. Simultaneously a new operating room suite, laboratories, and an X-ray facility were added, along with a school of nursing that would produce its first graduates a year later. Gradually Oklahoma City General Hospital's reputation for excellence increased, as did the number of its beds;

Mercy Hospital-Oklahoma City General was
purchased by the St. Louis province of the
Sisters of Mercy in 1947. Photo by Jim Argo

by 1947 it had 145. That year the institution was bought by
the St. Louis province of the Sisters of Mercy, who renamed
it Mercy Hospital-Oklahoma City General.

During the prosperity of the 1920s, the University of Oklahoma School of Medicine would get appropriations from the
legislature that brought expansion. Administrative offices and
nurses' quarters were added to University Hospital in 1921.
Seven years later came construction of the Crippled Children's
Hospital at the intersection of Kelley Avenue and Northeast
13th Street. Also opened in 1928 was the University of Oklahoma School of Medicine building, a structure of yellow brick
and limestone trim, on the corner of Phillips and Northeast
13th Street.

Thus two clusters of medical facilities gradually grew in Oklahoma City. Near downtown on the northwest side were St. Anthony, Wesley, and Oklahoma City General, while on the northeast side of town, just south of the state capitol, were University
and Crippled Childrens hospitals.

The Depression of the 1930s prevented additional growth

of Oklahoma City's health delivery system, just as did World War II. However, there gradually grew in the minds of some of the city's leaders, men such as Stanley Draper, managing director of the Chamber of Commerce, the idea of making Oklahoma City a major center for delivering health care and for scientific research in the health field. In February 1946 an effort began to raise $3 million for an Oklahoma Medical Research Foundation. This concept was given a tremendous boost that fall when President Harry S. Truman announced that a 500-bed veterans hospital would be built in Oklahoma City. Opened in 1953, it was adjacent to and closely affiliated with the University of Oklahoma School of Medicine and University Hospital.

The Oklahoma Medical Research Foundation, incorporated in August 1946, raised sufficient funds by 1950 to be able to open an $800,000 building, housing some 50 laboratories, adjacent to the university medical school. With private funds, it provided the research scientists and laboratories which the medical school needed, but which the state of Oklahoma was not able to finance.

By the mid-1950s, a great medical complex was taking shape in northeastern Oklahoma City. Located adjacent to each other were the University of Oklahoma School of Medicine, the University Hospital, the university's school of nursing, the Crippled Children's Hospital, a speech and hearing clinic, the Veterans Administration Hospital, and the unique Oklahoma Medical Research Institute. Added to this complex in the 1950s were an outpatient clinic building, constructed in 1951, and a radiology building, completed in 1959.

In the years after World War II, as Oklahoma City expanded and prospered, St. Anthony Hospital grew in order to give better care both to city residents and to the patients who increasingly came to it from the entire region. A three-phase building program began in 1955; this increased the enrollment capacity of the hospital's school of nursing, and then space for more than 200 beds was built as specialized departments in psychiatry, occupational therapy, pediatrics, and maternity were added. In the 1960s came yet more expansion as the addition of the northwest wing, the annex, and the east central tower brought the hospital to 684 beds. During all this growth and service, the Sisters of St. Francis have remained true to their vow not to turn anyone away while offering the finest medical care available anywhere.

Likewise becoming much larger was Deaconess Hospital. In 1955 came the Anna L. Witteman addition on the south side

FACING PAGE: Medical education in Oklahoma City is exceptional. Photo by Matt Bradley

St. Anthony Hospital opened its doors for health care in November 1899. Photo by Jim Argo

of the original building, raising the bed count to 40. In 1959 came construction of the emergency wing, in which were two emergency units. In 1964 came additional growth that raised the number of beds to 109, and then in 1971 two floors were added to the hospital at a cost of $2.68 million. In 1980, thanks to generous donors, work began on the Butterfield Wing, which would raise the number of beds to 250. Deaconess opened the first intensive-care unit in Oklahoma City in 1965, and it organized the state's first outpatient surgical facility. Today Deaconess is proud that it is considered the area's family practice hospital.

It was in the mid-1950s, during the era of rapid movement to the suburbs in Oklahoma City, that Baptist Memorial Hospital was founded as a nonprofit part of the Baptist General Convention of Oklahoma. After a statewide fund-raising effort, the hospital was built on a 62-acre site on the Northwest Expressway. When it opened in 1959, Baptist Memorial Hospital had 188 beds, a maternity ward, laboratory, pediatrics unit, physical therapy area, diagnostic section, emergency room, and surgery unit. So successful was this effort that the following year ground was broken for an adjacent four-story Doctors'

Medical Building. In 1965 a second phase of building was completed, raising the number of beds to 376 and adding an intensive-care unit, a coronary-care unit, a radioisotope laboratory, and an additional six stories to the Doctors' Medical Building. When a third phase of building began in 1972, the name of the institution was changed to Baptist Medical Center of Oklahoma in order to more accurately reflect the wide range of health-care services it offered. Phase 3 raised the number of beds to 563 in 1975.

In 1978 Baptist Medical Center ended its affiliation with the Baptist General Convention and became an independent, nonprofit corporation. In 1983 this became a subsidiary of the Oklahoma Health Care Corporation, under which the facility had continued to grow to serve the needs of Oklahomans. Today it provides a comprehensive approach to cancer treatment for patients and their families, and it is a center for heart and other organ trans-

Presbyterian Hospital was the recently acquired by the Hospital Corporation of America. Photo by Matt Bradley

plants at the Oklahoma Transplantation Institute, a subsidiary enterprise. Working with doctors at Baptist Medical Center in the effort to make this health-care facility a center of organ transplants has been the internationally famous pioneer of heart transplants, Dr. Christiaan Barnard. Baptist Medical Center now sponsors the Barnard Symposium, which attracts to the Sooner State some of the world's leading cardiovascular authorities.

In addition to growth at Baptist Medical Center, there was building on the southwest side of town in the early 1960s when South Community Hospital was incorporated. By 1976 its bed count had increased to 391. In Midwest City, on the southeast side of the metropolitan area, the Midwest City Hospital constructed 78 beds in the late 1960s and eventually grew to 110 beds.

In the 1960s, as Baptist and St. Anthony hospitals were growing and changing and as suburban hospitals were being constructed in other parts of town, some of Oklahoma City's civic leaders were considering the broad scope of health care in Oklahoma City. One problem area was Wesley Hospital. In 1961 it was acquired by the Wesley Hospital Foundation, and three years later it merged with the Washita Presbytery of the United

FACING PAGE: *Oklahoma City's Children's Memorial Hospital has recently undergone a $41-million renovation. Photo by Matt Bradley*

Presbyterian church; at that time the name of the institution was changed to Presbyterian Medical Center of Oklahoma, and plans began for constructing a new, modern facility. Similarly, the Sisters of Mercy were contemplating the construction of a new Mercy Hospital, for their facility no longer met public health standards. Both University and Crippled Children's hospitals were state-owned, and by the mid-1960s both had deteriorated to the point that only a dedicated staff was able to keep them open. Clearly these two aging state hospitals, along with the two private institutions considering a move, provided an opportunity for dramatic change in Oklahoma City's health-care system.

Early in 1965 Dr. James L. Dennis, dean of the University of Oklahoma School of Medicine, had a meeting with Stanley Draper, executive director of the Oklahoma City Chamber of Commerce, and with Draper's assistant, Paul Strasbaugh. Together they conceived the idea of an Oklahoma Health Sciences Center in which university, public, and private health agencies would work together. In turn, they convinced city civic leaders, such as E.K. Gaylord, Dean A. McGee, William T. Payne, and John Kirkpatrick of the value of their plan. The Chamber of Commerce cosponsored a trip by city leaders to look at the Texas Medical Center in Houston, and all returned enthusiastic about the concept. In the months and years that followed, the Health Sciences Center became a reality.

One of the first to agree to become part of this complex was Presbyterian Medical Center of Oklahoma. Its directors voted to construct a $36-million facility which, after a major fund-raising effort, opened in 1974 at Northeast 13th Street and Lincoln Boulevard. It has 407 beds and a staff of 500 physicians. This was followed in 1982 by a $6-million expansion. Presbyterian Medical Center recently was acquired by Hospital Corporation of America, the world's largest health-care provider.

With the backing of Oklahoma City's civic leaders, the legislature provided the funds needed to transform the university medical school and its teaching hospitals into one of the finest health-care facilities in the state—and in the nation. The Health Sciences Center grew to 200 acres with a complex of 22 buildings. Old University Hospital was renamed Oklahoma Memorial Hospital and given an extensive refurbishing.

Another teaching hospital is Children's Memorial Hospital (previously known as Crippled Children's Hospital). In 1973 this facility was transferred to the Oklahoma Department of Human Services because this state agency had tax monies ear-

The medical staff in Oklahoma City's hospitals maintain accurate records. Photo by Shelly R. Harrison

marked for it; state leaders felt this agency could invest the dollars necessary to transform it into the medical facility all Oklahomans wanted. Within a short time a $41-million renovation and expansion of the facility was undertaken, totally changing its appearance. A seven-story annex was added to the west of the original structure, and a new five-level addition was built on the east side.

By state mandate, Children's Memorial Hospital provides medical and dental care to patients under 21 years of age, and it offers treatment for diseases and abnormalities ranging from ordinary childhood illnesses to more complex and rare medical and surgical problems. Everything there is designed to help ease the fears experienced by young people in a medical setting.

Yet another of the teaching hospitals is the Child Study Center, which serves patients ranging from newborns through age 21. The Child Study Center was created in 1959 and housed in temporary quarters as a multidisciplinary unit to provide outpatient evaluation and treatment. In 1975 a separate two-story building to house the Child Study Center was erected one block east of Children's Memorial Hospital.

The fourth teaching hospital in the Health Sciences Center is the Don H. O'Donoghue Rehabilitation Institute, which opened in 1981 to provide both medical and rehabilitative services to physically disabled children and adults. This facility was named for a pioneer orthopedic surgeon in Oklahoma City and contains 120 beds. It is capable of providing occupational therapy, respiration therapy, and speech pathology. One of the special programs offered at the institute is training to enable the handicapped to live independently at home. This utilizes three self-contained apartments in which patients in the final phase of rehabilitative treatment practice the activities of daily living while a special team evaluates and assists them.

At the Health Sciences Center the first major construction began in 1970, with work on a $12-million, 8-level hospital structure named Everett Tower. Completed in 1973, it contains 30,000 square feet of space, nine operating suites, patient lounges on each floor, as well as the largest dietary facility in the state.

In 1973, control of Memorial Hospital was removed from the University of Oklahoma Board of Regents and given to University Hospitals and Clinics. Development of the medical complex has continued as the facility's equipment was upgraded. Part of this was construction of a 10-unit outpatient kidney dialysis center that allows kidney patients to be treated without hospitalization. In 1979 the Everett Tower was renovated, and a 10-bed coronary care unit was added to permit expansion in the treatment of heart disease. In 1979 work also began on a new building to house an emergency care and trauma center, as well as new clinical laboratories.

Not part of the Health Sciences Center but also serving to make Oklahoma City the center of health care in the state, are two other hospitals in Oklahoma City: Mercy and St. Anthony. It was the decision of Sister Mary Coletta, administrator of Mercy Hospital, that this institution should be located on the far northwest side of Oklahoma City, not in the downtown Health Sciences Center. Aided by civic leaders, such as William T. Payne, Robert E. Lee, Sylvan N. Goldman, and John Kirkpatrick, the Sisters bought a 40-acre tract on Memorial Road. Completed in 1974, the new Mercy Hospital and its Doctors' Tower were yet another jewel in Oklahoma City's health-care center.

By the 1970s the Health Sciences Center was becoming the great center for health care in Oklahoma that civic leaders had envisioned, the place to which those not able to be helped elsewhere were brought, the place from which new medical and dental personnel graduate to serve all Oklahomans. The building of this center has not been without controversy, and from time to time the legislature, the governor, and others aspiring to high office have injected politics into what perhaps should not be a political matter. But the Health Sciences Center has become a showplace in Oklahoma City for which all Sooners can be grateful.

To facilitate and speed the transfer of patients to the Oklahoma teaching hospitals, MediFlight of Oklahoma began in 1974. This employed two helicopters to carry patients whose survival depended on rapid transportation from any point in Oklahoma to the highly specialized medical treatment facilities available only in Oklahoma City. This service is available to physicians, community hospitals, ambulance services, and law enforcement agencies for stabilizing, treating, and transporting patients.

Oklahoma City indeed has become the major center of health care for the entire state.

Chapter Five

Education for Everyone

Most of those who made the run in 1889 would have agreed with British author and poet Joseph Addison's 1711 comment: "I consider an human soul without education like marble in the quarry, which shows none of its inherent beauty till the skill of the polisher fetches out the colours, makes the surface shine, and discovers every ornamental cloud, spot and vein that runs through the body of it."

The first residents of Oklahoma City wanted their children to shine with knowledge, but the legislation which opened the Unassigned Lands to settlement made no provision for education. Therefore parents with youngsters to educate for a time had to make do with subscription schools. Just a month after the great run, Mrs. L.H. North opened a subscription school in a tent and soon had a large number of pupils. Parents paid $1.50 or more per month depending on means and grade level. During that first summer, one school was said to be operating under the shade of blackjack trees. That same fall Jenny

McKeever opened her subscription school with 25 dollars' worth of desks, a stove, and chairs in the rear of a building on First Street; she taught the lower grades, while Professor Frederick H. Umholtz conducted the upper grades.

Public schools first opened in the fall of 1890 but they were severely underfunded. In 1890 Congress appropriated $50,000 to be used for all the schools in the Oklahoma Territory; part of the act making these funds available stipulated that teachers' salaries should be $25, $30, or $35 per month, depending on the grade taught. Oklahoma City supplemented its share of the federal money with local tax funds, but teachers were still paid in a specially printed currency—scrip—that had to be discounted when used to make purchases. That first year some 700 students were taught by 20 teachers, 7 of whom were men.

Classes for these first public school elementary pupils were held in rented quarters in each of the four wards, while the school superintendent, R.A. Sullins, taught older beginning students in a rented storeroom on North 1st Street. Secondary students met in what had been a military barrack. The ability to write clearly and speak forcefully was considered necessary in educated people at that time, so all students had to belong to a literary society and take part in its programs.

In 1894 Congress helped public education in Oklahoma City by giving it a plot of ground known as the Military Reservation. The money that derived in 1896 from selling the lots carved out of what was called Military Hill was used to build the first two schools, Washington and Emerson. Funds raised by a bond issue of $45,000 built three additional buildings—Jefferson, Lincoln, and Garfield—so that each ward would have its own elementary school, and there was a segregated school for all black children in town. The high school building opened in 1896 and would be used until 1937, when it burned (for a time it served as the temporary capitol of the state). By 1898 some 2,000 students were being served in the Oklahoma public schools. The first graduating class in Oklahoma City, six seniors, received their diplomas at a special ceremony held in the Overholser Opera House and attended by all town digni-

Yukon, Oklahoma, is the location of this elementary school classroom. Photo by Jim Argo

taries.

By the time of the great population boom that began in 1908, it seemed that the Oklahoma City Public School District had to erect a new building or two every year. Elementary schools sprouted like mushrooms in all quarters of the city, while new junior and senior high schools kept pace with the thousands of students who enrolled each year. The 1960s would see desegregation enforced, and a resulting integrated system.

ABOVE: *Students of chemistry prepare an experiment. Photo by Jim Argo*

BOTTOM: *This Oriental youth leads his class in the Pledge of Allegiance. Photo by Jim Argo*

Overseeing and certifying these schools has been the job of the State Department of Education, which moved from Guthrie to Oklahoma City in 1910 along with all other branches of the state government. As provided in the constitution, a six-member State Board of Education and the State Superintendent of Public Instruction provide and enforce guidelines for teacher certification, curriculum, and textbooks, as well as allocate the resources voted by the state for all school districts in Oklahoma. From the education buildings in the state capitol complex on North Lincoln come the leadership that urges excellence on teachers and students alike in all parts of the Sooner State.

Advocates for improved education have long had an impor-

tant resource in the public libraries. In 1898, with wooden shacks and tents still dotting the downtown landscape, the Philomathea and Sans Souci women's clubs organized the city's first library with 600 books. The one-room facility was soon overcrowded, so in 1901, with a grant from Andrew Carnegie and the leadership of Mrs. Selwyn Douglas, the territory's first Carnegie Library was built at the corner of Third and Robinson.

For the next 50 years the library expanded and branches

Old Central High School, Oklahoma City's first high school, located in the downtown area, is now the corporate headquarters for Southwestern Bell, Oklahoma Division. Photo by Jim Argo

were opened in various parts of town. The demand for books and programs accelerated even faster after World War II, and in 1950 voters approved a bond issue to build a new, enlarged library downtown and a branch library in Capitol Hill. That expansion was followed in 1965 by the Metropolitan Library Act, which established a city/county library system combining five libraries in Oklahoma City with libraries in Bethany, Del City, and Midwest City.

The recession of the early 1980s interrupted this pace of development by reducing library hours and staff, but the voters of Oklahoma County responded by approving an additional

$3.4-million library tax in 1982. By 1988, with a budget of $8.9 million and circulation of 3,350,000 books, the Metropolitan Library System had 11 branch libraries, 4 extension libraries, and 5 bookmobiles. Whether it was 1898 or 1988, the people of Oklahoma City considered books and knowledge a high priority.

In the area of higher education, Oklahoma City had a university operating before statehood. Methodists meeting in Oklahoma City in 1892 proposed what eventually would become Oklahoma City University. However, nothing came of that original recommendation. Then in 1900 came a call for a Methodist

Carnegie Library in Guthrie was the site for the swearing in of the last territorial and first state governor of Oklahoma. Photo by Jim Argo

school jointly sponsored by the two branches into which Methodism was then divided. This was approved, provided Oklahoma City donated 240 acres of land, 40 of them to be set aside as a campus and the other 200 platted and sold as town lots, the money to be used to erect a building and endow the school. Construction began some one and three-quarter miles northwest of downtown, and a 35-room building was completed in September 1903.

School opened at what was named Epworth University in September 1904 with 27 instructors and 175 students, a number that grew quickly as Epworth opened a school of medicine and a college of law. Epworth survived the Panic of 1907, but it could not survive the withdrawal of support by one branch of the Methodist Church. The doors closed in 1911 at the end of the spring semester. That fall an institution name Methodist University of Oklahoma opened in Guthrie, and there it would remain until 1919 when for financial reasons it was closed.

That same year, 1911, Oklahoma Methodists opened Oklahoma City College in temporary quarters. Eventually the trustees acquired a site at Northwest 23rd Street and Blackwelder, and there they began building a permanent institution of brick and stone—as well as a dedicated faculty and student body. During the postwar era the campus expanded, as did the class offerings with degrees in liberal arts, fine arts, law, and business. Especially noteworthy would be the law school, the business school, and the music department.

A second college in the Oklahoma City area likewise had a religious affiliation. Shortly after statehood the El Reno Interurban Railway Company was laying tracks west from Oklahoma City. To encourage the growth of population and business along its right of way, the firm offered 10 acres to the Church of the Nazarene, which had announced that it was looking for a site for a school. The church accepted the offer, and in the vicinity of the school the town of Bethany was platted. During the fall of 1909 the first building was completed at what was called Oklahoma Holiness College. In the 1920s the Peniel Nazarene College of Texas merged with Holiness College, and

the name was changed to Bethany Nazarene College. Located on what now is Northwest 39th Street, Bethany Nazarene College grew rapidly in enrollment after World War II, and new buildings were erected. Today it offers bachelor's degrees in religion, liberal arts, education, and business.

During the postwar prosperity and growth in Oklahoma City, several other private schools of post-secondary learning were established. Southwestern Bible College was founded in 1947 by the Pentecostal Holiness Church, and Midwest Christian College was established in 1946 at the corner of Northeast 63rd and Kelley; it grants a bachelor's degree in religion. Then in 1957 Oklahoma Christian College, affiliated with the Church of Christ when it was established seven years earlier, moved from Bartlesville to Oklahoma City. Situated on a 200-acre site on the north side of Oklahoma City and adjacent to Edmond, Oklahoma Christian College has attracted major endowment funds and has grown to a handsome campus of more than 30 buildings and an enrollment of some 2,000 students. It has become known nationwide for its commitment to free enterprise and for its pioneering work in the area of electronic media in teaching.

During the first years after the run, many of the teachers in the Oklahoma City public school system were trained at the Territorial Normal School, which was created by the first ter-

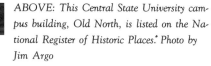

ABOVE: *This Central State University campus building, Old North, is listed on the National Register of Historic Places.* Photo by Jim Argo

TOP RIGHT: *Chrysanthemums bloom each spring on the south oval at the University of Oklahoma.* Photo by Jim Argo

ritorial legislature on December 24, 1890. The legislature provided that the institution was to be located at Edmond, just north of Oklahoma City, provided that Oklahoma County donate $5,000 in bonds; that Edmond donate 40 acres of land within one mile of town; that the land, except for 10 acres for the campus, be divided into lots; and that these lots be sold with the proceeds used to benefit the institution. These conditions were promptly met—and even exceeded by $2,000 in additional bond money.

Classes began at the Normal School on November 9, 1891, with 23 students meeting in the Epworth League room of the unfurnished building of the First Methodist Church, on the southwest corner of Broadway and Hurd. The school opened more than a month before any other public institution of higher learning, making this the oldest public college in Oklahoma.

Oklahoma City pioneer Anton Classen volunteered to donate the required 40 acres just northeast of downtown Edmond, an offer that was accepted by the Normal School Commission. Plans were drawn by an architect for a three-story building with a central section, two wings, and a bell tower. On January 3, 1893, the 3 instructors and 80 students of the Normal School moved into the structure, which became known as Old North

Tower. Subsequent appropriations by the territorial legislature allowed expansion of this building. By 1898 it had 15 classrooms and an auditorium that could seat 500. At statehood in 1907 this two-year teacher-training institution had an enrollment of 600—a figure that included those enrolled in its preparatory (high) school. A preparatory school was considered necessary to the survival of the college, for few students seeking teaching credentials were high school graduates. In short, Central Norman had to educate those seeking enrollment so they could qualify as freshmen.

In 1919 the State Board of Education changed the name of the institution to Central State Teachers College and authorized it to begin a four-year curriculum that would lead to a baccalaureate degree in education. This caused the student population to swell to 2,500 by 1923. In 1939 the legislature changed the name of the institution to Central State College and authorized it to offer degrees without teaching certificates. In the boom that followed World War II, Central State College emerged as a comprehensive college with offerings in business and the liberal arts as well as education, and then in 1954 it began offering graduate work to those needing advanced de-

En route to class, these students discuss an upcoming exam. Photo by Matt Bradley

grees. In 1971 the legislature recognized the changed nature of the institution and renamed it Central State University. As it approached its centennial, the university could boast an enrollment approaching 15,000 students studying in dozens of fields, some of them unique to this institution, on its 200-acre campus.

Central State University was not the first institution of higher learning created by the first territorial legislature. That honor belonged to the University of Oklahoma, which dates from December 19, 1890. Its purpose, according to the statute creating it, was "to provide the means of acquiring a thorough knowledge of the various branches of learning connected with scientific, industrial, and professional pursuits." The legislature stipulated that the university would be located in Norman, provided local citizens donated 40 acres within half a mile of the town.

Classes began in a rented rock building on Norman's Main Street with 119 students and 4 professors, including Dr. David Ross Boyd, the president, who was employed at a salary of $2,400 a year. To comply with the legislature's mandate regarding the financial contribution necessary from townspeople, local citizens raised $10,000. A 40-acre tract half a mile south of town was purchased for $1,500, and the remaining funds were used to construct the first building on campus. The first graduating class came in 1896 when two students received degrees in pharmaceutical chemistry. Two years later the first degrees in the area of liberal arts were awarded, and the first graduate degree was conferred in 1900.

Today the University of Oklahoma, after conferring more than 150,000 degrees in almost all fields of human knowledge, is a comprehensive institution of higher learning. It is recognized worldwide for its efforts in the area of energy, especially in geology and petroleum-related fields. The university campus in Norman covers more than 1,000 acres and its many buildings are valued in the hundreds of millions of dollars, while the Health Sciences Center and medical school in Oklahoma City, the dental college in Oklahoma City, and a college of medicine in Tulsa add to its size. More than 20,000 students are enrolled on its main campus.

The University of Oklahoma, in Norman, occupies more than 1,000 acres of land. Photo by Matt Bradley

Very few Oklahomans dreamed of going to a college or university during the territorial period and the early years of statehood. In fact, most never finished high school. Those who wished to better themselves often turned instead to one of the private business colleges, such as Hills Business College, which were established in Oklahoma City. For a fee, these trained ambitious young women in the arts of typing and secretarial skills, while young men learned bookkeeping, the use of business machines, or even secretarial skills in that era when many business executives still preferred male secretaries.

The good results achieved by those completing a course of study at a business college were attested by pioneers such as Clarence E. Page. Late in life he told how, after dropping out of high school in 1915, he enrolled at Draughton's Business College for a six-month course in bookkeeping. The owner, whom Page remembered as "Mr. Flannery," thought he was qualified to go to work after he had been studying for just three months and sent him to interview with the Oklahoma Refining Company. He immediately started at a salary of $65 a month, a tremendous sum for an 18-year-old youngster. Such examples led to the founding of yet other business schools and a flood of students taking their courses of study. In 1923 the city had four business colleges training more than 2,000 students. Business colleges would survive into the 1980s, but at a much-reduced level because of the competition they began to receive from an unexpected source.

Congress in 1917 passed the Smith-Hughes Act, which appropriated federal funds for what eventually became known as vocational education—industrial, home economics, and agricultural courses. For almost 50 years under the terms of the Smith-Hughes Act, vocational education was taught in Oklahoma City high schools and across the state. This consisted of trade and industrial subjects, such as carpentry, auto and aircraft mechanics, drafting, printing, electronics, and even training in firefighting and law enforcement. The programs were funded in part by the federal government and in part by state and local tax dollars, an expense that Oklahomans thought a wise investment in the future of their young people.

Then came passage in 1963 of the Vocational Education Act, which provided federal funding for area vocational-technical (vo-tech) schools. This called for the construction of separate school facilities where high school students and adults could take courses in traditional business college areas such as accounting, bookkeeping, typing, and secretarial skills, but also in new fields such as word processing, data processing, computer programming, and a host of new skill areas related to the electronic revolution of the 1980s. In just a few months a student can learn a skill that will bring employment at good wages. Oklahoma City is home to several of the state's best vo-tech schools.

The year 1961 brought the opening of yet another public institution offering technical and vocational training. Okla-

It's time to hit the books! Photo by Matt Bradley

homa State University Technical Institute opened in an abandoned public school building, with both day and evening courses of study that would lead to a junior college degree. Students could also merely take those courses they needed to learn a new skill or improve the skills they already had. So popular was OSU Tech, as the school was called, that in 1971 it moved to a new 60-acre campus on North Portland Avenue.

By the 1960s most Oklahomans believed they had a right to education beyond the high school level, more even than that offered in vo-tech schools, and they wanted easy access to such post-secondary education. The result was the creation of a number of municipal junior colleges, supported in part by tuition and in part by local taxes. When such support proved inadequate, the advocates of these schools began clamoring for the state to establish a system of publicly supported junior colleges. The result was the passage in 1968 of legislation calling for the creation of a system of community colleges.

Under the terms of this legislation, Oscar Rose Junior College was authorized in 1968; it was to be located in Midwest City, a suburb on the east side of Oklahoma City. Then in 1971 came authorization for South Oklahoma City Junior College. Both Oscar Rose, whose name subsequently was changed to Rose State College, and South Oklahoma City Junior College offer several types of programs. Two-year programs, complete with the junior college associate in arts degree, are available for those wishing to transfer to universities and complete a bachelor's degree there. There are also programs of shorter duration that carry college credits and lead to certification in many spe-

These students are the future leaders of Oklahoma. Photo by Jim Argo

cialties, such as cosmetology, the repair of air conditioning and heating equipment, television and radio repair, and numerous other specialties. Finally, there are noncredit courses of varying lengths in subjects of interest to the general public; most of these courses are offered in the evenings or on weekends and are designed for self-help or self-enrichment, courses such as aerobics, foreign languages, self-defense, or familiarization with basic automobile repair.

Overseeing the entire scope of higher education in Oklahoma is the state system of higher education and its board of regents. This system was mandated by a constitutional amendment passed in 1941 stipulating that all institutions of higher learning "supported wholly or in part by direct legislative appropriations" are part of "a unified system." It is the task of the chancellor and regents to avoid costly duplication and to coordinate degree programs. The State Regents for Higher Education maintain offices in Oklahoma City, and from this comes the leadership that keeps the entire system in harmony and operating at peak efficiency.

Oklahoma City and its suburbs thus are providing educational leadership for the entire state, both in the field of public schools and at the college and university level.

Oklahoma! *was presented by the Lyric Theatre in June 1988. Photo by Jim Argo*

Chapter Six

Bandstands to Ballet

Ask on the streets of New York about the image that Oklahoma City conjures up and you get a variety of responses, from cowboys and Indians to the musical *Oklahoma!* and Sooner football. True, the frontier legacy is still part of the city's collective personality, and football may reign supreme each fall, but life in Oklahoma City has always offered a rich tapestry of opportunities, especially in the worlds of entertainment and cultural pursuits.

The people who made the run of 1889 brought with them a keen interest in entertainment and community fun. While the tent town still looked like a "handful of white dice thrown across the prairie," in the eyes of one pioneer, community leaders organized a Fourth of July celebration with horse races, foot races, dances, and picnics.

Typical of the frontier hunger for entertainment, city father Henry Overholser proclaimed that "every town needs schools, churches, hotels and a theater. I'll build the hotel and theater." By September 1890 the Overholser

ABOVE AND RIGHT: *Children of all ages attend the annual Fourth of July parade in Edmond. Photos by Jim Argo*

Opera House was booking acts from local theatrical productions to traveling minstrel groups.

The streetcar system, installed in 1903, radically altered the development of Oklahoma City and opened new opportunities for recreation and entertainment. The streetcar offered access to two parks, the smaller of which was Wheeler Park, located directly south of the city on the banks of the river. The site consisted of 44 acres of grass and timber, a picnic area, and the city's first zoo.

The other new entertainment center was Delmar Gardens, a 140-acre amusement park located farther west and north on the river just beyond Western Avenue and south of Reno. The land was owned by Charles Colcord, while the concessions and amusements were operated by John Sinopoulo and Joseph Marre, who had worked at Delmar Gardens in St. Louis. Featured attractions at the park included a 1,200-seat theater, a scenic railway, a dance hall, a hotel, a restaurant, a swimming pool, and an outdoor refreshment and picnic area. Other than general recreation, visitors to the park attended car races, horse races, dramatic presentations, and vaudeville.

Responding to the surge in population between 1900 and 1910, other entertainment centers were opened. Belle Isle Park, located five miles from downtown at the head of the Classen trolley line, was a popular spot for swimming, boating, and picnicking. The State Fair of Oklahoma, created in 1907, was originally located on 160 acres of school land near Northeast 10th Street and Eastern Avenue. Then, in 1909 the city purchased right-of-way and created the Grand Boulevard, a "motor race-

This modern-day Betsy Ross was sighted at a flag ceremony in Edmond. Photo by Jim Argo

way" and touring road around the entire community that connected four large parks.

The largest of these was Northeast Park, which was improved with an unpaved road and a dam that created Northeast Lake for swimming and boating. In 1923, after flooding of the North Canadian River severely damaged Wheeler Park, the city moved the zoo to scenic Northeast Park. Eventually renamed Lincoln Park Zoo, the animal preserve became a major Works Progress Administration project during the 1930s and an internationally recognized zoological center by the 1980s.

Amusement parks, zoos, and swimming pools may have been popular at the turn of the century, but for explosive popularity the brightest new entry into the world of entertainment was the motion picture. The first silent pictures were shown in multipurpose theaters such as the Overholser Opera House, which had been rebuilt on a grand scale in 1903. Until World War I motion pictures shared equal billing with vaudeville acts and other live entertainment at theaters such as the Liberty, the Lyric, the Empress, the Folly, and the Palace.

During the 1920s the growing demand for motion pictures

BELOW: Goofy is one highlight of the Walt Disney Parade in downtown Oklahoma City. Photo by Jim Argo

ABOVE: "Oklahoma City is OK with me!" Photo by Matt Bradley

TOP: Fun rides are found in Frontier City. Photo by Matt Bradley

RIGHT: Fairgoers enjoy the Ferris wheel at the Oklahoma State Fair in Oklahoma City. Photo by Jim Argo

FACING PAGE: Fourth of July fireworks are held annually at the 89er Baseball Stadium. Photo by Jim Argo

was met with several "grand movie palaces" such as the Midwest, with its starlit ceiling and Moorish interior, and the Victoria, the first suburban theater on Classen Boulevard. The ultimate showplace, however, was the Criterion Theatre, located on Main Street between Robinson and Broadway.

The Criterion was constructed in 1921, a five-story building that cost $700,000. The facade was an intriguing mixture of neoclassical symmetry, Mediterranean details, and stained-glass panels. Inside, every comfort was provided, from smoking rooms and child care to chilled air and a tearoom. An evening at the Criterion was more than simply watching a movie; it was an experience in total entertainment.

As the Criterion was being built, yet another form of entertainment was offered to the people of Oklahoma City—radio. In 1921 radio pioneers Earl Hull and H.S. Richards received a radio license, the 11th in the nation and the first west of the Mississippi River. Their 20-watt station, located in Richards' garage, was given the call letters WKY.

Early programs consisted of weather reports, sports, news, and recorded music played on a Victrola. Every evening at 8:15 a special program was offered over the airwaves with popular guests such as the Bird-Six Piece Jazz Orchestra, the Deep River Orchestra, and local groups.

The station grew steadily in power and programming until 1928, when it was purchased by E.K. Gaylord and the Oklahoma Publishing Company. Gaylord bought new RCA equipment, moved the station to the new Plaza Court, and improved the quality and quantity of broadcasts.

In December 1922 the second station in Oklahoma City went on the air. KFJF, later renamed KOMA, began broadcasting with a 20-watt transmitter, but increased to 1,000 watts in 1927. Other early stations included what would become WNAD, started in Norman in 1921; KOCY, a church station that went on the air in 1925; and KTOK, which started broadcasting in 1927. By the 1980s more than 30 stations filled the airwaves of Oklahoma City.

An even more popular medium of entertainment and information was television. E.K. Gaylord, who owned WKY Radio, had established ties with RCA, the parent company of NBC and the industry leader in television broadcasting and equipment. In October 1948 WKY received the first shipment of equipment and set up a small studio in the Little Theatre at the Municipal Auditorium. On June 6, 1949, WKY-TV made its formal debut, broadcasting locally produced programs for the estimated 3,300 sets in the city.

BELOW: Summer concerts are commonplace in Oklahoma City. Here, a Country and Western singer is featured. Photo by Jim Argo

FACING PAGE: Youths of Oklahoma revelled at this "Beach Party '88." Photo by Matt Bradley

As more sets were purchased and the market expanded, WKY-TV increased its programming. In 1950 they went to seven days a week, with about 40 hours of on-air time. In 1951, its success assured, WKY-TV moved to new studios on North Britton Road and completed a cable hook-up with NBC network for live broadcasts direct from New York.

On December 20, 1953, the second television station in Oklahoma City, KWTV, went on the air from temporary studios at KOMA. Four months later the CBS affiliate broke ground for a new studio on North Kelley that included a 1,572-foot tower, the tallest structure in the world at that time. On October 16, 1954, the first regularly scheduled programming was transmitted from the new facility.

The third network affiliate in Oklahoma City was KOCO-TV, which began as a station in Enid in 1954 under the FCC's efforts to decentralize television broadcasting across the country. By 1958 the station had moved to Oklahoma City with studios in a converted grocery store in the suburban town of Britton. A year later the ABC affiliate moved to studios at 63rd and Portland. By the 1980s Oklahoma City had an extensive cable-television network, a statewide OETA educational station, and newer stations such as KGMC, KOKH, and KTBO.

Television made stars of entertainers such as Milton Berle, Sid Caesar, and Dinah Shore, but to many Oklahomans the most important stars were local men and women who provided live programming from Oklahoma City. The baby boomers grew up watching Steve Powell as Foreman Scotty and Ed Birchall as Ho Ho, while adults tuned in to shows hosted by Tom Paxton, Danny Williams, and Ida "B" Blackburn. These people established a strong and progressive television market in Oklahoma City and added a regional flavor to broadcasting.

Whereas radio and television transformed the world of entertainment gradually over a number of years, the history of Oklahoma City's cultural life changed much more suddenly. The turning point was 1937, the year when the Oklahoma City Symphony Orchestra was organized; the Public Works Administration (PWA) sponsored art, theater, and writers' projects;

ABOVE AND TOP: "Down on Second Street," held in May of 1988, was the fifth annual Charlie Christian Jazz Festival. Photos by Jim Argo

FACING PAGE: Red Earth, the world's largest Native American celebration, which includes over 100 sovereign Indian nations, gathered in downtown Oklahoma City in June, 1988. Photo by Jim Argo

ABOVE: *Each December in Guthrie, Oklahoma, local residents celebrate a Victorian Christmas. Photo by Jim Argo*

TOP: *The Oklahoma Historical Society Museum, founded in 1893, is located in the Wiley Post Historical Building, Oklahoma City. Photo by Jim Argo*

FACING PAGE: *The mansion of the governor of Oklahoma is open for tours one day a week. Photo by Jim Argo*

LEFT: *The Overholser mansion, located in the Heritage Hills section of Oklahoma City, is the property of the Oklahoma Historical Society. Photo by Jim Argo*

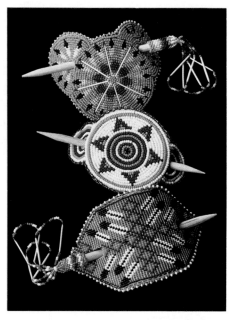

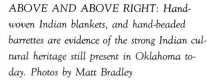
ABOVE AND ABOVE RIGHT: Hand-woven Indian blankets, and hand-beaded barrettes are evidence of the strong Indian cultural heritage still present in Oklahoma today. Photos by Matt Bradley

and local promoters booked six Broadway shows, international opera stars, and a host of popular performers. But of all the good news, all the dramatic headlines during that important year, nothing had a greater impact on the city's cultural life than the opening of the Municipal Auditorium.

The Municipal Auditorium was part of the civic center complex, a massive PWA project made possible by a $1.8-million bond issue and 45 percent funding through the federal government. Designed by J.O. Parr, the auditorium was six stories tall, with an exterior that was considered "modified classic." Like many other New Deal-era public buildings, the design was a subtle mixture of neoclassical and Art Deco features. Inside there was a large hall with seating for 6,200; a little theater with seating for 400; and several convention halls, conference rooms, and galleries.

The original objective of the design, according to Parr, was to provide a building that "could accommodate the various activities of a growing metropolitan city." Prior to that time, staged events were limited to facilities such as the Overholser Opera House or the India Temple Shrine Auditorium, which prevented booking big-name acts. With the seating capacity and elegance of the Municipal Auditorium, promoters quickly booked six Broadway productions, including *Tovarich* with Eugenie Leontovich; several opera performances, including Nino Martini of the Metropolitan Opera; and other productions featuring stars such as Lily Pons and Helen Hayes.

For the next 50 years the Municipal Auditorium helped lure

LEFT: *Western saddles and reins abound! Photo by Matt Bradley*

BELOW: *Western flavor is evident every-where in Oklahoma City. Photo by Matt Bradley*

117

Oklahoma City is the location of the National Cowboy Hall of Fame and Western Heritage Center. Photo by Jim Argo

the cream of cultural entertainment to Oklahoma City. In 1946 the musical *Oklahoma!* set a record with sales of 54,000 tickets; during the 1950s the Metropolitan Opera of New York established a regular series there; and the Ballet Russe de Monte Carlo made Oklahoma City a regular stop on its tours. More recently, stars from Carol Channing and Placido Domingo to Itzhak Perlman and Mikhail Baryshnikov have graced the stage at the renamed Civic Center Music Hall.

The Municipal Auditorium may have been an important outgrowth of the New Deal programs, but the cultural experiments of the 1930s went far beyond bricks and mortar. The Works Progress Administration established the WPA Theater Project in 1935. Supervisors searched the city for unemployed actors, then held rehearsals at 21 West Main. The troupes staged dramas, comedies, and musicals at a variety of locations and even performed on radio.

A similar contribution was made by the WPA Writers' Proj-

ect, which put unemployed playwrights, poets, and historians to work. The WPA Art Project, organized by longtime patron Nan Sheets in 1935, provided art instruction, sponsored shows, and established a permanent collection of art at the Municipal Auditorium.

Another WPA project that had a long-term impact was the music project, which organized Oklahoma City's Federal Symphony Orchestra in 1937. For the next five years the orchestra performed formal concerts at the Municipal Auditorium, "starlight" concerts at Taft Stadium, and "runouts" at small towns throughout the state. In 1942, when federal aid was withdrawn, local sponsors, led by Mrs. Merle Buttram, stepped in and secured the future of the Oklahoma City Symphony Orchestra.

Symphonic music was important to the people of Oklahoma City, but it shared center stage with a wide variety of sounds, from opera and jazz to rock and country. Oklahoma City had a band and even a small orchestra as early as 1890. From the

The Oklahoma State Firefighters Association Museum was built in 1969. Photo by Matt Bradley

1890s to the 1920s promoter Hathaway Harper booked popular singers such as Ellen Beach Yau and Madame Nordica, and others brought in bands and performers for a variety of entertainments.

Several well-known bands were based in Oklahoma City, including Clarence Tackett's Toe Teasers, the Bonnie Spencer Orchestra, and the regionally famous Blue Devils. The black community provided the stage for several jazz innovators, particularly Charles Christian, known in music circles as the "greatest of the jazz guitarists" who played with Benny Goodman and Lionel Hampton before his death at age 24. Playing at hot spots such as the Goody-Goody Cafe on California Avenue and Ruby's Grill on East 2nd, black musicians from Oklahoma City made important contributions to the development of popular music.

Whether it was art, music, or theater, the people of Oklahoma City proved time and again that they would support cultural endeavors. Nowhere has this commitment been more clearly demonstrated than through the variety and quality of museums in the community.

The first major museum in Oklahoma City was sponsored by the Oklahoma Historical Society, a private-membership organization and state agency that had been organized in 1893. In 1930 the society moved into its first permanent home on Lincoln Boulevard, where the staff developed exhibits and continued collecting artifacts. By the 1980s the State Museum of History offered new insights into the "Oklahoma experience" with galleries and exhibits on Indians, the land openings, art, transportation, military history, and the twentieth century.

In 1937 Nan Sheets, through the WPA Art Project, organized the city's first public museum dedicated to art. Located in the Municipal Auditorium, it consisted of five rooms, each 20 by 50 feet, providing public space for traveling exhibits and the permanent collection of 40 paintings, etchings, and lithographs that had been collected by the Art League since 1910. In 1958 the collection was moved to the new fairgrounds west of town and renamed the Oklahoma Art Center.

Another major art collection had its beginning in 1955 when

LEFT: A former armory, this building is now the home of the 45th Infantry Division Museum. Photo by Matt Bradley

BELOW: Don Fairchild poses with his Juke Box Hall of Fame. Photo by Jim Argo

17 western states voted to place the National Cowboy Hall of Fame in Oklahoma City. Ground on Persimmon Hill was broken in 1958, and after several delays were overcome, the unique museum opened in 1965. By the 1980s the National Cowboy Hall of Fame and Western Heritage Center had established an international reputation as a major center for the preservation and presentation of Western art and culture.

Perhaps inspired by that success, the community dedicated even more support for museums. The Oklahoma Firefighters Museum was built in Lincoln Park near the zoo in 1969, followed four years later by the National Softball Hall of Fame across the street. In 1971, under the direction of Stanley Draper, the Oklahoma Hall of Fame was renamed the Oklahoma Heritage Association and moved into the Hefner Mansion at 14th and North Robinson. The stately home is maintained as a museum and open to the public.

Other museums founded or expanded during this era included the Oklahoma Museum of Art, which moved into the Nichols Hills mansion of Frank Buttram in 1975; the 45th Division Museum, which opened in a former armory on Northeast

36th in 1976; the Overholser Mansion, a stately 1902-era Victorian mansion purchased by the Oklahoma Historical Society in 1971 and opened to the public in 1982; and Enterprise Square, U.S.A., a museum dedicated to the understanding of the free enterprise system, built on the campus of Oklahoma Christian College in 1982.

In 1978 the largest museum complex in the city, the Kirkpatrick Center, was opened near Northeast 50th and Martin Luther King Avenue. After a major expansion in 1983 the massive structure offers 352,000 square feet of gallery and storage space to several independent museums.

First to open was the Omniplex Science Museum, which incorporated the Kirkpatrick Planetarium. Then came the Center for the American Indian, the Aviation and Space Hall of Fame and Museum, the International Photography Hall of Fame and Museum, the Kirkpatrick Gardens, and the Green Arcade. By the late 1980s the entire complex included 17 galleries, a museum store, and an active educational outreach program.

If a community is judged by its support for the performing arts, the visual arts, and museums, then surely Oklahoma City takes its place among first-class cities. And if a community is judged on its variety of entertainment and amusements, again, Oklahoma City is out front. From amusement parks such as Frontier City and Whitewater to cultural institutions such as the Symphony Orchestra and Ballet Oklahoma, the entertainment and cultural opportunities in Oklahoma City contribute much to the quality of life in the city.

ABOVE: "Kidspace" is revered inside the Kirkpatrick Center. Photo by Jim Argo

BOTTOM: This astronaut in outer space is one display at the Air and Space Museum inside the Kirkpatrick Center. Photo by Matt Bradley

Football is a popular sport at the University of Oklahoma. Photo by Jim Argo

Chapter Seven

Spectators and Sports

When the first cool winds of autumn blow down across the plains and reach Oklahoma City, they bring a chill that begins to paint the leaves with shades of red, gold, and brown. Yet it is not this riot of color that constitutes autumnal splendor for most residents of the city. Rather than driving about the countryside to view fall foliage, Oklahomans turn their eyes 20 miles south of the city, to the suburb of Norman, where early September brings the first game of the season for "The Big Red Machine"—the football team of the University of Oklahoma.

As the annual football madness sets in, it brings out frenzied chants of "Go Sooners," red shirts and caps emblazoned with the "OU" logo, and a frantic bidding for season tickets, preferably between the 40-yard lines at Owens Field. However, this OU football frenzy has existed for only slightly more than four decades. Prior to World War II, football fever did not come in such virulent form. From the time of the run until the

This Sooner quarterback opts for a running attack. Photo by Jim Argo

mid-1940s, a crowd of 2,500 in Norman was considered large. Most Oklahomans thought autumn's mightiest legions were high school boys fighting on the gridiron for city honors.

The first football game on record in Oklahoma City was played on November 29, 1894 between a team organized at the high school, known as the "Boomers," and a team composed of town residents who previously had played the game and who called themselves the "Terrors." The high school boys won by a score of 24-0, playing before what was described as a large crowd. The following year the Oklahoma City High School gridiron legion defeated a team put together at the University of Oklahoma; the final score was 34-0. In the years that followed, football slowly attracted a small, enthusiastic following as the Oklahoma City High School team scheduled games with teams from surrounding towns.

As Oklahoma City grew and new high schools were built within its borders, crosstown rivalries became intense, and teams of astonishing excellence were produced. In 1933 the Capitol Hill High School Redskins were proclaimed the champions of the United States after they won 12 straight games, including a 55-12 post-season victory over Harrison Tech, the city champions of Chicago. Most of these early games were played at the Western League baseball stadium on Exchange Avenue. To get a football facility with a large seating capacity for high school sporting events, the Junior Chamber of Commerce began a fundraising campaign. When the Jaycees had collected 10 percent of the estimated cost of the facility, the Works Progress Administration (WPA) funded the remaining 90 percent, and Taft Stadium at Northwest 25th and May Avenue became a reality in 1937. In addition to serving area high schools, Taft became the site of college and professional football games.

College football came to Oklahoma City in the fall of 1921 when a team nicknamed the "Goldbugs" was organized at Oklahoma City College. Although there were only enough players to make one squad, the Goldbugs played a close game against the Bisons of Oklahoma Baptist University at the Western League Baseball Park. During the next 15 years the Goldbugs would win 72 games, lose 66, and tie 9. The glory era for the Goldbugs began in 1928 when Vivian "Vee" Green arrived as coach. His teams won 30 of their first 38 games, including a perfect season in 1931, and they attracted large, enthusiastic crowds. However, the college ceased to sponsor football during World War II.

The Sooner Schooner entertains the crowd at halftime. Photo by Jim Argo

Another institution of higher learning with a football team in the Oklahoma City area was Central State Normal College, eventually to become Central State University. Located in Edmond, a suburb on the north side of Oklahoma City, this institution began early to field a varsity 11 that competed against teams from colleges in Oklahoma and surrounding states. However, despite attracting some outstanding players and even winning the national championship in their class, the Central State "Broncos" have never been able to attract large crowds, nor to win the allegiance of Oklahoma City fans. The University's stadium would remain small and its athletes free from any taint of re-

cruiting violations as the team continued a tradition of quiet excellence. Several of its players have graduated to renown in professional ranks.

It was the success of the Oklahoma City College Goldbug team of 1931 that led to the formation of Oklahoma City's first professional football team. In 1932, after many of the members of that great team had graduated, they formed the Oklahoma City Indians. The team also included a professional baseball player, a former football player from the University of Oklahoma City, a pro wrestler, and several other great athletes. Under the direction of Wes Fry, the Indians won 8 of their 10 games in 1932—and the players made three dollars each per game. The Indians struggled through one more season before disbanding for financial reasons.

In 1966 and 1967 Tommy Pearson made an effort to organize a semiprofessional football team, the Plainsmen. At the heart of this group were former players from Capitol Hill High School. In 1968, affiliated with the Professional Football League of America, the Plainsmen played their home games at Taft Stadium, but financial problems plagued the effort. When the Plainsmen disbanded, some of the players joined in an attempt to form yet another local professional team, the Midwest City Falcons, but that effort lasted only a year. Then in 1973 came the formation of the Oklahoma City Wranglers, a team that played in the Southwest Professional League. This conference scheduled its games in the spring and summer so that it would not compete with high school and college games. Yet it too failed after slow ticket sales and labor disputes. A women's professional football team formed in the 1970s was no more able to attract a sufficient number of ticket buyers to succeed.

The only football team in the entire state of Oklahoma able to gain and hold the loyalty of fans and to attract crowds of 75,000 and more to every home game has been that of the University of Oklahoma. Regularly scheduled football games began at the university in 1897; the team joined the Southwest Conference, then moved to the Missouri Valley Conference, and finally in 1927 became part of what was then called the Big Six Conference (which eventually would become the Big Eight), consisting of the University of Oklahoma, Oklahoma State, Kansas State, University of Kansas, University of Missouri, University of Colorado, Iowa State, and University of Nebraska.

The goal of becoming a major football power was a decision made consciously at the University of Oklahoma in 1945. The president at that time, Dr. George Lynn Cross, later wrote that he and the regents felt the university should seek to build a winning football team in order to lift morale and bring pride to all Oklahomans. Coach Jim Tatum, hired to achieve this goal, stayed just one year, but with returning veterans forming the nucleus of his team, he took the Sooners to the Gator Bowl in Jacksonville. When he left to become head coach at the University of Maryland, the regents voted to hire Tatum's chief assistant, Charles "Bud" Wilkinson, as head coach.

When Wilkinson resigned as coach in 1964 after 17 seasons, he had accomplished everything the president and the regents of the university had hoped. His record was 145 wins, 20 losses, and 4 ties; he had taken the Sooners to 8 bowl games, of which he had won 6. His teams had set an all-time national record for consecutive wins—47—a record of such stunning proportions that most coaches say it will never be broken. During Wilkinson's 17 years as head coach, the Sooners had won 13 conference championships and had tied for a 14th. To contain the crowds that came to see their beloved Sooners play, the university had found it necessary to expand the stadium—and then to expand it again and again.

Wilkinson indeed had dispelled the image of "Poor Okies" given the state in John Steinbeck's novel *The Grapes of Wrath*. So great was the university's reputation in football that President George Lynn Cross, in asking the legislature for a larger appropriation for academic programs, jestingly commented in February 1950, "I would like to build a university of which the football team could be proud." After Bud Wilkinson left, the university was fortunate in eventually replacing him with another great coach who would continue the winning tradition, Chuck Fairbanks. When Fairbanks departed to coach a team in the National Football League, Barry Switzer became the head coach at the University of Oklahoma. In the decade and a half that followed, Switzer's winning percentage would be the highest of any coach at a major football power in the United States. Oklahoma was indeed a winner.

In the postwar years, attendance at University of Oklahoma home football games became a regular part of the social tradition of Oklahomans. By the 1950s it had become customary for groups to band together in order to lease a bus to make the trip to Norman in comfort and with ease. Such groups would leave their cars and board a bus at the Oklahoma City Country Club or downtown at one of the banks. During the trip to Norman they would sing and tell stories, and afterward there would be parties to celebrate yet another victory.

A major focus of the football tradition at the University of Oklahoma has been the annual contest against the University of Texas, played each year for many decades at the Cotton Bowl in Dallas. For these games groups would likewise lease buses for the trip south, usually leaving on Thursday and coming back on Sunday. In Dallas there would be a round of parties at the downtown hotels where they stayed, and when the Sooners won, the celebrating would continue during the return trip. Sometimes there was celebrating even when the Sooners lost, for just to be at the game somehow seemed a victory of sorts.

In the early years in Oklahoma City baseball overshadowed football. Just days after the run of 1889, a baseball field was "constructed" just outside the original city limits. The stands were crude, constructed of beer kegs and two-by-twelves, but fans swarmed to see the three teams that had been organized play each other or out-of-town teams. The first successful professional baseball team in Oklahoma City was the Metropolitans, organized in 1904. That year they won the title in the Southwestern League, which comprised only Oklahoma teams. Then for five years the Mets, as they were called, played in the Western Association, a Class C professional league. Briefly the Mets were part of the Texas League, then fell back to the Western Association until they disbanded during World War I.

After the war the Oklahoma City Indians were formed as part of the newly organized Western League, which was

These amateur cyclists participate in the Sooner State Games. Photo by Jim Argo

Class A. Their games were played in Holland Stadium, located at Northwest 4th and Pennsylvania. In 1931 they became part of the Texas League, which was Class 2-A. This team, which did not play during World War II, was affiliated with the Cleveland Indians and was able to win the Texas League and the Dixie Series in 1935. On that team was Carl Hubbell, who would go on to fame in the National League. However, by the 1950s the Indians, like other minor-league teams, were having problems with attendance, and in 1958 the team disbanded.

Civic leaders in Oklahoma City wanted to continue an association with professional baseball, and in 1961 the city built a new stadium at the fairgrounds. In 1962 the 89ers were formed as a part of the Houston organization. They became part of the Triple-A Class Pacific Coast League, and in 1963 they won the pennant in that league. In 1970 the 89ers became part of the American Association, still at the Triple-A level, and switched to become once again part of the Cleveland Indians' organization. Still later they joined the Texas Ranger system. Many major-league players played in Oklahoma City just before moving up to the big leagues, and on occasion the 89ers

ABOVE AND FACING PAGE: This Aerospace America Air Show, held at Will Rogers World Airport, was sponsored by the Oklahoma City Chamber of Commerce in 1988. Photos by Jim Argo

play exhibition games against major-league clubs, thereby enabling Oklahomans to enjoy the thrill of eating ballpark hot dogs and booing the umpires as they watch live baseball of high caliber.

Games between the youngsters of Oklahoma City began on vacant lots in the early summer of 1889, but not until the 1920s was the Junior Baseball League organized. The games in this league were played at Rotary Park, named for the civic club which supported the organization. American Legion baseball came to Oklahoma City in the early 1930s, with teams supported by local merchants. Still other civic and charitable organizations began sponsoring baseball for youngsters. Eventually these leagues acquired land on which they built their own diamonds for play, many of them lighted, and they were used almost every night from spring to autumn.

Oklahoma City has been called the softball capital of the

nation because of the many people involved in playing this amateur sport. The sport began here in the mid-1930s, and soon there were numerous lighted playing fields located in all parts of the city. Teams were organized for men, women, boys, and girls. Eventually an Oklahoma City Amateur Softball Association was formed, which grew to claim many thousands of members and several hundred teams, some playing fast pitch and some slow pitch. The season begins on May 1 and lasts until Labor Day, with games every evening of the week. Because Oklahoma City is so active in this sport, it was chosen as the site for the National Softball Hall of Fame, which is housed in a building completed in 1973 in the Lincoln Park area on Northeast 36th Street.

Baseball was the spectator sport of choice for most Oklahomans prior to World War II, with football second—and gaining. Meanwhile, basketball had a slow beginning. Oklahoma City College took up the sport in 1920, but after the first 15 years it was played there, the record stood at 97 wins and 142 losses. However, the OCC women's team won the na-

The National Finals Rodeo was held in the Myriad Convention Center for years before relocating to Las Vegas. Photo by Jim Argo

tional championship in 1933 and was invited to play exhibition games at the Chicago World's Fair that year.

Basketball in Oklahoma City, and the entire state, received a great boost in 1936 when the Milk and Ice Fund of the Oklahoma Publishing Company sponsored an All-College Tournament to raise funds for its charitable work. That year 16 teams were invited, 12 of them from Oklahoma. Although that first effort lost money, the All-College Tournament proved popular with coaches, and in 1937 22 teams were invited to what then and thereafter proved to be a financial success.

When the Oklahoma Publishing Company dropped its Milk and Ice Fund in 1957, fans clamored for the tournament to continue. Therefore the Sports and Recreation Council of the Oklahoma City Chamber of Commerce formed the All Sports Association to continue sponsoring the tournament, as well as other sporting events in Oklahoma City. At first these contests were held in high school gymnasiums. Then in 1937, with completion of the PWA-sponsored Municipal Auditorium, the tournament shifted there to take advantage of its greater seating capacity. Next it moved to the State Fair Arena at the state fairgrounds, and then in 1972, with completion of the Myriad Convention Center in downtown Oklahoma City, the tournament was moved there. By the 1980s the All-College Tournament was still operated with four outstanding teams invited to participate.

Basketball also became popular with noncollegians in the 1920s, and in 1926 an amateur team was formed to play in the Missouri Valley AAU Basketball League. First sponsored by Sterling Milk Company, this team was active into the 1930s when gradually the concept of adult, company-sponsored teams began to wane.

Classen became the first high school to gain prominence in basketball. Under Coach Henry P. "Hank" Iba, Classen High's "Comets" won the state championship in 1929 and then was one of the 40 teams invited from across the country to the Stagg Invitational Tournament, a national high school play-off championship sponsored by the University of Chicago. Classen won second place in the tournament, thereby stimulating high school basketball in the Sooner State. Other high schools would take up the sport, and interscholastic league play would become a regular part of the athletic scene. High school girls likewise took up the sport, but with a slight variation; they had six players on a team, half of them playing at one end of the court on offense and the other three playing on the other half of the court on defense. This variation proved so popular that there would be a round of play-offs each year to determine a state champion in each class of play (determined by the size of the high school).

Yet other sports have come to Oklahoma City. In the mid-1930s the Oklahoma City Warriors were formed, a professional hockey team that played its games at the Stockyards Coliseum. The Warriors failed after two seasons, and professional hockey did not return for almost three decades. In 1965 the Oklahoma City Blazers, a farm club of the Boston Bruins, was formed to play in the Central Hockey League. The Blazers played their games at the All-Sports Arena at the fairgrounds and would draw more than a million fans in six years, but this still was not enough to make the Blazers a financial success, and the team was disbanded. Then in 1972, after the Myriad Convention Center opened, the Ontario team of the National Hockey League agreed to sponsor a team in Oklahoma City in the Central Hockey League. However, the sport of hockey has never attracted a wide following in Oklahoma City.

Residents of all ages find fun and frolic in Oklahoma City. Photo by Jim Argo

Rodeo came to Oklahoma City in the early 1900s when a contest was held at Colcord Baseball Park, and soon large prizes were being offered for riding and roping. The State Fair Rodeo was a major attraction each September, drawing the top riders and ropers from across the nation. With a public hungry for rodeo, the Chamber of Commerce recruited the National Finals Rodeo from San Francisco to Oklahoma City in 1965. Each year the top 15 cowboys and cowgirls in the 7 major rodeo events congregated in Oklahoma City, for 10 performances that culminated in the crowning of national champions. Until this event moved to Las Vegas in 1986, it annually attracted tens of thousands of avid rodeo fans to Oklahoma City.

Another sport which came early to Oklahoma City was golf. At a total cost of $15, a 9-hole course with sand greens was built at Northeast 12th and Stiles in the summer of 1900. A newspaper account indicated that the first course champion was Frank Butts, whose score was 53. The sport grew gradually, and by 1910 there were four courses in Oklahoma City. The following year the Oklahoma City Golf and Country Club was formed, and within a decade it had 840 members.

By 1928 the sport was so enthusiastically supported that the Professional Golfers' Association (the PGA) held a national tour event in Oklahoma City, but after two years the match died because of the hard times generated by the Depression. In the 1930s some national matches, such as the PGA National Championship Tournament in 1935, were held at the Twin Hills Golf and Country Club, and a national amateur contest was played there in 1934. Area golfing enthusiasts organized the Oklahoma City Golf Tournament in 1938, and it quickly grew into a major amateur event in the state. Other PGA matches came to the city in the 1950s and 1960s, while the national Amateur Championship Tournament of the U.S. Golf

BELOW AND FACING PAGE: Quail Creek Golf and Country Club is the location of the Silver Pages Golf Tournament, a tournament for senior professional golfers. Photos by Jim Argo

Association was held at the Oklahoma City Golf and Country Club in 1953. At a development in Edmond known as Quail Creek, two championship courses were built in the 1960s that enticed the PGA to hold one of its annual events there in the 1980s.

Tennis has also been popular in Oklahoma City. Courts were built in the first years of statehood. The best of these early facilities was a four-court complex near Classen and Western. A privately owned complex, it nevertheless was the site of several school tournaments and gave great encouragement to tennis at the high school level. In the 1920s and 1930s there were several great players at the University of Oklahoma and in Oklahoma City, who toured the country winning matches and bringing distinction to the city and state. Today there are lighted tennis courts in all parts of the city.

Bowling came to Oklahoma City in 1901 when an alley was opened in a tent near the downtown area. As the sport gained in popularity, other alleys were opened in the downtown area, and local youngsters earned money by setting pins. In 1933 the Oklahoma City Men's Singles Classic was organized, and a bowling craze swept Oklahoma. Bowlers from across the state converged on Oklahoma City in 1937 when the Municipal Marble Tournament was held. In the postwar era, with the move to the suburbs, the downtown alleys closed. They were replaced with large alleys in residential areas, each featuring the latest automatic equipment, the best hardwood lanes, and large parking facilities. In 1976 the American Bowling Congress held its annual tournament in Oklahoma City, setting up its own specially constructed lanes and automated equipment in the Myriad Convention Center and attracting 80,000 bowlers to what proved to be a three-month event.

Yet another minor sport in Oklahoma City has been drag-racing. When this sport first became popular in the early 1950s, some enthusiasts raced their vehicles on city streets because there seemed to be no other place for them. To halt such dangerous activity, the Junior Chamber of Commerce in 1956 built a first-class drag-race strip at the fairgrounds, and regular racing

began there on Sunday afternoons. In 1957 the national hot-rod championship races were held at the fairgrounds on Labor Day.

Fishing was a sport that gave relaxation to many pioneer residents of Oklahoma City—and put food on the tables of some of them. As the population of the city swelled, however, fishing holes were drained and streams dried up as the water table dropped. In 1917-1918 came the damming of the city's first municipal reservoir, Lake Overholser; when it filled its 1,700-acre capacity, it became a place for fishing and boating. Another reservoir was built on Bluff Creek. After completion in 1943, this structure was renamed Lake Hefner. Then in 1964 came completion of Stanley Draper Lake, Lake Thunderbird was constructed on the east side of Norman, and in the 1980s Arcadia Lake opened on Oklahoma City's northeast side.

ABOVE: Skydivers jump near Norman. Photo by Jim Argo

FACING PAGE: Ballooning in Oklahoma City is an uplifting experience! Photo by Jim Argo

These man-made reservoirs have become the scene of many aquatic sports, including fishing and boating. Every weekend during summer months, sailboats are impressive as their colorful sails catch Oklahoma City's notorious winds and thrust white craft across the blue surface. And dozens of water-skiers leave a white wake behind them on every lake.

A sport that is unknown in the Sooner State today was popular in Oklahoma City during the territorial years. Dog racing drew crowds as large as 5,000 or more to some races. Greyhounds were pitted against each other in contests held north of Council Grove. In 1903 the National Coursing Association held its annual Waterloo Cup meet in Oklahoma City, bringing enthusiasts from across the nation to watch 250 dogs in national competition. With the coming of statehood and laws against gambling, the running of dogs ceased.

The other major sport at which large-scale betting took place

ABOVE: Lake Hefner is a popular location for wind-surfing enthusiasts. Photo by Jim Argo

RIGHT: Another day draws to a close at this local marina. Photo by Matt Bradley

in territorial days was horse racing. Many of those who dashed for land in 1889 did so on the back of a favorite horse, and arguments about who had the best animal often led to races on which large sums were staked. In 1893 a horse race was a featured part of the territorial fair, the race taking place at the fairgrounds. When Kramer track was built in the city, it was described by a newspaper as the best racing course in the territory. In 1900 a reunion of Teddy Roosevelt's Rough Riders, nationally famous for their part in the Spanish-American War, was held at Kramer Park, and in 1903

ABOVE: Speed boats race at Lake Over-holser. Photo by Jim Argo

BELOW: Pam Waterman congratulates her World Champion Appaloosa. Photo by Jim Argo

FACING PAGE: Oklahoma City is a major host city for quarter horse, Arabian, and Morgan horse shows and competitions. Photo by Jim Argo

a harness race was held there.

With the coming of statehood and subsequent legislation, however, gambling and pari-mutuel wagering became illegal. Horse and dog tracks closed. Because of the ranching tradition in Oklahoma, many fine animals, both thoroughbreds and quarter horses, continued to be raised in the Sooner State. Those who raised these animals were proud of them, and horse shows and sales became a regular feature at various places in Oklahoma City. For example, the National Championship Arabian Horse Show became an annual event at the Oklahoma State Fairgrounds in 1969.

Then in 1982 the voters of the State of Oklahoma approved

pari-mutuel gambling on horse racing. After a state racing commission was named, approval was granted for the construction of a $90-million track in Oklahoma City, to be known as Remington Park. Opened in 1988, this is one of the finest racing facilities in the nation, and it immediately began attracting some of the finest horses in America to compete there. Once again Oklahomans can legally wager on their knowledge of horses.

Whether it be grandstand or personal participation, the greater Oklahoma City area offers the best in sports and recreation. Camping, boating, and fishing are available on area lakes. Area golf courses challenge the greatest golfers in the nation, while duffers find satisfaction at several country clubs and on the city's many inexpensive public courses. Almost every park in the city has tennis courts at which enthusiasts can demonstrate their skills, while bowlers find some of the nation's best facilities within easy distance. City parks provide walking and jogging paths—or room to throw a Frisbee or hold a pickup touch-football game.

For those whose taste in sports tends to the spectator side, Oklahoma City offers professional baseball at the Triple-A level, where major-leaguers of the near future demonstrate their skills. University baseball teams from the Big Eight Conference frequently hold their post-season tournament at All-Sports Stadium at the state fairgrounds, and the All-College Basketball Tournament each year showcases the best round-ball talent in the national. The great golfers of the Professional Golfers' Association tour make periodic stops on the city's courses.

And then there is the spectacle, the pageantry, and the "Sooner-mania" of University of Oklahoma football. On cool autumn afternoons, Sooner fans gather in Norman to be lifted up into a frenzy of joy as their red-clad legions battle the best football teams from across the nation. With pennants fluttering and band playing, Owens Field rocks to the shouts of "Go Big Red," "Go Sooners"—and all Oklahomans stand a little taller and feel a mite prouder. The price of oil and agricultural commodities may be low, unemployment may stalk the land, and taxes may be increasing, but all's well when the Big Red takes the field for 60 minutes of high drama and excitement.

ABOVE: Betty Burns enjoys her flowers in Norman. Photo by Jim Argo

FACING PAGE: Running off into the sunset, this local resident finds health and happiness. Photo by Jim Argo

The state capitol of
Oklahoma, located in
Oklahoma City, was
dedicated in 1917.
Photo by Matt Bradley

Epilogue

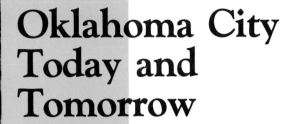

Oklahoma City Today and Tomorrow

Born in a dramatic run, Oklahoma City bypassed the slow formative years most major cities were allowed in their infancy. In just 21 years it changed from prairie to capital city of a thriving state. It underwent recurring cycles of boom and bust as the headquarters of oil firms that rode the roller coaster of petroleum prices. It was the marketing center for farmers tied to world price fluctuations and the vagaries of Oklahoma's weather—farmers who produced food, fiber, and livestock so abundantly that their surpluses brought them recurring depressions.

The Oklahoma City celebrating its 100th birthday on April 22, 1989, is a dynamic, modern metropolitan center with almost a million people in and around it. The Oklahoma City area, which at times has been one of the fastest growing metropolitan areas in the nation, stretches from Norman on the south to Edmond on the north, or more than 40 miles, and another 40 miles from El Reno to Harrah. Within its metropolitan area are almost a score of incorporated towns and villages.

The pioneers who settled this region indeed "builded better than they knew." Oklahoma City of 1989 is the chief market for the state's livestock industry and has major processing plants for both livestock and agricultural products. It is the point where the multilane divided ribbons of concrete and asphalt known as Interstates 35, 40, and 44 come together, and numerous other highways radiate outward, making Oklahoma City the hub of a great trucking industry; railroad tracks, like highways, converge at Oklahoma City, bringing dozens of freight trains through daily; and cargo and commercial planes land at the two major airports, named for two of Oklahoma's best-known and best-loved citizens, Will Rogers and Wiley Post. Thanks to truck, railroad, and air cargo facilities, Oklahoma City is the major wholesaling and jobbing center for the entire state and region.

Greater Oklahoma City has known several oil booms in the immediate vicinity, while giant petroleum firms and related service industries have established national or regional headquarters in its downtown and suburban offices. Oil field supply firms with their vast yards of pipe and drill bits and assorted machinery have come to Oklahoma City to manufacture and distribute the tools and equipment needed in the oil patch. Other manufacturing firms include electronics, automobiles, airplanes, and dozens of assorted items which make this a manufacturing hub for the great Midwest. Aviation and Oklahoma City have been almost synonymous from the earliest days, and in the late 1980s the city boasts the air logistics center at Tinker Air Force Base with its huge air force and civilian workforce as well as the Mike Monroney Aeronautical Center where the Federal Aviation Administration trains air traffic controllers and maintains research and records facilities.

Oklahoma City has become the cultural hub of the Sooner State with its symphony orchestra, theater groups, university students, touring groups that play in the Civic Center Music Hall, and Myriad Convention Center. The State Fair of Oklahoma is held each September at the fairgrounds on the west side of Oklahoma City, while rodeos and horse racing attract tens of thousands of Sooners and out-of-staters to Oklahoma's capital city. Every autumn there is University of Oklahoma football, a spectacle that guarantees that Sooners everywhere, both inside and outside the state, feel more than a twinge of pride. Baseball, basketball, field and track, and numerous other major sporting events are held in Oklahoma City at the university and professional levels. Oklahoma City is the health center of the state with its Health Sciences Center, the Medical Research Institute, Veterans Hospital, and numerous other health facilities.

Oklahoma City is where visitors come to see the great National Cowboy Hall of Fame, Lincoln Park Zoo, the Oklahoma Historical Society, the National Softball Hall of Fame, the Firefighters Museum, the 45th Infantry Division Museum, the Air Space Museum, and the Kirkpatrick Center's numerous exhibits and attractions. The state capitol itself, with an oil well on the grounds, is visited annually by thousands.

Downtown Oklahoma City is a city reborn—like the phoenix of ancient times, rising young again from the ashes of its previous life. Thanks to the planning of a dedicated Chamber of Commerce and the leadership provided by its staff and other civic leaders, Oklahoma City has cleared out that which had deteriorated and has preserved that which was usable to make a new city. Today's central business district gleams with several new and many refurbished skyscrapers.

The Myriad Convention Center each year attracts hundreds of thousands to Oklahoma City thanks to its excellent convention facilities, while the Myriad Gardens and the other features of the Pei city redevelopment plan have transformed downtown into a place of beauty. Statues and other monuments are here to commemorate those who made the run and those who dreamed and built this great city of steel, brick, concrete, mortar, and heart.

Oklahoma City has come far in just 100 years—thanks to its great people. Through good years and bad, Oklahoma City has been served by talented men and women. Some were pioneers or the descendants of pioneers, while others moved here from elsewhere after the run. Each year there have been a few who tired of the fight for progress, but fortunately there were always new leaders who were optimistic and who undertook the tasks that had to be done. In every period of economic downturn, there have been those who knew that the

This sculpture in red accents the urban landscape. Photo by Matt Bradley

hard times were but a wintry season and that a new springtime lay ahead. Always they kept in mind the lessons learned from the past, knowing that the Panic of 1893, coming just after Oklahoma City was born, proved to be the harbinger of the great boom years of 1898 to 1901; that following the Panic of 1907 came years of tremendous growth; that the Great Depression of the 1930s was but the forerunner of World War II's prosperity and the great postwar surge. There were those who believed that the downturn in oil and agricultural prices that began in 1982 would precede yet another era of growth for those who do not shrink from challenges.

Every generation has been faced with hardships to be overcome and goals to be set and accomplished. Oklahoma City is 100 years old, but there is still a spirit of youth, not of age, about it. As the poet Robert Browning said, "The best is yet to be."

Oklahoma City by night, or by day, is an outstanding urban center. Photo by Matt Bradley

Part
Two

Partners
in Progress

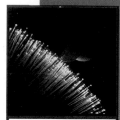

Networks

O klahoma City's energy, communication, and transportation providers keep products, information, and power circulating inside and outside the area.

SOUTHWESTERN BELL TELEPHONE COMPANY

On June 15, 1893, barely four years after the Run of 1889, the first local telephone exchange was opened for business in Oklahoma City.

Serving 50 subscribers, the Missouri & Kansas Telephone Company—the predecessor of Southwestern Bell Telephone in Oklahoma—operated out of the second floor of a building at Northwest Main Street and Robinson Avenue. Published rates for service at that time were $2.25 per month for business customers and $1.15 per month for residence customers.

In 1905, after a series of mergers, Pioneer Telephone & Telegraph Company became part of the Bell System.

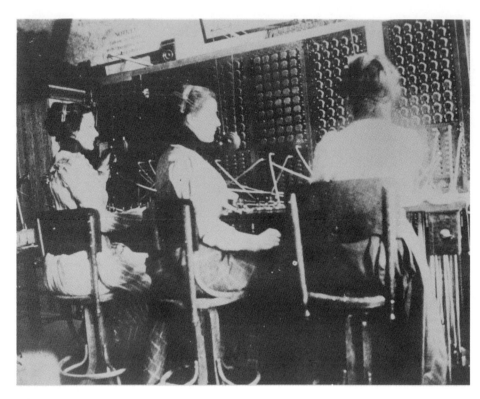

The Pioneer Telephone Building, erected in 1908, and the 16-story Southwestern Bell Administration Building, on the right, were landmarks in downtown Oklahoma City.

In 1900 three operators could handle all the calls for the few hundred Pioneer Telephone & Telegraph customers in Oklahoma City. Pictured here (from left) are Ella Davis, Mayme Gibbons, and Anna Loughmiller.

Three years later the newly constructed, seven-story Pioneer Telephone Building, located at Northwest Third and Broadway, was opened and quickly became a landmark in downtown Oklahoma City. However, booming business forced Southwestern Bell to lease space in several other nearby locations until 1928, when a 16-story administration building was completed at 405 North Broadway. Both buildings are still in use.

As the city continued to grow, Southwestern Bell kept pace with the demand for expanding communications needs. By 1987 there were 29 central office equipment locations, serving 430,000 main-access lines to businesses and homes in the metropolitan area, and five office buildings housing 1,951 employees in downtown Oklahoma City.

About the same time telephone service made its debut in the city, plans also were being laid for one of the city's most acclaimed historic landmarks—

Oklahoma City's first high school, which was completed in 1910 on Robinson Avenue between Seventh and Eighth streets. A massive Collegiate Gothic building of limestone exterior, the structure was a landmark in downtown Oklahoma City for three-quarters of a century with its massive bell towers, battlements, large pointed windows, and compound-arched entries. Then, in 1984, after more than three years of planning and construction, it became the corporate headquarters of the Oklahoma Division of Southwestern Bell Telephone Company. The transformation of this aging structure into a nationally acclaimed historic landmark is a fitting tribute to the heritage of Oklahoma City's Central High School and Southwestern Bell Telephone. The newly renovated school was named One Bell Central.

Southwestern Bell Telephone was a part of the AT&T family of companies until 1984, when an eight-year antitrust suit brought against the Bell System by the Department of Justice ended with AT&T agreeing to divest itself of 22 Bell operating companies. To fill the vacuum, Southwestern Bell Corpora-

One Bell Central was originally constructed in 1910, and the renovation of the structure in the early 1980s won nationwide awards for Southwestern Bell in the field of historic preservation. Courtesy, Jim Argo

tion, headquartered in St. Louis, Missouri, was formed as the parent company to provide overall financial management and strategic planning for Southwestern Bell Telephone and three other principal subsidiaries—Southwestern Bell Publications, Southwestern Bell Telecom, and Southwestern Bell Mobile Systems.

Southwestern Bell's divesture from AT&T created a new environment and a new set of challenges for the company, which forged a new course into the information age. Although the divestiture revolutionized the national telecommunications industry, Southwestern Bell Telephone's commitment to provide the best possible service to customers—a commitment that requires the company to remain in the forefront of technological advancement in the telecommunications industry—remained unaltered.

As a part of this effort to remain

a leader in telecommunication technology, Southwestern Bell Telephone installed a light-wave communications system within metropolitan Oklahoma City in April 1983. Carrying signals on beams of pulsed light, this fiber-optic cable network relays voice, data, and video transmissions over hair-thin fibers of glass by laser light pulses at a speed of 45 million bits per second, and 6,048 simultaneous conversations are transported on a single pair of fibers. By the end of 1987, 87 percent of customers in Oklahoma City were served by offices with fiber-optic interoffice facilities.

The first major installation of fiber-optic cable on a larger scale was laid between Oklahoma City and Ponca City in 1987 at a cost of approximately $4.7 million. Capable of accurately transmitting information and voice across the country and around the world, this project enables Southwestern Bell Telephone to meet the projected demands for service in central Oklahoma for the next two decades. It also provides a vital asset to the promotion of Oklahoma City as an attractive place to locate new industry.

Since the early 1960s Southwestern Bell Telephone's statewide network has been evolving from analog to digital technology. Analog transmission originally was developed to carry voice communications over wire, a miracle in its earliest development; however, analog systems are not compatible with the intelligent network of the future.

In 1985 the company decided to move full-speed ahead toward a total digital network. State-of-the-art digital technology affords customers a myriad of options for basic telephone and data transmission services. Coupled with 99.5-percent error-free transmission over fiber-optic cable, digital technology is capable of providing more than adequate service from the basic to the most sophisticated needs. Lower cost, absolute reliability, higher speed/capacity, enhanced security of data traffic, and synergy of communication and computers are standard features of the digital network.

No longer are businesses forced to

The interior of One Bell Central shows the restored auditorium. Courtesy, Jim Argo

make the usual capital investments for telecommunications requirements in order to receive special services. Customized office communications requirements from two to 400 lines are provided from a dynamic menu of Southwestern Bell Telephone service offerings—Plexar[SM], Megalink[SM], and Microlink[SM], which are designed to grow with businesses into the future as their needs dictate. With service to multipoint private line operations at speeds of 2.4, 4.8, 9.6, and 56 kilobits per second and up to 1.544 megabits per second, customers are able to transmit large volumes of data and/or voice, slow scan video, electronic mail, and facsimile. Amazingly accurate, reliable, and flexible, this cost-efficient, intelligent network is maintained and monitored 24 hours a day and is capable of repairing itself before a problem is detected.

With the foundation for the Integrated Services Digital Network (ISDN) already in place, a number of services are available to customers in Oklahoma City. End-to-end digital transmission and access to multiple services over a single telephone line are just a short time away. Application of this advanced network architecture—

transporting of voice, text, and images over one line—simply means customers will be able to plug their telephone set, data terminal, personal computer, facsimile, or even an alarm system into a standard telephone jack. The Southwestern Bell Telephone network then provides the service as easily as an electrical wall outlet handles appliances. In the home, ISDN will provide easier and less-expensive access to mainframe computers and data bases for work-at-home applications, banking, shopping, and a wide range of other services.

With ISDN, internal rearrangement of telephones and terminals no longer will require the complicated procedure of placing orders with Southwestern Bell Telephone and other vendors and rewiring of existing cable. Users merely will indicate to the switch, through standard interfaces, what changes are being made. This can be done quickly and inexpensively, providing the user with more control and eliminating the concern for equipment obsolescence.

Because of Southwestern Bell Telephone's commitment to a total digital network, the company is poised to usher Oklahoma City into the information age. The company prides itself on

envisioning the future of telecommunications. In fact, as far as digital technology is concerned, Oklahoma City is ready for the future—now.

While a dynamic telecommunications network is an attractive asset to any city, Southwestern Bell Telephone's vision for the future encompasses more than simply providing state-of-the-art technology. The firm also understands its partnership role with other corporate and civic leaders in making Oklahoma City an economically attractive location. Helping to bring new business opportunities to the community is a mutually beneficial endeavor. To that end, Bell management expertise is freely shared in collaboration with organizations and agencies whose agenda include improving the quality of life in Oklahoma City.

Aggressive community participation coupled with financial support is a well-known Southwestern Bell Telephone tradition. Annual corporate contributions average more than a half-million dollars for the arts, education, human welfare, medical research, youth programs, and charitable organizations. Company-initiated projects have earned national recognition for excellence as well. The company recently was awarded first place among 137 major businesses reviewed annually by *The Community Relations Report,* a nationwide publication that monitors and evaluates corporate community relations programs. Southwestern Bell Telephone's statewide program was acclaimed by the organization as "by far the best organized and most successful" in the promotion of economic development, education, tourism, recreation, and cultural enrichment in the

A circuit board. Photo by Don Carroll

Robert George Young fibre optics.

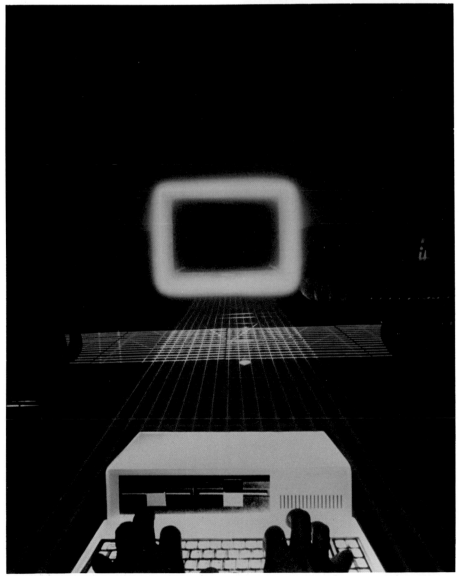

communities it serves.

Another element in the promotion of any city is its work force. Providing quality telephone service is a deeply ingrained tradition fostered through generations of Southwestern Bell Telephone employees; however, beyond this spirit of service to customers, Southwestern Bell Telephone also demonstrates responsible citizenship with exemplary leadership and participation in community affairs. The company sponsors nearly 300 employee memberships in 100 community, civic, business, and professional organizations in Oklahoma City. Organizations such as the Telephone Pioneers of America and Community Relations Teams extend to employees opportunities for showing compassion for human need, serving as volunteers, and sharing talents or personal resources. Company employees may be found in every strata of Oklahoma City's community and public service arena.

Growing with Oklahoma City for nearly a century, Southwestern Bell Telephone Company's innovative technological advances and solid corporate citizenship are the foundations upon which the company will build another century of dependable telephone and community service.

FLEMING COMPANIES, INC.

While the heart of the Fleming Companies, Inc., organization is the coast-to-coast network of affiliated retail food stores in 37 states, the hub of the operation is the firm's corporate headquarters at 6301 Waterford Boulevard in Oklahoma City. From there the corporate staff provides valuable technical and professional expertise to associates at each Fleming division that are not possible to have on site at each location. Such support services allow efficient store development and planning, and the creation of successful marketing and merchandising programs.

In maintaining the company's ongoing commitment to improving the distribution system for the retailers it serves, Fleming maintains what almost could be defined as a retail service center in Oklahoma City. Five separate but closely cooperating departments—Procurement, Demographic Marketing, Consumer Affairs, Retail Electronic Services, and Food Marketing—provide invaluable support for retail stores nationwide. Other corporate activities, such as companywide distribution management and facilities engineering, human resources and management development, communications, labor relations, insurance, and corporate control and accounting, also are headquartered in the Oklahoma City facility.

Distribution is the foundation upon which the success of Fleming has

Fleming Companies' corporate headquarters, located at 6301 Waterford Boulevard in Oklahoma City, is the hub of its operations.

been built, and to ensure the continued growth of the firm, a state-of-the-art computer system makes the corporation one of the most technologically advanced in its industry.

Constructed in 1978, the 400,000-square-foot Oklahoma City distribution center, located at 10 East Memorial Road, was built at a cost of more than $15 million. The first to operate with a mechanized order-selection system backed by a computer to stream-

line the entire process of procurement and distribution, it remains a model distribution facility in the food distribution industry.

The Oklahoma City distribution center is but one of 33, with a total of 18 million square feet of warehouse space spread throughout the United States. Each provides a full line of products to retailers in its area. In addition, Fleming operates specialized warehouses that distribute such perishables as frozen foods, meats, dairy and deli products, and general merchandise. To ensure prompt service, Fleming's truck fleet travels more than 78 million miles annually, using on-board computers to make the most effective use of drivers and equipment.

Fleming, Oklahoma's second-largest publicly held company in total revenues, began in 1915. Five years later Ned N. Fleming joined his father, O.A. Fleming, a founder of the Fleming-Wilson Mercantile Company, in the management of the small wholesale grocery firm in Topeka, Kansas. At the same time the food-purchasing system in America entered a new era. Instead of a housewife ordering from a local grocery store, meat market, or bakery,

Fleming's truck fleet travels more than 78 million miles annually, using on-board computers to make the most effective use of drivers and equipment.

158

which delivered to her house and extended credit, chain stores appeared with their philosophy of mass marketing and corresponding lower costs. Threatened with a loss of customers, independent grocers banded together to form voluntary group organizations allowing members to become more competitive through mass marketing, widespread advertising, and more efficient operational techniques. The goal was to attract the customer into the store with lower prices and a wider range of products.

Ned Fleming was one of the first food distributors to understand this shift in the food-purchasing habits of Americans, and he expanded the operations of the Fleming Company, as the firm was renamed, to meet the expanding needs of independent grocers. As the trend toward large-volume grocery stores accelerated, Fleming Company embarked on a policy of active acquisition to keep pace. As a part of its expansion, Fleming acquired the Carroll-Brough-Robinson Company of Oklahoma City in 1941.

Three years later the Oklahoma

Distribution is the foundation for the success of Fleming Companies, Inc. With a total of 18 million square feet of space located nationwide, Fleming operates full-line centers as well as specialized warehouses that distribute such perishables as frozen foods, meats, dairy and deli products.

City operation moved to new quarters at 3500 North Santa Fe. That structure, which was to remain the hub of Fleming's Oklahoma operations for more than 35 years, was expanded six times during the decades to follow. During those years Fleming-served retailers gained strong market shares in Oklahoma, and the company became a major economic force in the state, with total assets growing to more than $1.3

The heart of Fleming is an extensive network of affiliated retail stores in 37 states.

billion.

In 1972 the corporate staff was moved to Oklahoma, and by the mid-1980s the employees in both Oklahoma City facilities had grown to 750 with an annual payroll of nearly $27 million. Under the direction of R.D. Harrison, chairman and chief executive officer from 1966 until 1988, and E. Dean Werries, current president and chief executive officer, Fleming Companies has become a national leader in the wholesale food distribution industry, serving affiliated retailers with sales in excess of $16 billion. If combined, these Fleming-served stores would rank as the third-largest supermarket chain in the nation. Fleming's customer base is varied, serving independents such as IGA, Thriftway, Piggly Wiggly, United Supers, and Big T, and chain stores such as American Stores and Kroger's. These retail outlets include some of the nation's most successful and progressive supermarkets, and the goal of Fleming Companies is to help all its customers succeed in an increasingly competitive environment.

WM. E. DAVIS & SONS, INC.

A full-line, private-label, quality distributor that offers its customers the greatest value, Wm. E. Davis & Sons, Inc., was built on a philosophy that success is based on providing customers with consistent quality, in both products and support services, coupled with dependable delivery. Initially organized in 1953 as a partnership between William E. "Bill" Davis and his wife, Margaret, the corporation is committed to the institutional food-service business.

Davis, experienced in food-service distribution, and his wife first operated out of the basement of the Bekins Moving and Storage warehouse on Main Street in downtown Oklahoma City, where they rented 2,500 square feet of space. Davis was the firm's only salesman, while his wife handled all the bookkeeping and ordering.

Occupying a vital nitch in the food-distribution industry, the partnership thrived, and within a year had outgrown its original location. To provide adequate space for the expanding business, the Davises moved to a 7,500-square-foot warehouse at Fifth Street and Indiana. Although the move tripled the available space, the firm was forced to move again by 1959, this time to a 13,000-square-foot facility at 6700 North Hudson. That same year the firm was incorporated as Wm. E. Davis & Sons, Inc. Although the company added another 6,000 square feet of warehouse space to the North Hudson location, by 1969 it was inadequate to serve the firm's rapidly growing list of customers, and 10 acres of land were purchased at the junction of Broadway Extension and 122nd Street in far north Oklahoma City.

A state-of-the-art 45,000-square-foot distribution center and company headquarters was opened in 1970, with a 6,000-square-foot refrigeration unit. The rapid growth continued, and by 1988, after several expansions, Wm. E. Davis & Sons occupied a 150,000-square-foot facility with 40,000 square feet of refrigerated space.

During the nearly four decades since its founding, the firm expanded from a staff of two to 60 full-time sales representatives and approximately 300 employees serving a marketing area stretching throughout Oklahoma and from central Texas through southern Kansas and into western and central Arkansas and southwest Missouri. Sales grew from $100,000 annually in 1953 to $102 million in 1987. The corporation maintains a fleet of 46 refrigerated tractor-trailer rigs and numerous smaller produce vehicles to serve its 4,000 customers with the highest level of service. All orders are handled by a sophisticated computer system that provides maximum efficiency in both inventory control and delivery requirements.

Customer service means more than just offering a full line of quality products. Wm. E. Davis & Sons' staff of 60 sales people, 8 managers, and 5 specialists all work to assist customers in terms of new products, marketing ideas, and market availability. The company's staff dietitian and PC specialist are available to provide customers with menu, recipe, and cost-containment programs. The firm also publishes a

A family-operated business for nearly four decades, Wm. E. Davis & Sons, Inc., was built on a philosophy of providing its customers with consistent quality and dependable delivery. Pictured here (from left) are William E. Davis, Charles T. Davis, Richard C. Davis, and Margaret H. Davis.

quarterly, 24-page newspaper for customers that gives information concerning the company, its customers, market analysis, new product information, and marketing ideas. Davis conducts one of the nation's largest trade shows; it is annually attended by more than 2,000 customers to provide them with the latest information on new products and marketing developments in the food-service industry. All these programs make Wm. E. Davis & Sons, Inc., one of the most aggressive food-service marketing organizations in the nation.

A full-service company, Wm. E. Davis & Sons provides its customers with a complete line of products, including general grocery, fresh produce, fresh and frozen meats, frozen foods, dairy products, sanitation supplies, and small equipment and supplies. In addition to the nationally known labels offered to customers, the firm also carries its own private labels of merchandise. "There are no disappointments in quality," Bill Davis explains, as the company constantly monitors and controls the quality of its products in it own test kitchen.

Believing that the corporation's success is based on a dedication to integ-

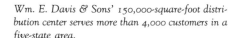

Wm. E. Davis & Sons' 150,000-square-foot distribution center serves more than 4,000 customers in a five-state area.

rity, honesty, and fairness, Davis insists that the company gives its customers the finest service from an attitude of flexibility and partnership. Since the formation of Wm. E. Davis & Sons, the food-service business has changed rapidly from a nation of small family restaurants to a network of chains and profusion of sophisticated independent establishments. Through a policy of forecasting and planning ahead, Wm. E. Davis & Sons changed with the times. It has been this ability to adapt that has contributed to the outstanding growth of the company.

As consumer purchasing trends have changed, so have the products offered by the firm. As a part of this flexibility, Wm. E. Davis & Sons owns and operates Chef's Market, located just south of the corporate headquarters and warehouse. Catering to retail and wholesale customers, Chef's Market offers a multitude of gourmet and im-

One of central Oklahoma's favorite specialty stores, Chef's Market's selection of worldwide food items attracts customers from throughout the region.

ported items not available at local food outlets. Canned wild boar, Swedish cookies, and King Crab legs are but a few of the specialty items available.

Throughout its history Wm. E. Davis & Sons has remained a family-operated business. In addition to Bill and Margaret, their six children—Charles, Richard, Porter, Elizabeth, Ann, and Marnie—worked with the company while they were young. Their three sons actively became involved in its management team in the early 1970s. Although Porter departed when he was elected to serve in the state legislature, Charles and Richard remained and today serve as president and vice-president, respectively, while Bill is chairman and Margaret is secretary/treasurer. The White Swan Company of Fort Worth, Texas, formerly owned by the Fleming Company, recently purchased the Wm. E. Davis and Sons Co., but the Davis Company is still operated separately from the other White Swan divisions. The Davis Company does have the advantages of using the expertise and buying power of the White Swan Company, which now has sales of $525 million.

Believing that Wm. E. Davis & Sons, Inc., is an integral part of the community, the firm maintains an active role in local affairs, supporting numerous civic programs. In addition, the corporation was an early participant in area food banks, providing surplus

Wm. E. Davis & Sons' fleet of company-operated vehicles ensures prompt delivery of products within the firm's 300-mile sales radius.

Chef's Market, located across the street from the corporation's headquarters and distribution center, provides a unique shopping experience ranging from bulk-food items, party products, fresh fish, and meat, to an extensive selection of frozen, gourmet, and imported items.

food for numerous charitable organizations. In so doing, the firm stresses its commitment to the local community as a locally owned, locally operated business that has served the food-service industry for nearly four decades.

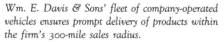

OKLAHOMA GAS AND ELECTRIC COMPANY

The Oklahoma Ditch and Water Power Company, OG&E's forerunner, 1889 hydroelectric generating plant along the North Canadian River in Oklahoma City. Unfortunately, most of the water needed to drive the turbines was absorbed by the sandy soil before it reached the generating station.

The Oklahoma Gas and Electric Company traces its roots to 1889, the year of the Run, when the Oklahoma Ditch and Water Power Company was organized to produce electricity for Oklahoma City. A second firm, the Oklahoma City Light and Power Company, was formed to distribute the electricity. After an ill-fated attempt to produce hydroelectric power, the two companies placed a steam-generating plant on line in September 1892, and for the next decade struggled to become established. Finally, in 1902, two of the principal investors in Oklahoma City Light and Power, G.E. Wheeler and E.H. Cooke, sold their interest to F.B. Burbridge and Harry M. Blackmer, who reincorporated the business as the Oklahoma Gas and Electric Company (OG&E).

Established five years before statehood, OG&E is Oklahoma's oldest state-chartered corporation. It received its first franchise from Oklahoma City in February 1902. Two years later C.B. Ames and Dennis Flynn acquired control of OG&E and brought H.M. Byllesby into the corporation. Under their direction, OG&E increased its generating capability from 700 kilowatts to 4,050 kilowatts, and expanded its distribution lines from 76 miles to 227 miles during the following five years. Correspondingly, the number of OG&E's customers jumped from 1,400 to 4,500.

Encouraged by this growth, OG&E expanded outside the Oklahoma City metropolitan area in 1910 and purchased the El Reno Gas and Electric Company. Additional expansion extended OG&E's service to Britton, Norman, Enid, Chandler, Byng, Shawnee, Ada, Guthrie, and other communities. As corporate expansion continued in the ensuing decades, OG&E extended its service area to include more than 640,000 customers spread across 30,000 square miles of Oklahoma and western Arkansas.

OG&E sold its natural gas properties in 1928; however, its name remained the same. That same year the firm expanded into western Arkansas. Also in 1928 OG&E became the first investor-owned electric company to develop performance data on natural lake cooling for generating stations. This was the first of many innovations that characterized the firm in the following decades: In 1935 OG&E was the first in the nation to use recarbonation of circulating water to reduce scale formations in condensers; in 1949 it was the first American company to use gas turbines combined with steam turbines to produce electricity; in 1959 OG&E introduced single-phase service, which was more economical for consumers than any previous method; in 1963 the company built the world's largest combined-cycle generating unit at Horseshoe Lake Station; and in 1971 OG&E became the first electric company in Oklahoma to open one of its cooling reservoirs, Lake Konawa, to the public. In 1979 Sooner Reservoir, on the Arkansas River north of Stillwater, also was opened to the public.

In 1977 OG&E placed a modern coal-fired generating plant, Muskogee 4, into operation and eased the firm's reliance on natural gas. The plant also produced fly ash as a useful by-product. That same year OG&E placed on-line a Supervisory Control and Data Acquisition system to control substations by a centrally located computer. This allows the more rapid transfer of power throughout the system. In 1983 OG&E introduced computerized me-

James G. Harlow, Jr., chairman of the board and president of Oklahoma Gas and Electric Company, the state's oldest state-chartered corporation.

ter reading, which made meter reading and billing faster and more efficient. In recognition of its corporate leadership in technological innovations and service to the citizens of Oklahoma, *Electric Light and Power* magazine named OG&E the Utility of the Year in 1983.

In late 1986 OG&E diversified for the first time in its history, when it acquired Mustang Fuel Company. Reorganized as Enogex Inc., a wholly owned subsidiary of OG&E, Enogex oversees the operation of a 3,000-mile-long pipeline network serving all seven of OG&E's gas-fired power plants. The pipeline allows OG&E to assure its self-dependency by controlling all four aspects of natural gas-generated electricity—gas in the field, transportation of the gas to generating plants, the generation of electricity, and the distribution of electricity to customers. In addition, Enogex Products Corporation owns

OG&E's Seminole Power Plant, the last large gas-fired unit constructed by the corporation, is capable of producing 1.556 million kilowatts from four natural gas power turbines.

and operates four gas-processing plants. The acquisition has saved OG&E customers millions of dollars.

Under the direction of James G. Harlow, Jr., chairman of the board and president, OG&E underwent a complete reorganization in 1987 to streamline operations and reduce the cost of electricity to customers through the more economical use of company assets and the elimination of duplication of services within the corporate structure. This reorganization, along with such energy-saving projects as Peaks, Award, Echo, and Hand-N-Hand programs, which reduce electric use at high-demand periods, reflects the Oklahoma Gas and Electric Company's ongoing commitment to provide the best possible service at the lowest possible cost.

OG&E's corporate headquarters is located at 321 North Harvey in downtown Oklahoma City. The company provides electric service to customers in a 30,000-square-mile area.

The turbine floor of OG&E's ultramodern, coal-fired Sooner Plant. More than 800,000 tons of coal are required annually to power the plant's huge electric-generating turbines.

DEVON ENERGY CORPORATION

The Ross Well, in which Devon Energy Corporation has an interest, was drilled in February 1988 in southeastern Oklahoma. ©Christopher Weeks

Devon Energy Corporation, an independent oil and natural gas exploration and production company, was formed in 1969 as a privately held corporation by John W. Nichols, the firm's chairman of the board. Nichols has long been a force in the international energy industry, having been a pioneer in 1950 with the first syndicated oil and gas drilling program registered with the Securities and Exchange Commission, and with the first international royalty fund in 1971. His innovative financing has opened previously untapped reservoirs of capital for America's oilmen.

When Devon was formed in 1969, it had only a corporate charter, a negative net worth, and virtually no oil or natural gas properties; its only significant asset was a $6-million tax loss that could be applied to shelter future income—if the company was to ever generate any. From this inauspicious beginning Devon has grown in less than two decades into a force in international financial circles, responsible for attracting more than $150 million from primarily foreign sources for direct investment in the American oil and natural gas industry.

Primarily engaged in the acquisition of existing producing oil and gas properties and the exploration for and development of new oil and gas production, Devon and its affiliates own interests in 3,500 producing wells located

on 1.67 million acres in 14 states. In addition, the Devon group owns interests in 167,000 acres of undeveloped leases. Operations are conducted mainly in the Mid-Continent, Gulf Coast, Rocky Mountain, and Appalachian areas of the United States. Total reserves as of January 1, 1988, were 2.9 million barrels of oil and 70.4 billion cubic feet of natural gas. To oversee these operations, Devon employs approximately 120 people, and maintains not only its headquarters in the Mid-America Tower in downtown Okla-

homa City, but also a district office in Denver, Colorado, and individual field offices in Oklahoma, Louisiana, and West Virginia.

Two years after its formation Devon Energy found a creative use for its $6-million tax loss. Devon Energy combined this tax loss with the financing horsepower of a major European marine shipping company and created Devon International Royalties Limited, the first international royalty fund. This fund was creative not only because it was the first of its type, but also because it had a unique advantage—the first $6 million of its earnings would be free from income taxes. From 1971 to 1977 Devon International Royalties Limited expended approximately $74 million to acquire producing oil and gas properties, gas-processing plants, oil and gas products transportation systems, and marketing outlets throughout the United States.

From 1978 to 1982 Devon formed a series of business ventures with other European and American financial and business institutions that resulted in another round of acquisitions of oil and gas properties. Because these arrangements were structured so that the institutions furnished most of the funds used for the purchases, nearly $88 mil-

Pictured here is Devon Energy Corporation's senior exploration geologist for the Mid-Continent region. Behind him is a geologic map showing the United States' major oil- and gas-producing regions.

lion of foreign-based, nonenergy-related capital was poured into the American petroleum industry.

Revealing a corporate commitment to the state, whenever possible Devon has funneled the funds through Oklahoma financial institutions and into the state's economy. Though the Devon group's oil and gas operations are conducted in 14 states, Oklahoma represents the single-largest concentration of properties. In fact, nearly 52 percent of the group's oil and gas reserves are located in its home state. The Sooner Trend, which extends 100 miles through the north-central portion of Oklahoma, and the Quinton South and Blocker Southeast fields in the southeastern part of the state are notable portions of the Devon group's properties. Devon also participated in the first significantly successful well drilled in the Ivanhoe field in the Oklahoma panhandle. The company now operates the majority of the wells in this field. Devon's #1-7 Thomas and #1-8 Dickenson wells were the initial discovery wells for what is now the Chickasha field in south-central Oklahoma.

The continual acquisition and development of new oil and gas reserves is an absolute necessity for Devon's success in the future. By their very nature, firms such as Devon, whose primary business is the extraction of oil and natural gas, are self-depleting unless there is continuous reinvestment to create

new reserves.

Devon has not only replaced its reserves over the years, it has also caused these reserves to multiply many times. Devon's success has been guided by three basic business principles. First, be contracyclical. Devon is not so large that it can create trends in an industry somewhat dominated by billion-dollar, multinational companies. Rather, Devon must make itself the beneficiary of those trends—and usually this has meant being contracyclical.

In 1979, two years before the deep Anadarko basin of Oklahoma became the hottest onshore exploration play in the United States, Devon purchased oil and gas drilling rights in the area for around $100 per acre. In 1981, when drilling reached feverish levels, Devon sold one-half of its interests in some of these leases for $5,000 per acre, netting a total of $3 million in profits. In other words, Devon was a buyer when there were few that wanted to buy, and it was

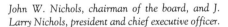

John W. Nichols, chairman of the board, and J. Larry Nichols, president and chief executive officer.

In this boardroom scene, an actual negotiating session is under way involving the financing of an acquisition. The participants are senior officers of the company and some of its investment bankers.

a seller when virtually everyone wanted to buy.

Second, maintain flexibility. The economic rewards available by either acquiring existing production properties or by drilling on previously unexplored properties have been different in any given year. Thus, Devon has been alternately either an acquirer of or an explorer for oil and gas reserves depending upon the relative risk/reward of each. Most energy companies Devon's size are either exploration or acquisition oriented, but few are equally prepared to do both. This flexibility has allowed Devon to take advantage of opportunities no matter what their origin. The access to the many sources of capital referred to above has also enhanced Devon's flexibility. Very few of Devon's corporate peer group in 1971 have consummated $200 million of acquisitions or enjoyed an aggregate exploration budget exceeding $80 million by 1988.

Third, strive for diversity. Though Devon maintains a significant portion of its properties in Oklahoma, no single property, well, field, or asset dominates the company. No single oil or natural gas purchaser has been allowed to become critical to the firm. Thus, Devon has been able to avoid or reduce the economic squeeze many of its peers have endured caused by the failure of a single major property or the refusal of a major product purchaser to honor its obligations.

Devon Energy Corporation and its affiliates—committed to sound business practices and committed to Oklahoma.

KERR-McGEE CORPORATION

Innovation and hard work. No traits have contributed more to Kerr-McGee Corporation's success in finding and developing natural resources.

These attributes can be traced to the company's founding in 1929. At that time two young Oklahomans formed a small firm to drill oil wells. Robert S. Kerr and James A. Anderson were short on cash but long on ambition.

Kerr-McGee Corporation, the company that grew from that partnership, today ranks as a major producer of crude oil, natural gas, industrial chemicals, and coal. Kerr-McGee also refines petroleum, markets petroleum products, and operates a fleet of offshore drilling rigs.

With assets of more than $3 billion, the company transacts business worldwide from its headquarters in downtown Oklahoma City. Kerr-McGee Center spreads across one square block and is anchored by the 30-story McGee Tower. Across the street lies Kerr Park, an oasis of fountains, trees, and flowers that the firm donated to the city and continues to maintain.

Kerr-McGee realizes that success in

business brings with it a responsibility to its employees and communities. The company actively supports education, medicine, the arts, and other worthwhile endeavors in Oklahoma and its other areas of operation.

Kerr-McGee's primary business is exploring for and producing crude oil and natural gas in selected areas around the world. The company has earned success by relying on both the tools of science and the skills of individuals.

Kerr-McGee's most profitable producing area is the Gulf of Mexico, where the firm holds interests in several hundred oil and gas wells. Since launching the offshore petroleum industry in 1947, Kerr-McGee has earned a leadership role in Gulf Coast exploration and production.

The company also holds significant interests in the North Sea, where Kerr-McGee and its partners have overcome technological challenges and stormy weather to operate successfully. The firm's Beatrice Field has won environmental awards for safeguarding delicate habitats near the Scottish shore.

Kerr-McGee's other international holdings include properties in the Arabian Gulf and Malaysia. Onshore North America, the company explores for petroleum in nine states and in northwest Canada.

Kerr-McGee Refining Corporation operates refineries at Corpus Christi,

McGee Tower, 30 stories tall, anchors the block-square Kerr-McGee Center in Oklahoma City. In the foreground lies Kerr Park, a downtown oasis of fountains, flowers, and trees. The company maintains the park and sponsors musical performances from spring through fall.

At a Kerr-McGee coal mine in Wyoming, electric shovels standing six stories tall carve coal from a seam. The coal will be processed and shipped to utility companies for use in generating electricity.

Texas; Wynnewood, Oklahoma; and Cotton Valley-Dubach, Louisiana. End products from these plants include liquefied petroleum gases, gasoline, home heating oil, diesel fuel, solvents, petrochemicals, and asphalt.

Kerr-McGee Refining also offers a complete line of branded petroleum products, while its Triangle Refineries Division sells primarily in the unbranded market. The company markets gasoline and other automotive products through more than 1,900 service stations, primarily in the central United States.

A subsidiary of Kerr-McGee Refin-

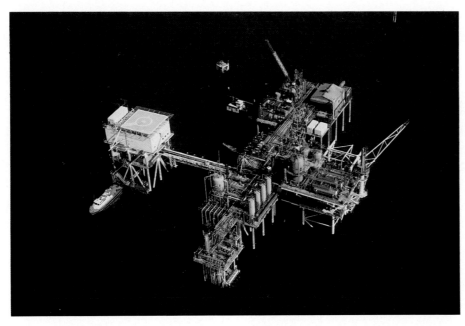

Offshore Louisiana, Kerr-McGee operates a massive facility that processes oil and gas from more than 130 wells in the Breton Sound Field. The Gulf of Mexico ranks as the company's chief source of domestic oil and gas production.

ing, Cato Oil and Grease Co. is a leading producer and packager of high-quality lubricating oils and specialty greases, specializing in custom packaging and lubricating grease technology.

Transworld Drilling conducts offshore contract drilling worldwide. This subsidiary's foundation was laid in 1947, when Kerr-McGee pioneered methods of drilling in open waters. The firm conceived using a platform accompanied by a rig-tender vessel to drill the world's first commercial oil well out of sight and safety of land.

Transworld innovation continues today. Its fleet of 19 rigs gives the company the capability to work in shallow waters or to venture to 2,000-foot waters. Searching for oil and gas worldwide, Transworld can drill to 30,000 feet deep—nearly six miles.

Kerr-McGee Chemical Corporation produces and markets industrial chemicals, specialty chemicals, and forest products. The company's largest operation lies in Searles Valley, California. A three-plant complex produces soda ash, used to make glass; potash, a fertilizer raw material; boron chemicals, needed in ceramics and electronics; and salt cake, used in detergents.

At other plants in Mississippi, Alabama, Nevada, and Idaho, Kerr-McGee produces chemicals with uses ranging from strengthening steel to bleaching wood pulp. Kerr-McGee markets its chemicals nationwide and in more than a dozen foreign countries, and also licenses its technical processes to firms in the United States and abroad.

The company's Forest Products Division ranks as a leading supplier of treated railroad crossties. Supplying part of the division's raw timber needs is company-owned forest land in the Ohio and Mississippi river valleys.

Kerr-McGee Coal Corporation ranks as one of the nation's major coal companies. Most of its production comes from the coal-rich Powder River Basin in Wyoming, where Kerr-McGee owns two surface mines. There, massive electric shovels remove rock and soil covering thick coal seams. After coal is mined and processed, it is shipped by train to utility companies for use in generating electricity. Kerr-McGee carefully contours and reseeds the mined areas.

In southern Illinois, the company operates the underground Galatia Mine. Coal is mined several hundred feet below the surface and carried by conveyor to above-ground facilities that process the fuel and ship it to a utility company.

In all of its mining activities, Kerr-McGee Coal is committed to providing a safe work place and protecting the environment.

Common to all Kerr-McGee operations is a management philosophy that stresses developing new approaches to producing natural resources, growing through diversification and acquisition, operating safely, protecting the environment, and serving its communities. These challenges require innovation and hard work—the hallmarks of Kerr-McGee Corporation since 1929.

Working around the clock, a Kerr-McGee chemical plant in Mississippi manufactures titanium dioxide pigment. The white pigment is a key ingredient in paints and plastics.

OXY USA INC.

OXY USA Inc. is a new name to the Oklahoma City oil patch, but it is certainly not a new company. OXY USA Inc. is marking its sixth decade in the Oklahoma City community. Known for some years as Cities Service, the firm has changed its name to OXY, a name of strength, a name of the future, and a name that signifies the corporation's affiliation to its parent, Occidental Petroleum Corporation, one of the world's leading industrial firms.

OXY USA Inc. seeks to build on the success of its past affiliates. The company and its predecessors and subsidiaries were among the giants of the Oklahoma oil boom era, and were responsible for many major discoveries and firsts in the industry.

The Phoenix Oil Company, which was merged later to form Indian Territory Illuminating Oil Company, pioneered the development of the prolific Osage Nation. The Indian Territory Illuminating Oil Company (ITIO) became a subsidiary of Cities Service Oil and Gas Company and was a major developer of the Greater Seminole Oil Region and drilled the discovery wells of the Bowlegs Field, the Little River Field, and the Seminole City Field— Bowlegs and Little River, respectively, ranked 55th and 61st among the nation's largest finds in the first half of the twentieth century. ITIO also drilled the discovery well of the huge Oklahoma City Field, the fourth-largest oil find in America prior to 1950 and one of the world's largest producers of crude oil and natural gas.

These discoveries have brought Oklahoma City world fame as a major energy center. As oil derricks once dotted the capital lawn, OXY USA Inc. moves aggressively to position itself to meet the challenge of the years ahead.

While the petroleum industry works to stabilize following the dramatic decline in crude oil prices in 1986, OXY USA Inc. is working to further its ability to increase its strong reserve position and to continue the successful development and production of oil and gas reserves.

To accomplish the successes of today and the opportunities of the future, the company has chosen to maintain its presence in Oklahoma City as the home office for directing a major portion of its exploration and production operations, ranging from the Midwest through parts of the Southwest and

Drilling throughout the United States, OXY USA Inc. is building a strong energy reserve for the American public.

from the Rocky Mountains to the West Coast.

Some 250 employees work out of OXY USA Inc.'s Oklahoma City office. They come with experience gained in other U.S. oil patches, such as Bakersfield, California; Denver, Colorado; and Midland and Houston, Texas. They come from the city of Tulsa and the oil-rich plains of Kansas. They come to Oklahoma City, one of the nation's oldest oil patches, to continue the tradition of an experienced oil and gas producer.

They also come to Oklahoma City to continue the commitment of support for community, cultural, educational, and charitable endeavors. For more than six decades OXY USA Inc. and its predecessors have helped provide for the growth of universities, hospitals, schools, community services for the needy, and arts and cultural events.

Recognizing the significance the community has played in its development, the corporation relocated to a newly constructed, modern office complex in north Oklahoma City—Quail Springs Parkway Plaza II—in 1988, thus marking a positive move in firmly establishing Oklahoma City as a base of operations for OXY USA Inc.'s continuing search for, development of, and production of oil and gas.

OXY USA Inc. is also continuing a tradition of community involvement, support, and commitment.

Top left: OXY USA Inc.'s 250 Oklahoma City employees work hard to protect America's energy future.

Top right: OXY USA Inc.'s belief in the American free enterprise system has created a faith for a bright future for the nation's oil and natural gas producers.

Right: A Christmas tree on one of the thousands of OXY USA Inc. wells spread throughout the United States.

KWTV-9

KWTV, Channel 9, the CBS television network affiliate in Oklahoma City, signed on the air December 20, 1953. Originally, the late John Griffin, along with a small group of broadcast pioneers, purchased the station as a group; Griffin later acquired sole ownership, and for more than 3.5 decades it has operated as a part of the Griffin Companies. When Griffin died in 1985, his widow, Martha Griffin, became chairman of the board of KWTV and the other the Griffin Companies. She is an

Duane Harm, president and chief executive officer of KWTV-9.

Oklahoma native and lives in Muskagee.

Oklahoma City has always been a very prominent television market, with KWTV-9 leading the way with many broadcasting firsts over the years. Most notably, TV-9 was the first commercial television station in America to actively use Doppler Weather Radar, which, along with the utilization of other sophisticated equipment by TV-9's mete-

KWTV is located in northeast Oklahoma City. The broadcast facility and production studios are combined at the site established by the company's founder, the late John Griffin.

The number-one-rated news team in Oklahoma.

orologists, has greatly improved the advance warning of impending severe weather and has saved hundreds of lives. Other firsts, such as hour-long newscasts, regular editorials, company-owned helicopter and aircraft, live eye broadcasts, and satellite uplink, are examples of this station's broadcast leadership.

Duane Harm, a 28-year veteran broadcasting executive, is president and chief executive officer of the Griffin Companies. He managed TV sta-

recently launched TV 9 Productions. This $2.5-million addition to the station represents a commitment to the highest-quality broadcast production available in this part of the country. Staffed with professionals and outfitted with the finest equipment, it was built to satisfy the demanding needs of the television industry and is the equal in broadcast technology of the major television production centers located on the East and West Coasts.

TV 9 Productions features the highest-quality broadcast production in this part of the country.

tions from Michigan to Hawaii for other major networks before taking control of Griffin TV in 1980. In addition to KWTV in Oklahoma City, the Griffin Companies includes KPOM-TV, the NBC affiliate in Fort Smith, Arkansas; various real estate holdings; ranching interests; and the Griffin Food Company, located in Muskogee. Griffin Foods manufactures many different food products and packages much of the jams and jellies marketed throughout the Southwest by the Kraft Food Company. In all, the firm employs more than 400 people in Oklahoma and Arkansas.

Continuing its role as a leader in innovative high technology, KWTV

KWTV is especially well known for outstanding news and community service. Channel 9 consistently ranks number one in the state of Oklahoma as the most watched newscast on the air. The station is dedicated to going anywhere in the world with the best equipment to bring the news to Oklahomans. It has received a number of awards, both nationally and locally, over the years for its efforts, and plans to make news and community involvement its number-one goal throughout the remainder of this century.

KWTV continues its commitment to community service with food drives, teen drinking awareness programs, and telethons to name a few. KWTV anchors Jack Bowan and Patti Suarez pose with Crystal Rushing at a recent Easter Seal Telethon.

CLEAR CHANNEL COMMUNICATIONS
KTOK-1000 AM RADIO KJ-103 FM RADIO

Serving the people of Oklahoma for more than six decades, KTOK Radio signed on the air in 1927 as KGFG, a small 50-watt religious broadcast station operated by the Full Gospel Church and located at 10th Street and Phillips Avenue near downtown Oklahoma City. Today KTOK is a part of the Clear Channel Communications family of 16 radio stations stretching from Oklahoma and Texas to the East Coast. Operating out of a state-of-the-art studio at 50 Penn Place in Oklahoma City, KTOK's issue-oriented format is available to 3.35 million Oklahomans, broadcasting with 5000-watts and a five tower transmittor.

Highly successful in appealing to the adult market, KTOK leads the list of radio stations in the Oklahoma City metropolitan area reaching adults 18 years of age or older with combined household incomes exceeding $50,000 annually and who have completed four years of college or graduate school. This success has been built around an informative format designed to provide KTOK's listeners a forum on contemporary local, national, and international issues. With such on-the-air personalities as Bob Durgin, Oklahoma's premier issue-oriented radio spokesman; Billie Rodely, who provides a feminine touch to exciting and interesting topics; and Bob Riggins, who has been Oklahoma's best-known radio talk personality for two decades, KTOK is the region's most listened to issue-oriented station.

Acutely aware of its commitment to the community it serves, KTOK is one of the most respected public service stations in the state. In a region where severe weather poses a major threat, KTOK is the first source of weather information, whether during the emergency situation of an Oklahoma tornado, a frigid norther, or the blistering, sweltering heat of summer. Eleven times daily on a regular basis and whenever needed during severe weather, KTOK's meteorologist, Rick

Tasetano, keeps listeners up to date on the changing weather picture and provides emergency storm warnings

should life-threatening weather appear.

Anchored by Jackson Kane, one of the state's most respected newsmen

Headquartered in Oklahoma City, KTOK Radio has been serving the people of Oklahoma City for more than six decades.

and the recipient of numerous awards for his reporting and editorials, KTOK is one of the most highly regarded news sources in the nation. A vital part of statewide news coverage, the Oklahoma News Network (ONN), provides state news to approximately 40 radio stations throughout Oklahoma. KTOK is also the flagship station to the ONN's Sooner Football Network which is the second-largest radio network in the nation, with stations stretching from the East Coast to Hawaii and often worldwide on the Armed Forces Network. In addition, KTOK's Agrinet provides up-to-the-minute agriculture news, including futures markets, farm and ranch prices, and major farm legislation.

KTOK's sister Oklahoma City station, KJYO-102.7 FM (KJ-103), also a part of Clear Channel Communications, is the region's number-one-rated contemporary, hit-oriented FM station. Its popular features, such as Shadoe Steven's "American Top Forty" broadcast, consistently place KJ-103 at the top of the ratings lists. In addition, the highly successful "KJ Comment"

KTOK is one of the most highly regarded news sources in the nation—a vital part of statewide news coverage. KTOK's issue-oriented format is available to 3.35 million Oklahomans.

feature serves as an effective format of increased community awareness.

Much of Clear Channel Communications' success at KTOK and KJ-103 is the result of providing listeners with consistent programming, programming that the public wants to hear. Programming with a popular, community-oriented, public awareness format.

THE JOURNAL RECORD PUBLISHING COMPANY

Back in the 1890s, before Oklahoma City even existed, a young attorney named Dan Hogan became known as "Sycamore Dan" in western Arkansas because of the editorials he wrote for local newspapers.

He wrote for the *Alliance Banner*, which was published in Mansfield, Arkansas, for the Farmers Alliance. Then he became editor of the *Huntington Herald* and attorney for the United Mine Workers of America, District 21.

That was the start of the remarkable careers of Hogan and his daughter, Freda, two careers that were destined to leave a heritage that continues to this day in Oklahoma City.

The Hogans moved to Oklahoma City in 1920 to start Leader Press, Inc., and the *Daily Leader* newspaper with Oscar Ameringer. Freda, who grew up working in the Huntington print shop, married Oscar in 1926.

Stacks of copies of the Oklahoma City Advertiser *await distribution by this unidentified carrier and others. The* Advertiser *was launched in 1931 and was an early part of the Journal Record Publishing Company; it ceased publication in 1968.*

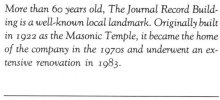

More than 60 years old, The Journal Record Building is a well-known local landmark. Originally built in 1922 as the Masonic Temple, it became the home of the company in the 1970s and underwent an extensive renovation in 1983.

Though Oscar Ameringer died in 1943, Freda continued to operate the *Daily Law Journal Record*, a forerunner to the present *Journal Record*, until 1972. At that time the firm was taken over by her nephew, Dan Hogan III.

Hogan is the grandson of "Sycamore Dan" and today is chairman of the Journal Record Publishing Company and publisher of the *Journal Record*. Hogan is the first to admit that the Journal Record Publishing Company's growth has outpaced his fondest dreams from those days in the early 1970s.

In 1977 events took place that reshaped the entire company. First, the building at 621 North Robinson was purchased from the Home State Life Insurance Company and renamed The

Journal Record Building. The corporate headquarters was moved into the new downtown location from the old building at 4515 North Sante Fe. Hogan sees moving back downtown as a major step forward for the company. "Moving back downtown was important. It allowed us to be near the center of the business and financial community," he says. The next major change was establishing the expanded format of the newspaper, with a business news section published for the first time together with the well-established legal news section.

As for the growth of *The Journal Record*, this business and legal newspaper has nearly quadrupled its circulation since 1980 to more than 6,000 with a readership of approximately 20,000 executives and professionals in the business and legal community in central Oklahoma. As the readership of business news grows and as Oklahoma City grows, there is extensive potential for

The Journal Record is central Oklahoma's only daily business newspaper and is relied upon by professionals and executives as their main source of state and national business news.

growth of *The Journal Record.*

Through the leadership of Dan Hogan, the company has grown and diversified within the marketplace. The Journal Record Publishing Company also prints and distributes the *Tinker Take Off* newspaper for the Tinker Air Force Base. This weekly publication is one of

The Komori Lithrone press is a state-of-the-art sheet-fed press and the only five-color press in Oklahoma City.

the largest of its kind in the United States.

The Journal Record Press is the commercial and financial printing division of the company. The recent purchase of the Komori Lithrone five-color sheet-fed press makes it the leader in commercial printing in central Oklahoma. Financial printing is a very specialized area of printing. Companies turn to Journal Record Press for dependability and experience in the printing of annual reports, prospectuses and other financial printing.

For more than 50 years the Journal Record Publishing Company has been the official publisher for the Oklahoma House and Senate. At the peak of congressional session, up to 1,000 pages of important legislative information are typeset and printed overnight.

The Journal Record Publishing Company owns and manages the building and handles the leasing of the office space at this prestigious downtown location. The company also owns its own garage, which offers full mechanics services to its employees and building tenants.

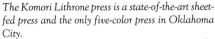

OKLAHOMA NATURAL GAS COMPANY

The Cimarron gas-processing plant.

There were those who thought it was a questionable undertaking back in 1906. A group of pioneering businessmen decided to form Oklahoma Natural Gas Company for the purpose of building a 100-mile pipeline from the producing fields of northeastern Oklahoma to Oklahoma City.

The questions long ago vanished.

There was a risk, to be sure. Around the turn of the century natural gas was regarded by some as little more than a nuisance. And there were other risks to be faced at that time, not the least of which was statehood itself. But as Oklahoma established itself and prospered, so did Oklahoma Natural Gas. It has been a shared relationship through the years; it continues to be today.

From that bold start in the days before statehood has grown one of the state's premier energy providers. Nearly 2,000 employees operating a system of more than 16,000 miles of pipeline bring natural gas to the homes and businesses of more than 2 million Oklahomans in two-thirds of the state—at some of the lowest rates in the country.

Oklahoma Natural Gas Company and ONG Transmission Company are divisions of ONEOK Inc. of Tulsa, and engage in the purchase, transmission, storage, and distribution of natural gas in Oklahoma. The third ONEOK division, the Energy Companies of ONEOK, conducts operations in natural gas liquids extraction, oil and gas exploration and production, and contract drilling. In addition to the three divisions, there are several subsidiaries, including Thermal Systems, Inc., which provides steam and chilled water to a number of downtown buildings in Tulsa and Oklahoma City, and operates a cold-storage warehouse in Tulsa.

A trademark of Oklahoma Natural Gas Company during its more than 80 years of service has been innovation—and the ability to change with changing market conditions. In addition to being a leader in creating pricing and transportation programs that enable state businesses and industries to operate successfully in a time of economic difficulty, the firm continues to play a major role in the state's economic development effort. Through a program of national advertising, companies searching for potential industrial sites have learned that they can rely on ONG as a clearinghouse of accurate information. Through this service and others, ONG has been instrumental in the arrival of several important industries in recent years.

Oklahoma Natural Gas Company also takes seriously its commitment to the communities it serves. One outstanding example of that commitment: Since 1983 Oklahoma Natural and the Salvation Army have jointly sponsored the Share The Warmth program. ONG customers and stockholders have contributed more than $1.5 million to assist Oklahomans facing difficulty in paying home heating costs.

Oklahoma Natural Gas Company is proud to be a vital part of Oklahoma and Oklahoma City's business community.

A natural gas drilling rig.

Photo by Jim Argo

Manufacturing

Producing goods for individuals and industry, manufacturing firms provide employment
for many Oklahoma City residents.

Photo by Jim Argo

UNARCO COMMERCIAL PRODUCTS

Unarco Commercial Products, headquartered in Oklahoma City since the company began in 1937, is today a leading supplier of essential equipment for the mass-merchandising retail store industry worldwide—manufacturing and marketing shopping carts, merchandise display equipment, stock-handling trucks, and a complete line of specialized equipment for preparing, storing, stocking, and moving food in supermarkets.

The company was founded more than 50 years ago to make and market the first shopping carts—shopping carts that changed the way people shop and created a revolution in the traditional retail distribution of food products. Today shopping carts are critically necessary for self-service store operations of every kind everywhere. It's hard to imagine a supermarket or any other mass merchandiser without them. In fact, this Unarco product is now a basic part of the giant food-marketing industry and all mass retailing—a basic part of American life and commerce.

Products of Unarco are the heart of mass merchandising store operations. Under the direction of Marvin Weiss, company president, Unarco Commercial Products is the nation's largest manufacturer of shopping carts, plus a wide

Unarco shopping carts are a basic tool for American consumers in supermarkets and mass-merchandising stores of every kind everywhere.

variety of other merchandise-moving equipment. The firm's headquarters is located in downtown Oklahoma City at Century Center. In announcing the company's 50th anniversary in 1987, Weiss said, "Unarco has a unique partnership with America's mass-merchandising industry. The first shopping carts from Unarco were the equipment needed to make self-service a success in food retailing. More than anything else, it's the shopping cart that's made possible the growth of early-day supermarketing into the gigantic mass-merchandising retail store industry we know today."

One of the key factors in the growth of Unarco is its continuing commitment to this partnership—its commitment to providing products of superior craftsmanship, durability, and quality; its commitment to reliability in on-time delivery of equipment that's essential for stores operations; its commitment to active programs for product development and innovation to fulfill changing needs in store operations; as well as expansion of its manufacturing facilities as needed to keep pace with

the market requirements for its products and advances in production technology. The firm observes a policy of open communication between its customers and its top executives to ensure that management is market responsive. By maintaining close contact with a changing marketplace, Unarco has greatly expanded its product lines that complement the shopping cart and meet additional needs of retailers and consumers. Today a wide range of other Unarco products, as well as shopping carts, contribute to the success of supermarkets and mass-retail stores of all kinds.

Unarco Commercial Products manufactures virtually every type of equipment used to move merchandise through the store—from the point of delivery at the back door to the point of sale, to the checkout, and out to the customer's car in the parking lot. Unarco shopping carts move billions of dollars in sales from shelf to cash register in the many different kinds of mass-merchandising stores evolved by retailers in recent years.

The firm offers a wide variety of shopping cart models and accessories developed for particular needs in store operations: carts for scanner checkouts, large-capacity carts for warehouse stores, carts for sloping parking lots, and carts to inhibit pilferage at the checkout. Unarco's Vendall display systems of stacking or continuous baskets and mobile bins are widely used for jumbled stocking to cut labor costs and stimulate impulse sales.

Unarco product lines provide specialized carts and trucks for the full range of stock-handling tasks in all departments of the store. The company markets a broad line of containers and carts to move and store them, and processing tables and storage racks for in-store food preparation and presentation (meat, produce, bakery, deli), wherever sanitation and durability are requirements. Unarco Commercial Products is committed to its tradition of product development to anticipate needs and provide quality products at competitive prices—equipment that contributes to efficiency and profitabil-

Unarco plants produce the shopping carts and wide variety of specialized stock-handling and display equipment needed by America's mass retailers to keep merchandise moving through the stores.

ity of mass merchandising retail store operations.

The company, which is one of several steel-fabricating divisions of publicly owned UNR Industries, Inc., has a significant role in the economy of Oklahoma. In 1986 Unarco made a multimillion-dollar investment in its new manufacturing plant at Wagoner, Oklahoma. This centrally located plant, with state-of-the-art metals fabrication and finishing facilities—together with the company's other strategically located plants and distribution centers in Memphis, Tennessee; Allentown, Pennsylvania; and Sacramento, California—positions Unarco for further diversification and expansion of product lines to serve growing national and international markets for store equipment. Unarco operations now employ more than 500 Oklahomans in the Oklahoma City offices and Wagoner plant in addition to personnel at its other locations. The Unarco family of employees everywhere takes pride in working together to maintain the Unarco tradition of excellence in service to its customers.

For the future, Unarco Commercial Products is positioned for growth, building on its acknowledged leadership in its present principal market and expanding its product lines for new markets and new business opportunities.

GREAT PLAINS COCA-COLA BOTTLING COMPANY

WHAT IS COCA-COLA?

Coca-Cola was invented in 1886 by Dr. John S. Pemberton, an Atlanta, Georgia, pharmacist and great-grandfather of Art Pemberton, owner and operator of Oklahoma City's exclusive Crescent Market grocery store.

Company letterheads around the turn of the century stated that Coca-Cola is a beverage based on "the tonic properties of the wonderful Coca Plant and the famous Cola Nut."

According to a booklet produced by The Coca-Cola Company in 1916, Coca-Cola is "pure water sterilized by boiling sugar-granulated—best quality, flavoring extracts and caramel. Caffeine—the active principle of tea, citric, and phosphoric acids."

In 1931 *Fortune* magazine claimed that Coca-Cola is 99-percent sugar and water. The other one percent, it maintained, is caramel; fruit flavors; phosphoric acid; caffeine from tea, coffee, or chocolate; "Merchandise No. 5," three-parts coca leaves (decocainized) and one-part cola nut; and a secret ingredient, "7X."

Other ingredients that outsiders have claimed to have found in Coca-Cola are cinnamon, nutmeg, vanilla, and glycerine. To this day the product's formula remains a secret.

Coca-Cola contains less than one-fourth the caffeine found in coffee. When it comes to "Soda Pop," Coca-Cola is The Real Thing, but when it comes to sodium or salt content, Coca-Cola is classified by the Food and Drug Administration as containing "very low sodium." The exact sodium level found in Coca-Cola is dependent upon the local water from which it is made. In Oklahoma, it would take three cases of 6.5-ounce bottles to extract one teaspoon of sodium.

The Coca-Cola Company maintains the secret formula for Coca-Cola in concentrate form, which it sells to franchised bottlers. Coca-Cola syrup is made from concentrate by bottlers in 5,000 gallon batches, with each batch containing 28,000 pounds of sweetener; finally, Coca-Cola is one ounce of Coca-Cola syrup and 5.5 ounces of carbonated water mixed together and served chilled.

In 1982 cane sugar was replaced with high-fructose corn sweetener, which is the same substance chemically but more plentiful and, therefore, less expensive. The "original formula" for Coca-Cola remained unchanged until 1985, when Great Plains Coca-Cola Bottling Company became the first bottler to introduce "New" Coke.

Today Coca-Cola Classic is the same "original formula" that Art Pemberton's great-grandfather concocted in 1886.

Today Great Plains produces more bottles of Coca-Cola in one day than were produced for the entire year in 1922. Current management includes Virgil Browne's grandsons, Henry Browne and Bob Browne, as well as Bob Upton and Ed Dyer.

panies in Oklahoma and each of the surrounding states. These sales outside the franchise area boost the corporation's totals to nearly 70 million gallons per year. To accomplish this thirst-quenching feat, Great Plains employs more than 800 Oklahomans in Oklahoma City and seven sales centers in Enid, Stillwater, Vinita, Chickasha, Ardmore, Tulsa, and Bartlesville. The containers (glass, aluminum, and plas-

Oklahoma's Coca-Cola plant was located near Third and Broadway when this photo was taken in early 1920. The two men in the inset are founder Virgil Browne (left) and his son Henry, who ran the company from 1937 to 1980.

Great Plains Coca-Cola Bottling Company is more than "your local Coca-Cola bottler." The company's products include Dr Pepper, 7Up, Sunkist, Welch's, Barq's, and Canada Dry, to mention just a few of its 40-plus well-known soft drink brands. Today the company's franchise territory includes 40 Oklahoma counties and more than 2.5 million Oklahomans. In 1987 each of these customers drank an average of about one-half gallon of the company's products every week—enough to keep Great Plains number one in Oklahoma.

Great Plains also produces soft drink products for other bottling com-

tic) for these products also are made in Oklahoma by still more Oklahomans.

Since 1967 the company's headquarters have been located in the 160,000-square-foot plant located at 600 North May Avenue. In 1975 the company established Oklahoma Canning Company, a wholly owned manufacturing division in Oklahoma, which has added more than 250,000 square feet to the Great Plains operations. In 1978 another 100,000-square-foot distribution facility was added as a result of the acquisition of Dr Pepper and 7Up. Since 1975 the company has constructed new buildings for five of its sales centers. In 1988 Great Plains acquired the Coca-Cola franchise territories for Bartlesville and Tulsa, Oklahoma. Today, if Great Plains was under one roof, it would cover more than 20 acres.

The Oklahoma City franchise for

Great Plains Coca-Cola Bottling Company's headquarters is now located in this modern facility at 600 North May Avenue.

Coca-Cola first was incorporated and named the Oklahoma Coca-Cola Bottling Company in 1903. In 1922 a group of businessmen headed by Virgil Browne purchased the company, which at that time was located on the ground floor of the Havilin Hotel at 27 Third Street in downtown Oklahoma City.

Browne, at the age of 44, moved to Oklahoma City from New Orleans, Louisiana, "for a year or two to get the business established," but he stayed on to become one of the city's most prominent civic leaders. He served as director and officer of the Oklahoma City Chamber of Commerce for 26 consecutive years. Both he and his wife, Maimee Lee, were inducted into the Oklahoma Hall of Fame.

Virgil Browne was able to give so generously to the city's growth because his son, Henry Browne, Sr., took charge of the company's operations in 1937. Virgil Browne lived to be 102, and Henry ran the business until 1980.

In 1980 Henry's sons, Bob and Henry Jr., together with other investors, purchased the company and changed its name to Great Plains Coca-Cola Bottling Company. Bob Browne became chairman and chief executive officer; Henry Jr. became the vice-chairman; and Henry Sr. was named chairman emeritus. Bob Upton, chief operating officer, and Eddie Dyer, chief financial officer, round out the company's executive management team.

Three generations of Pembertons, Robert, Art L., and Art E., descendants of Coca-Cola's inventor, stand before a display of Great Plains products in their Crescent market—Oklahoma City's oldest grocery store.

GULFSTREAM AEROSPACE TECHNOLOGIES CORPORATION OF OKLAHOMA

A stretch press with skins forming.

Gulfstream Aerospace Technologies, a wholly owned subsidiary of Chrysler Corporation, has been an important part of central Oklahoma's economy for nearly four decades, and when the company's Oklahoma City-based facility, under the direction of its president, R.N. Buckley, reaches its full production potential, it will employ nearly 1,000 individuals and fill a vital niche of the American general and military aviation industry.

As the production of aircraft has become more specialized and rapid technological advancements have become commonplace in the 1980s, many of the larger aircraft production companies have divested themselves of much of their production capabilities. In so doing, they have avoided the costly outlay of capital necessary to open new plants. Instead they have turned to such corporations as Gulfstream to fill the gap. This is precisely the role that Allan Paulson, the chairman and chief executive officer of Gulfstream Corporation, and A.H. Glenn, the president of Gulfstream's U.S. operations, wish to fill.

Originally incorporated as Aero Design and Engineering, Inc., on December 21, 1944, in Culver City, California, Gulfstream, headed by Ted Smith, was organized specifically to develop a twin-engine airplane for executive business needs to meet the demands of an increasingly aviation-conscious society. Four years later, on April 23, 1948, the prototype Aero Commander made its first flight. Fulfilling all the expectations of its designers, providing twin-engine safety with comfort, economy, and speed, that aircraft is now on permanent display at the State Fair Grounds in Oklahoma City.

In September 1949 two Oklahoma City contractors, Rufus T. and W.D. Amis, and a Philadelphia engineer and pilot, George T. Pew, provided sufficient capital to allow the Aero Commander to be certified by the Civilian Aviation Agency. The following month the engineering work was started to provide the required data for a Type Certificate, and flight tests began in April 1950. With their successful completion, the CAA issued a Type Certificate for the Aero Commander on June 30, 1950.

Six months later, in October 1950, Aero Design and Engineering, with the assistance of the Oklahoma City Chamber of Commerce, moved its operations to Tulakes Airport in Oklahoma City and began production of the Aero Commander 520 under Type Certificate No. 6Al. The first production model rolled off the assembly line on January 30, 1952. It was the first twin-engine aircraft designed exclusively for business use, the first pressurized business light twin aircraft, and the first civilian aircraft to use a three-blade propeller. A later model, the 560A, was the first civilian aircraft designated "safe enough for the president" by the Secret Service and the Air Force, and an order for 15 of the aircraft was received from the federal government.

As sales increased Aero's Research and Development opened an adjunct facility at Max Westhermer Field in Norman in September 1954. However, wishing to concentrate the production facilities in a single site, ground was broken for a new and expanded operation at Northwest 15th Street and West Avenue in Bethany in May 1956. Although a fire destroyed the Tulakes plant before the Bethany facility was online, management and production personnel joined together and on December 20, 1957, the first production model came off the new assembly line.

A windshield retainer G4.

In 1964 Aero Commander entered the jet age with the introduction of the Jet Commander, the first aircraft designed specifically as a business jet to be produced by a general aviation manufacturer. A revolutionary aircraft, the Jet Commmander set 25 international flying records. The following year the Turbo Commander, another aviation innovation, was introduced.

Between the late 1950s and the late 1980s Aero Design and Engineering changed ownership several times. It was acquired by Rockwell-Standard Corporation in 1958, and as a wholly owned subsidiary in October 1960 the name was changed to Aero Commander. Three years later it became a division of Rockwell-Standard. Rockwell-Standard merged with North American Aviation Corporation in 1967 to form North American Aviation, and, as a part of the transaction, the Jet Commander was sold to Israel Aircraft Industries, Ltd. Later North American Rockwell was reorganized as Rockwell International Corporation, and the Oklahoma City facility became a part of the General Aviation Division of Rockwell International.

In February 1981 Gulfstream American Corporation, the world's largest privately held general aviation manufacturer, purchased the Okla-

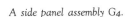

A side panel assembly G4.

homa City plant. In December of the following year the Gulfstream American Corporation name was changed to Gulfstream Aerospace Corporation, and in April 1983 the company went public with its stock. In August 1985 Chrysler Corporation acquired Gulfstream Aerospace Corporation as a

The wiring of a breaker panel G4.

wholly owned subsidiary.

Unfortunately, owing to a general downturn in the civilian aviation industry, Gulfstream announced in January 1985 that it was discontinuing production of the Aero Commander line. However, four months later, with the huge success of the new Gulfstream IV, one of the most modern and efficient general aviation aircraft available, the Oklahoma City plant was reactivated as a support facility to produce many of the integral parts of Gulfstream's newest aircraft. The success of the Gulfstream IV, coupled with the shift of many aircraft production companies to contract instead of in-house production, drastically increased the Oklahoma City plant's value. As a result, in September 1986 the Oklahoma City facility was reorganized as Gulfstream Aerospace Technologies Corporation of Oklahoma.

Leading the way in the new marketplace of aircraft production, Gulfstream Aerospace specifically was designed to fill the needs of aircraft production companies. In so doing it again assumed a leadership role in the American aviation industry.

CAIN'S COFFEE COMPANY

In conjunction with the Centennial of the Run of 1889, Cain's Coffee Company, which blends, roasts, and grinds more than 20 million pounds of coffee annually, will celebrate seven decades of continuous operation. Its corporate history parallels the birth and growth of the Sooner State and is the story of a homespun Oklahoma company.

Its founder, William Morgan Cain, arrived in Oklahoma in the late 1890s with his widowed mother and eight brothers and sisters in a horse-drawn wagon. Pausing in Oklahoma City for the winter, the family decided to remain and supported itself with whatever jobs became available. With the outbreak of World War I, Cain enlisted in the United States Navy, and shortly afterward the idea for Cain's Coffee was born. What sparked his suc-cess was the visit of a ship in Brazil, where Cain was awed by the enormous piles of newly picked coffee awaiting shipment. He was so fascinated by the sight that he decided to become a part of the chain that brought coffee from its native lands to the palates of Okla-homans.

Recognizing that he lacked experi-ence in the food-marketing industry, Cain obtained employment with the A&P Company after he was discharged from the Navy. A little more than a year later he felt sufficiently confident to embark on his own venture and purchased the Western Tea and Coffee Company in Oklahoma City. Establishing himself as a one-man operation, Cain roasted his coffee, ground it, packed it, and then sold it from a basket over his arm throughout the community's business district.

From the beginning Cain paid particular attention to retail markets, and one of his first steady customers was a local cafeteria. As a result of this initial success, he became heavily involved with the hotel and restaurant trade. One of Cain's most successful innovations in this aspect was the pioneering of portion-controlled packages of coffee for use by restaurants.

In addition to coffee, Cain expanded his operation into the marketing of tea and spices. Continually searching for additional markets, Cain developed the one-quart-size tea bag, packed in its own filter paper. A complete spice line is sold throughout its retail marketing area in grocery stores and to more than 20,000 food-service establishments now encompassing a 12-state area.

Cain's Express

Cain's Delivers Freshness.

With increased sales and growth, Cain's Coffee Company was officially incorporated in 1923, and Cain's built a new corporate headquarters near downtown Oklahoma City. In later years the firm moved into larger facilities along the Santa Fe Railroad on Northeast 12th Street, and then into existing corporate headquarters at 13131 North Broadway Extension in northern Oklahoma City in 1964.

Early in his career Cain embarked on a policy of expansion and acquisition. The Tulsa Coffee Company was integrated into Cain's operations in 1941, and many others followed, including the Wilson Coffee Company of Fort Smith, Arkansas; the Manhattan Coffee Company of St. Louis, Missouri; the Yarbrough Company of Corpus Christi, Texas; the Golden Light Coffee Company operating in Amarillo and Lubbock, Texas; and the Star Coffee Company of Little Rock, Arkansas. Eventually more than 20 businesses

were brought under Cain's corporate umbrella, with expansion via acquisition and market penetration an ongoing "modus operandi."

Cain's has continued to stress personal contact with its clients. More than 50 salesmen continually ply Oklahoma's streets and highways, personally servicing accounts and delivering products. They are backed up by sales specialists who seek out new opportunities, and by divisional sales managers who oversee sales operations in Oklahoma, Kansas, Arkansas, Mississippi, New Mexico, Texas, Missouri, Louisiana, Colorado, Indiana, Illinois, and Iowa. Also of importance was Cain's concern with community involvement. He became one of the leaders of the local business community, supporting the progressive growth of the state and Oklahoma City.

After William Morgan Cain's retirement, the company became a subsidiary of Nestle Foods Corporation in

1960 under the direction of Jack Durlund, ushering in another era of growth and expansion, and the firm continues to flourish. Its current president, Tom G. Donnell; executive vice-presidents Harlan Clonts, Ray Robinson, Bob Millspaugh, and Ewart Vaughan; and treasurer, Mark Hoehner, have perpetuated the same basic ideals of the firm's founder.

As a result, Cain's Coffee Company has grown from a one-man operation to become the employer of more than 500 individuals, with an annual payroll in excess of $11 million. By the late 1980s Cain's had become the major brand of all coffee and tea consumed in Oklahoma. Equally important, more Cain's coffee is sold to Oklahoma restaurants and hotels than all other brands combined, and its complete coffee line, consisting of ground roast, soluble, and freeze-dried, continues to grow with retail consumers in the state's supermarkets.

CONTROL DATA CORPORATION SMALL DISK DIVISION

When the first computers went on-line in the late 1940s, they weighed 30 tons, were as large as a gymnasium, used 18,000 vacuum tubes, and required 130,000 watts of electricity to operate. Their magnetic-tape storage devices—which had a capacity of 10,000 characters per second—required 50,000 watts of electricity for power and occupied as much space as six modern refrigerators.

Four decades later computer systems with the same capabilities are small enough to fit on a desk top, utilize microcircuits instead of vacuum tubes, and require a mere 200 watts of electricity to operate. Today's disk storage units, which can fit into the palm of a hand, require only 20 watts of electricity for power and are capable of storing more than one billion characters of information on magnetic disks.

A *Fortune* 500 business operating in 33 countries, Control Data has been a high-tech pioneer since the earliest stages of the computer era. A part of the firm's Data Storage Products Group, the Oklahoma City-based Small Disk Division began in 1963 as a segment of General Electric's Military

Communication Division. Today it is the world's leading OEM supplier of high-performance, high-capacity, 5.25-inch rigid disk drives, known as the WREN™ series, and America's only remaining OEM manufacturer of same.

Headquartered at 10321 West Reno in the extreme western section of Oklahoma City, the Small Disk Division employs 2,000 Oklahomans who produce approximately 500,000 WREN™ disk drives annually, which are shipped throughout the world to original equipment manufacturers of

World competitive, Control Data's Small Disk Division is the leading supplier of high-performance, high-capacity 5 1/4-inch rigid disk drives to original equipment manufacturers. It offers a full line of WREN™ disk drives in both half height (on the right) and full height models, which incorporate the latest in computer disk drive technology.

advanced computers systems. Its contribution to the local economy exceeds $70 million annually.

The Small Disk Division's WREN™ product line consists of a full range of full-height and half-height models ranging in capacity from 48 megabytes (a megabyte is one million characters of information) to more than one gigabyte (one billion characters). The WREN™ 5.25-inch disk drives also have the fastest seek time in the computer industry: 14.5 milliseconds. Consequently, the most advanced WREN™ disk drive is capable of recording the entire text of 200 Bibles and of reading each complete Bible in less than two seconds. In addition, the WREN™ line's more than 50,000 hours meantime between failure rates is among the industry's highest.

Clearly recognized as the technological leaders of the disk drive industry, the Small Disk Division's engineers and technicians have introduced such inno-

Robert K. Maeser, Jr., vice-president of Oklahoma City operations, (right) received a Commendation of Excellence Award from Governor Henry Bellmon for Control Data Small Disk Division's continued contributions to Oklahoma's high-tech industry.

vations as the straight-arm rotary actuator, zone bit density recording, thermal compensation, and adaptive slimming—all industry firsts.

To produce the most reliable product possible, WREN™ disk drives are assembled by highly trained technicians in Class 100 clean rooms. The atmosphere in these rooms contains no more than 100 particles three-tenths of a millionth of an inch or smaller in each cubic foot of air. This ultraclean environment is approximately 10 times cleaner than a hospital operating room.

To remain competitive in America, the Small Disk Division incorporates many advanced design and manufacturing concepts. One of the most successful is the just-in-time material concept, which eliminates the cost of warehousing and allows the division the flexibility of incorporating the latest technological advancements into its line without having a backlog of outdated merchandise. In addition, the latest in manufacturing automation is represented by the Small Disk Division's use of 25 robotic cells and a complete in-house surface-mount technology assembly line for the placement of components onto the electronic circuit boards.

The company also utilizes business center team concepts that bring employees into the day-to-day decision-making process, which has resulted in a number of cost-saving and quality-improvement innovations. Another part of its competitive edge is the alliance the Small Disk Division has formed with state educational institutions, which has been successful in maintaining the highest-possible technical skills of its employees.

"World competiveness in the international market for small computer disk drives is the key to the Small Disk Division's success, and continued innovation is the key to our future," according to Robert K. Maeser, the Small Disk Division's vice-president, who has more than a quarter-century of experience in the computer industry.

"The demand for high-performance, high-capacity 5.25-inch rigid disk drives is increasing rapidly," Maeser points out. "However," he is quick to add, "with the caliber of employees that we have at Control Data Small Disk Division in Oklahoma City, I am confident we will meet the challenge. We have what it takes to be the best, anywhere in the world."

NORICK BROTHERS, INC.

When the capital of Oklahoma was moved from Guthrie to Oklahoma City in 1910, George A. "Lon" Norick mortgaged his home; purchased two small hand-fed presses, a hand cutter, and a limited supply of type; and opened a print shop. Once he had secured the necessary equipment, the entrepreneur convinced his brother, Henry, to quit his $15-per-week job and become a printers devil in his enterprise for three dollars a week. Henry eventually purchased a one-third interest in the company.

The two men first conducted business in a small frame structure next to a blacksmith shop. Sometimes, when the smithy was shoeing a horse or mule, the animal would kick the wall and send a shower of plaster and dust falling on the printers. Of greater concern was the multitude of small print shops that appeared in the capital city; the limited amount of work available made competition keen. Often the Norick brothers had to mortgage their equipment in order to pay creditors. On other occasions they had to suspend operations and take a job with the Oklahoma Publishing Company until they accumu-

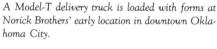

A Model-T delivery truck is loaded with forms at Norick Brothers' early location in downtown Oklahoma City.

lated sufficient capital to reopen.

The tremendous competition forced the partners to be innovative. They realized the business would have to specialize, but in what? Then George purchased an automobile in 1917 and discovered that the booming automobile industry lacked a uniform accounting system to handle the upsurge in sales. In the following weeks George and Henry designed a simple form that could be adopted by all automobile agencies. Several months passed before the first forms were printed.

Deciding to market the forms statewide before any competition could de-

velop, the Noricks mailed samples to Oklahoma's 252 Ford dealers. Realizing that many dealers did not bother with records of any kind and therefore might not recognize the potential of their product, George and Henry spent several anxious days. Within three days they received their first order. With more following the next day, it became obvious that the product had filled a vital need. Within a short time the demand for Norick Brothers forms made it imperative to expand the business.

Initially Norick Brothers was strictly an Oklahoma enterprise—but after officials of Ford Motor Company took notice of the forms and began encouraging its dealers nationwide to adopt the system, orders poured in. At the same time Norick Brothers initiated an aggressive publicity campaign to encourage adoption of the forms by other automobile dealers. The mail campaign was augmented by traveling salesmen who demonstrated the advantages of the Norick system.

The major drawback the firm's salesmen reported was the scarcity of adequately trained automobile accountants. Rather than miss the opportunity to acquire a new customer because that particular dealer did not have an effi-

Ronald (left) and James Norick, two generations of leadership at Norick Brothers and for Oklahoma City. Ron Norick, as mayor of Oklahoma City, will oversee the community's celebration of the Centennial of the Run of 1889.

One of the modern rotary presses at the Norick Brothers' facility in Oklahoma City.

cient accountant, Norick Brothers employed six traveling accountants who offered free training to any bookkeeper whose employer utilized the Norick system. Another endeavor, implemented in 1922 as part of the firm's continual training program, was the publication of *Service News,* an automobile dealership periodical that explained new additions to the system and answered common questions. *Service News,* which changed its name to *Motor Dealer,* grew to more than 50,000 subscribers before it was discontinued in 1955.

By the time George retired because of ill health in 1936, Norick Brothers was marketing forms to handle nearly all makes of American and foreign automobiles sold in the United States. Under Henry's direction the firm continued to expand. A series of branch offices and manufacturing plants were opened, and by the mid-1980s the company had facilities in north Las Vegas, Nevada; Chicago, Illinois; and Kings Mountain, North Carolina, as well as its corporate headquarters in Oklahoma City. To accommodate the expanding network of customers, Norick Brothers organized a private trucking system to provide rapid delivery of orders throughout the country.

In 1953 the firm was reorganized as Norick Brothers, Inc., with Henry Norick retaining the presidency. Three of his children—James H. Norick, Marjo-

rie Norick, and Dorothy Norick Patton—were elected vice-presidents, and another daughter, Frances Norick Lilly, was named secretary. Six years later James H. Norick became president, serving in that capacity until 1980, when he was made chairman of the board and his son, Ronald Norick, assumed the presidency.

While he was building Norick Brothers into the success it is today, James Norick played an ever-increasing role in community activities. He was elected to two terms as mayor of Oklahoma City, 1959 to 1963 and 1967 to 1971. The Norick family's involvement in community affairs was carried on by his son, Ronald Norick, who was elected mayor of Oklahoma City in

1987 and as such will oversee the celebration of the Centennial of the Run of 1889.

In 1959 Norick Brothers, Inc., moved into its current headquarters at 3909 Northwest 36th Street in Oklahoma City. To meet the demand created by the adaption of computers for record keeping by many automobile dealers, the firm created Norick Data Systems in 1975. The new software was produced in a plant just to the north of the corporate office and in the following years expanded its line of software to include insurance ratings, which allowed insurance agents to select the best-possible source of coverage for their customers. In 1986 Norick Data Systems became an independent operation. Norick Brothers also expanded to meet the new demands created by computer technology, increasing its line of products to include numerous computerized forms.

By the time of Oklahoma City's centennial, under the direction of Ronald Norick, the firm's uniform system of accounting for automobile dealers was recognized as the most widely adopted program among the nation's car dealers. To handle its operations, which extended to all 50 states and several foreign countries, Norick Brothers' Oklahoma City plant and corporate headquarters employed 300 workers. Another 150 employees were located across the country.

The Norick Brothers' warehouse, located in the Annex Building just north of the main plant, houses the thousands of specialized forms used by the firm's multitude of customers.

Business

Building on the past while planning for the future, Oklahoma City's business community launches its second century in the forefront of technological innovation and financial leadership.

Photo by Matt Bradley

OKLAHOMA CITY CHAMBER OF COMMERCE

Founded in 1889, shortly after the land run that caused Oklahoma City to be "born grown," the Oklahoma City Chamber of Commerce has consistently been the most effective organization promoting economic growth and development in central Oklahoma.

For example, the chamber played a major role in the creation of the city's meat-packing industry in 1911, supported and encouraged the drilling of the Oklahoma City oil and gas field and related petroleum industries, promoted the community as a major transportation and distribution center, and established Oklahoma City as a center of both military and civil aviation. Through direct chamber action—under the leadership of Stanley C. Draper, Sr., and other dedicated civil leaders—Tinker Air Force Base, Will Rogers Bomber Base (later to become the FAA Center), Wiley Post Airport, and Clarence Page Airport all were established in 1942.

Following World War II the chamber expanded the scope of its activities. Its leaders worked diligently to see that both Interstate highways 35 and 40 passed through Oklahoma City. Economic development efforts contin- ued to expand so that by 1988 it was estimated that the organization had generated at least 95,000 jobs in central Oklahoma.

The important and challenging nature of the chamber's mission is reflected in the loyalty and dedication of the staff and volunteer leadership. Four active staff members have a combined total of 161 years of experience with the organization: Paul Strasbaugh and Arch Jack, each with 42 years; Clayton Anderson, 40 years; and Stanley Draper, Jr., with 37 years.

By 1988 the chamber had evolved to the point where its board of directors oversaw 17 different divisions— Administrative, Agriculture Development, Beautification, Centennial, Convention and Tourism, Economic and Community Development, Economic Research, Education and Community Services, Energy, Government Relations, Health Development, Membership Development, Metropolitan Activities, Metropolitan Development, Public Relations, Public Safety, and U.S. Olympic Festival—with each division containing one or more councils. The Convention and Tourism Division receives much of its funding from the city room tax and is operated by the chamber under contract with the City of Oklahoma City.

Throughout its history the chamber has managed to involve outstanding citizens in its leadership structure. Among its current officers are chairman Clyde Ingle and vice-chairmen Ray Ackerman, Robert H. Anthony, Clay Bennett, G.T. Blankenship, Wm. Kenneth Bonds, Andrew H. Coats, John C. Dean, Edwin deCordova, Ted Gumerson, Stanley Hupfeld, Steve Lynn, Edmund Martin, Frank A. McPherson, Ed Miller, William N. Pirtle, William W. Talley II, and C. Rainey Williams. Other officers are William E. Durrett, treasurer; Lloyd J. "Jimmy" Lyles, Jr., president; and Dean Schirf, corporate secretary.

With its immediate focus on the Oklahoma City Centennial Celebration, the Oklahoma City Chamber of Commerce is poised to promote a second century of economic development and improvement in the quality of life in central Oklahoma.

Oklahoma City, planning for the future. Courtesy, Ray Jacoby Photography

OKLAHOMA CITY ECONOMIC DEVELOPMENT FOUNDATION, INC.

Founded in 1981 as a nonprofit organization by several members of the Oklahoma City Chamber of Commerce, the Oklahoma City Economic Development Foundation is designed to work closely with the chamber to promote the overall economic development of Oklahoma City and to work cooperatively with other central Oklahoma communities.

The chamber, which was founded in 1889 and celebrates it centennial along with the Run of 1889, has always been in the forefront of Oklahoma City's growth and development and is one of the main reasons that the community is a major financial, manufacturing, and business center in the Southwest. The Economic Development Foundation also aids various governmental, business, and industrial elements that play key roles in the economic development of Oklahoma City and the state.

The idea of an economic development foundation developed in 1979, when chamber officials first began planning the centennial of the Run of 1889.

It was not until two years later, however, that the movement gained emphasis with the effort to prevent the National Cowboy Hall of Fame and Western Heritage Center from relocating. Plans for a nearby federally sponsored housing project had caused concern among officials at the Hall of Fame as to the future of its Oklahoma City site. To ensure the continued development of the area as a major center of tourism and recreation, the economic development foundation raised sufficient funds to purchase the affected property.

Soon afterward, planning for the centennial of the Run of 1889 began in earnest. With the foundation providing the staff, financing, and overall coordination, a major effort was made to attract international attention to the first century of Oklahoma's growth by hosting a world's fair. Although the plan was not fulfilled, the information gathered became the basis for much of the centennial celebration.

One of the key elements to the celebration is the 1989 United States Olympic Festival, one of the nation's premier sporting spectaculars. The foundation provided the necessary financial support for special materials, studies, and travel expenses to lure the festival to Oklahoma City, and also organized Oklahoma Centennial Sports, Inc., to oversee the event. In addition, a myriad of other centennial activities are sponsored by the foundation, including a greatly expanded State Fair of Oklahoma and numerous special projects planned by institutions and organizations throughout central Oklahoma.

Responsibility for marshaling the efforts of central Oklahoma for the centennial celebration belongs to G.T. Blankenship, president, and Paul Strasbaugh, executive vice-president, of the Oklahoma City Economic Development Foundation, Inc. Joining with them to make the celebration a success are a host of civic-minded individuals and corporations, who share the goal of ensuring another century of growth for Oklahoma City and the surrounding area.

OKLAHOMA CITY ECONOMIC DEVELOPMENT FOUNDATION, INC.
BOARD OF DIRECTORS

Ray Ackerman	James G. Harlow, Jr.	John Parsons
Bob Anthony	Richard D. Harrison	William Pirtle
Rex M. Ball	Dan Hogan	Lowe Runkle
G. T. Blankenship	Don Hotz	Lee Allan Smith
James D. Blanton	Clyde Ingle	Chris Spelingene
Wm. Kenneth Bonds	Donald S. Kennedy	Paul B. Strasbaugh
Richard H. Clements	John Kilpatrick	Bill Swisher
Edwin deCordova	Robert E. Lee	James Tolbert, III
Don Douglas	M. Stanley Lee	Morrison G. Tucker
C. Richard Ford	Frank McPherson	James E. Work
Richard Gaugler	Edmund Martin	Ray A. Young
Edward L. Gaylord	Jerry Metcalf	Stanton L. Young
Brooks Hall, Jr.	William V. Montin	

CRESCENT MARKET

Throughout his two-thirds of a century in the grocery business, Art L. Pemberton, Sr., stressed the maintenance of a friendly, family-style grocery store catering to the individual customer. It is this philosophy that has made Crescent Market, located at 6409 Avondale Drive in Nichols Hills Plaza, the success it is today. The emphasis on serving the individual, instead of the mass marketing of pre-packaged food products, has created an attractive atmosphere for three generations of Oklahoma Citians.

Founded on the day of the Run, April 22, 1889, Crescent Market is the only business in continuous operation celebrating its centennial with Oklahoma City. Initially a partnership between John D. Thomas and Joe Rucks, Crescent Market began in a dirt-floored tent in downtown Oklahoma City stocked with merchandise hauled from Kansas by wagon. Three months later it moved into its first permanent structure, a clapboard wooden building with a sheet-iron roof. Although it occupied several locations, the enterprise remained in downtown Oklahoma City until 1928, when it moved to the Plaza Court Building on Classen Drive. In 1942 the market was purchased by Pemberton, who had been in the grocery

Left to right: Art E. Pemberton, Art L. Pemberton, Sr., and Robert A. Pemberton, three generations of the family engaged in the management of Crescent Market. They are seated on a priceless Belter-carved divan, one of many antiques displayed throughout the store.

business for many years in Muskogee. Crescent Market remained at Plaza Court until 1963, when Pemberton moved it to its present location.

Born in 1906, Pemberton is still active in the family-owned business, visiting the market daily; preparing a column, "Art Says," for the market's weekly newspaper advertisment; and serving as consultant. However, most of the day-to-day operation has been turned over to his son, Art E. Pemberton, who serves as president. The third generation of Pembertons joined Crescent Market when Robert A. Pemberton completed his education and entered the family business as vice-president. It is not unusual for the three generations of Pembertons to serve three generations of customers, calling many by name as they shop in the store.

In explaining Crescent Market's 100 years of successful operations, Art Pemberton, Sr., remarked, "Never sell something you would not eat." In keeping with this tradition, Crescent Market maintains eight full-time butchers who custom cut meat to customers' orders so they obtain the "best value received for good food." Meat and produce are the only two items you can improve after it reaches the store, the elder Pemberton explains, and in order to provide the highest grade of beef possible, Crescent Market pays a two-cent-per-pound premium selection for choice meat and ages the beef 28 days in an on-site cooler before preparing it for sale.

While the meat department produces 30 percent of Crescent Market's annual sales, the produce department also specializes in individual service, and accounts for 12 percent of total sales. Two shipments of fresh fruits and vegetables, which are not available on the local market, are received weekly from the West Coast. Other out-of-season fruits are air freighted into Oklahoma City from South America. It is the only store in Oklahoma City, and one of few west of the Mississippi River, to operate a special ripening room with controlled humidity and temperature, to allow fruit to ripen to

Founded on the day of the Run of 1889, Crescent Market is the only business in continuous operation celebrating its centennial with Oklahoma City.

perfection before being sold. In addition, fresh herbs, instead of dried, are available to customers, and such items as pineapples are peeled and cored in the store for sale. These innovations allow Crescent Market to present the freshest-possible products to its customers.

In addition to produce and meat, Crescent Market handles a variety of specialized products. More than 400 varieties of domestic and imported cheeses are offered. All are purchased in large wheels and then individually cut in the store. More than 200 specialty frozen-food items are stocked, and fresh orange juice and peanut butter are produced daily in the store. All specialty items are easily located in with the standard products on the market's shelves, so that a shopper might find a jar of imported caviar next to a can of Vienna sausages.

These specialty items, plus health and beauty aids, comprise one-quarter of Crescent Market's sales. Meat produces another 30 percent, and produce, 12 percent. The remaining 33 percent of sales is made up of staple products.

During the holiday season Crescent Market also offers a wide variety of food items as gifts. Smoked turkeys are a favorite, with 500 to 600 sold annually. Other popular items are gift packages of cheese and gourmet steaks. All gifts are packaged and shipped for the customer in his own name.

As a part of being a family grocery store where customers can do all their food shopping, Crescent Market maintained for years an extensive charge account system that allowed customers to order by telephone. Dry ice was used to keep frozen food and ice cream frozen as deliveries were made to customers' homes. Although home deliveries were discontinued in 1975, walk-in customers are still treated to cookies, candy, and hot coffee, and immaculate rest rooms are maintained for their convenience. Checks are cashed and stamps sold at the market's courtesy office, and friendly clerks always are available to help find a particular item. The carpeted shopping aisles, which are vacuumed daily and steam cleaned monthly, are specially designed so that shoppers may view the shelves on both sides, while being wide enough to allow two shopping carts to easily pass.

Adding to the family atmosphere is the prominent display of fine antiques. Presented alongside the 20,000 items offered for sale, the antiques break the monotony associated with average grocery store shopping. A priceless John Belter-carved divan, Victorian desk, grandfather clock, and other items are

Featuring out-of-season fruits and other produce not available on the local market, the produce section of Crescent Market, through the use of a special ripening room, provides customers with the freshest-possible fruits, vegetables, and herbs.

attractively displayed along with the firm's coat of arms, which features a crescent, the age-old symbol of food; a beef; and a horn of plenty together with a monogrammed "C.M."

By catering to individuality instead of mass marketing, Crescent Market grosses $6 million annually from a sales area of 20,000 square feet. When the hours of operation are considered, from 9 a.m. to 6:30 p.m., six days a week—the store is closed on Sunday and all recognized holidays—the ratio of sales to the square footage make Crescent Market one of the most successful grocery operations in the nation. Art Pemberton believes the combination of quality products and competitive prices, presented to individual customers, has allowed Crescent Market to prosper for 100 years.

LIPPERT BROS., INC.

A diversified general contracting company and utilities firm, Lippert Bros., Inc., was founded in Boone, Iowa, in 1920 by two brothers—Erick W. and Walter H. Lippert. Both were brick masons. Initially they specialized in residential chimney and basement construction and such outside concrete work as sidewalks and driveways. However, within a short time they expanded into complete commercial and industrial building projects. As the business grew, three other brothers—Lewis T., Reuben C., and Leo J.—joined the firm. All were either trained masons or carpenters.

Eight years after the partnership was formed, Lippert Bros. entered the field of large-scale sewage- and water-treatment facilities. With the move came rapid expansion and diversification, and by the outbreak of World War II the firm was a recognized leader in the construction industry. Quickly entering the nation's war effort, the brothers constructed numerous projects throughout the Midwest for the military training command. One of their first projects was the construction of the sewage-treatment plant at the newly opened Tinker Army Air Corps Base near Oklahoma City. In a more direct contribution to the war effort, Erick's sons, Donald E. and Robert L.,

served in the Navy during the war.

Donald and Robert returned home in 1946, completed their college educations, and joined the family business. With their successful completion of the Tinker project and other efforts, Erick Lippert, together with Donald and Robert, decided to permanently move to the Sooner State. To handle the expanded operations, they incorporated as Lippert Bros., Inc., in 1947. The Iowa-based portion of the family business remained separate from the Oklahoma operation. Since that time Lippert Bros., Inc., has been a driving force in the state's economy, and as the business grew the firm eventually expanded its operations into eight surrounding states—New Mexico, Texas, Colorado, Nebraska, Iowa, Missouri, Kansas, and Arkansas.

To enable the corporation to retain a broad base, Donald, Erick, and Robert formed Utilities Engineering and Construction Co. (UEC) in 1953 to provide specialized services for public works projects. The move allowed Lippert Bros., Inc., to retain its identity as a leader in the general building contracting business, while diversifying the family's operations into the field of public works projects, such as the 30-million-gallon-per-day addition to the Lake Hefner Water Treatment Plant in Okla-

Built by Utilities Engineering and Construction Co., a subsidiary of Lippert Bros., Inc., specializing in public works projects, the Lake Arcaida Water Treatment Plant is capable of providing 12 million gallons of water daily for the citizens of Edmond.

homa City.

Other UEC Oklahoma projects include the $16.2-million Arcaida Lake Water Treatment Plant, the $5.8-million Del City Waste Water Treatment Plant, the $3.6-million Shawnee Waste Water Treatment Plant, the $11.3-million Lawton Waste Water Treatment Plant, the $11-million Cow Creek Waste Water Treatment Plant for Oklahoma City, and the $5-million Midwest City Water Treatment Plant.

In the meantime Lippert Bros., Inc., successfully undertook a variety of general building projects, such as office buildings, churches, and industrial and commercial facilities. Within Oklahoma City, the firm's most visible projects include Oklahoma City University's Gold Star Memorial Library, the Draper Lake Water Treatment Plant, Citizens Tower, the First Presbyterian Church, the National Cowboy Hall of Fame and Western Heritage Center, and the Myriad Gardens' Crystal Bridge. One of the corporation's most unique undertakings was the historical renovation and transformation of Oklahoma City's old Central High School into One Bell Central for Southwestern Bell, a nationally recognized, award-winning example of historic preservation and the modification of classic structures for modern usage.

Lippert Bros., Inc., has also been highly successful in the construction of education facilities, having built projects for the Oklahoma City Public Schools, Oklahoma City University, Oklahoma State University, the University of Oklahoma, Oklahoma Christian College, Rose State College, Central State University, Iowa State College, Colorado State University, St. John's College, John Brown University, and the University of Nebraska. Other areas of specialization include the firm's work in broadcast facilities for KAUT-TV, KOCO-TV, KWTV, and KTVY in Oklahoma City, as well as health care construction for the State of Oklahoma's Department of Health Building, Edmond's Memorial Hospital, Woodward Hospital, Oklahoma

City's Bone and Joint Hospital, and Children's Memorial Hospital in Oklahoma City.

In 1964 Donald and Robert Lippert assumed management of the corporation, becoming president and executive vice-president, respectively. A family-owned and -operated business since its inception, Lippert Bros. continues with the third generation of the family now entering the business. It is this corporate structure, combined with a base of satisfied customers and a reputation for performance and quality work, that has contributed to the continued overall success that Lippert Bros., Inc., has enjoyed for more than seven decades.

One of a disappearing breed of contractors, the firm possesses a large field staff and the appropriate field equipment capable of structural excavation, concrete reinforcing, miscellaneous steel installation, carpentry, specialty installation, equipment installation, and site utilities work to support its staff.

Completing between $20 million and $30 million worth of construction projects annually in the Southwest, Lippert Bros. employs hundreds of local workers on a myriad of individual projects, basically in Oklahoma.

Guided by a basic business philosophy of utilizing the appropriate personnel within the corporation to provide the needed experience and knowledge for specific individual projects, the firm prides itself on conducting its operations efficiently. As Don Lippert points out, "The quality that goes into construction is not just depicted on plans and specifications, it is reflected in our people's performance on the job," and Lippert Bros., Inc., takes great pains to use the best people for a particular task.

Lippert workers completing the concrete work on the grandstand for Remington Park, a multimillion-dollar horse racing facility in north Oklahoma City. Lippert Bros., Inc., was responsible for nearly 19,000 cubic yards of concrete used in the grandstand's construction.

YORDI CONSTRUCTION, INC.

Yordi Construction, Inc., combines 12 years of quality construction, a team of highly skilled personnel, and an outstanding reputation for professionalism and performance. This reputation is the foundation upon which Yordi Construction will build its future in Oklahoma City.

A civil engineering graduate from the University of Oklahoma, Ronald N. Yordi founded Yordi Construction, Inc., in 1976 and continues today as president of the company. The firm is headquartered at 13415 North Santa Fe in Oklahoma City and specializes in a broad variety of commercial and industrial work. Yordi Construction has built such projects as historical renovations that had to be completed to exacting detail, airport terminal work that had to be planned around automobile and pedestrian traffic, hospital renovation work that could not interfere with patient treatment, and other work that other contractors were hesitant to undertake for various reasons.

Recognized as an industry leader, Yordi Construction, Inc., has received numerous awards for its multitude of projects. Among them was being named the Outstanding Oklahoma Contractor in 1987 by the Central Oklahoma Chapter of the American In-

College of Pharmacy Building, University of Oklahoma Health Sciences Center. Courtesy, Jack Mills Productions, Oklahoma City, Oklahoma

stitute of Architects. Numerous safety awards have been received, and they are the recognition in which the greatest pride is taken.

The company consists of professional engineers, project managers, licensed architects, marketing experts, certified public accountants, superintendents, and office and field personnel who are heavily recruited, well trained, and highly accomplished in their areas of expertise. It blends these individuals into a team that provides the most economical and highest-quality construction for the customer.

Members of the firm are active in Leadership Oklahoma City and Leadership Oklahoma, the Associated Gen-

eral Contractors, United Way, and Allied Arts. Various Yordi personnel volunteer their time by serving on the boards and committees of numerous social services and arts agencies.

Much of the success enjoyed by the firm is the result of its philosophy of business, which is to provide the best-possible professional services and not just sell a product. By offering a diversity of professional skills, Yordi Construction is committed to being known as the company that can complete the difficult jobs on time and on budget.

By relying on the experience of the management team—Ronald N. Yordi, George W. Todd, James A. Pickel, and Sam B. Smith—and refusing to compromise professional pride in the company's work, Yordi Construction's reputation has grown. The annual dollar volume of work contracted by the firm has increased each year since its founding.

Yordi Construction does not stay on budget the easy way, by stripping a project of its quality finishes and unique design features. The use of innovative construction techniques and economical systems and materials for the nonaesthetic portions of a project saves the owner money. Other savings are realized by Yordi Construction's involvement as a part of the owner-architect team during the design phase of a project, when the construction time frame can be cut by ordering long-lead items and implementing phased construction that allows work to continue at the full, 100-percent level.

Yordi Construction, Inc.'s, project

Will Rogers World Airport, Oklahoma City. Courtesy, Jack Mills Productions, Oklahoma City, Oklahoma

list includes numerous banks and financial institutions, medical facilities, churches, schools, airports, office buildings, government agencies, housing, and industrial work. Recent work at Will Rogers World Airport has included the East Terminal addition, the West Terminal addition, the air cargo building, and the land-side access project. Yordi Construction has been an active force in the construction of Will Rogers World Airport as its growth has escalated.

A $6.5-million job at the Mike Monroney Aeronautical Center is a massive renovation of the Federal Aviation Administration's headquarters facility at Will Rogers World Airport. This 140,500-square-foot remodel will upgrade this facility to today's modern standards and strengthen Oklahoma City's commitment to the aviation industry.

A recent list of financial projects includes the First Interstate Bank branch in the Waterford complex, the Bank of Edmond, N.A., the drive-thru banking facility for Century Bank, N.A., and The Fort Sill National Bank in Fort Sill.

Medical facility projects include several St. Anthony Hospital renovations and additions, the Pasteur Medical Building, the Dental Specialties Center, and the College of Pharmacy

Building on the campus of the University of Oklahoma's Health Sciences Center.

Some of Yordi Construction's other recent projects include the Baden Building remodel in Bricktown, Westminster Presbyterian Church, Bethany First Church of the Nazarene, Northeast Missionary Baptist Church, the West Gallery of the National Cowboy Hall of Fame, and the OG&E generator building in downtown Oklahoma City.

Yordi Construction solicits new projects through the traditional methods of bidding, negotiating, and design/build. Although each method has its advantages, the design/build approach has offered Yordi's clients the greatest savings of time and money. By developing a team consisting of the owner, architect, and contractor, savings can be

West Gallery, National Cowboy Hall of Fame, Oklahoma City, Oklahoma. Photo by Bob Shimer, Hedrich-Blessing, Chicago, Illinois

St. Anthony Professional Building, Oklahoma City, Oklahoma. Photo by R. Greg Hursley, Inc., Austin, Texas

realized throughout a project. This method enabled Yordi Construction to build the $11-million St. Anthony Professional Building and parking garage in only 11 months and realize a substantial monetary savings.

As a community service, Yordi Construction provided construction management for the Mayfair Center—a facility for the administrative offices of five social service agencies and a community center for the Mayfair neighborhood. A former elementary school, the Mayfair Center required special attention be given to the specific needs of the elderly while closely monitoring a very tight budget.

Yordi Construction, Inc., is also assisting in the planning stages for the renovation of another vacant building, the Stage Center at Festival Plaza in downtown Oklahoma City. When the Arts Council of Oklahoma City purchased this building after it had been closed due to massive energy bills, Yordi Construction started working as a team with the new owner and the architects and engineers to develop energy-efficient systems, handicap access, and user-friendly features.

Whether the project is an exacting medical facility, a complicated airport expansion, or an office to provide services for senior citizens, Yordi Construction strives to provide the best-possible professional services. With its impressive base of repeat customers, a skilled staff of professionals, and a strong commitment to Oklahoma City, Yordi Construction, Inc., is looking forward to the future—a future of continued growth in a city that continues to grow.

USPCI, INC.

Headquartered at 2000 Classen Center in Oklahoma City, USPCI, Inc., founded in 1968, offers its customers the entire spectrum of industrial waste removal and treatment.

The firm's technicians can examine a client's industrial waste, analyze it for potential hazardous content, and classify it according to the latest federal, state, and local guidelines. Once this has been accomplished, company specialists can remove the dangerous material in complete safety without causing environmental damage, transport it to one of the firm's disposal or treatment facilities, and either store the hazardous waste in such a way that it poses no threat or treat it to render it nonhazardous.

USPCI's services start at the firm's National Analytical Laboratories (NAL) in Tulsa, where a modern,

A subsidiary of USPCI, Hydrocarbon Recyclers, Inc., maintains a state-of-the-art treatment and recycling facility in Tulsa. This is just one of USPCI's hazardous waste-management, treatment, and recycling plants located nationwide.

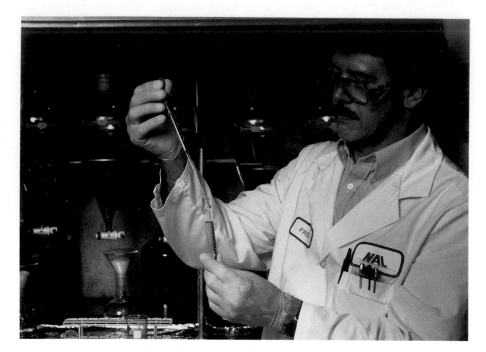

One of the National Analytical Laboratories' chemists analyzing a client's hazardous waste.

15,000-square-foot state-of-the-art laboratory enables the company's technicians to determine quickly a customer's needs. Under provisions of the federal Superfund Project, the corporation also has the primary responsibility for analytical services in case of an emergency or initial response to hazardous waste contamination.

In transporting the hazardous waste for its customers, USPCI uses a fleet of company-owned tractors, trailers, solid-waste containers, and a number of specially designed railroad intermodal containers. This equipment enables the firm to provide the most cost-effective method of transporting hazardous waste to one of its industrial waste-treatment and disposal facilities. At each location, laboratories and administrative offices carefully monitor and control all incoming waste to ensure its safe and effective handling.

The company also maintains a network of waste-treatment facilities that render hazardous waste safe for recycling or disposal. A wholly owned subsidiary, Hydrocarbon Recyclers, Inc., (HRI) in Tulsa, oversees USPCI's recycling operations, which are designed to extract commercially usable products such as fuel oil from waste material.

USPCI also spends a significant amount of its resources in emergency response to accidents and remediation projects. These investigatory and remedial action services were initiated as a service to customers and local and state agencies faced with potentially hazardous situations. The firm's Special Services Division technicians are on 24-hour call to provide rapid response to hazardous waste emergencies and offer a full range of on-site waste-management services.

In 1984 USPCI launched an aggressive expansion program based on selected acquisitions and aimed at making the company North America's foremost hazardous-waste-management firm. Among the acquisitions were PPM, Inc., specializing in the chemical destruction of polychlorinated biphenyls (PCBs), and JTM, Inc., a marketer of combustion and mineral processing by-products designed to turn a client's liability into an asset. The new expansion program also has propelled the organization into new technologies such as incineration—which promises to be the most profitable, efficient, and preferred method of hazardous waste disposal in the future.

With gross income in excess of $83 million for 1987 and more than 800 employees, almost half of whom are located in Oklahoma, USPCI has an important impact on the state's economy. Because of its unique services and nationwide reputation, the firm also serves as an effective lure for other industries seeking cost-effective solutions for a safe environment.

Chapter Eleven

Professions

Greater Oklahoma City's professional community brings a wealth of service, ability, and insight to the area.

Photo by Matt Bradley

205

FIRST INTERSTATE BANK OF OKLAHOMA

Bank on Opening Day

When Richardson's application for a federal bank charter was approved on August 20, 1890, the Oklahoma Bank was renamed the First National Bank of Oklahoma City. Rapid growth continued, and in 1893 a three-story stone building was completed. Following a policy of aggressive acquisition, the First National Bank eventually ac-

Left: Texas bankers T.M. Richardson, J.P. Boyle, and George T. Reynolds set up an office in a makeshift tent on April 20, 1889, to accommodate the first customers of the Oklahoma Land Run.

Below: The Oklahoma Bank moved to a temporary building on April 23, 1889, the day after its opening in a makeshift tent.

TEMPORARY BANK, 106 W. MAIN 1889

THE OKLAHOMA BANK

The forerunner of what today is First Interstate Bank of Oklahoma, a part of First Interstate Bancorp, opened for business on April 22, 1889. Almost a century later First Interstate is one of the state's most successful financial institutions, with six bank offices scattered throughout the Oklahoma City metropolitan area and a capital base in excess of $80 million. First Interstate Bank of Oklahoma is an affiliate of First Interstate Bancorp, one of the nation's top 10 banking companies with total assets approaching $60 billion. As an affiliate, it is an integral part of a nationwide network of financial institutions operating in 19 states with 1,100 offices located in 600 communities.

Originally called The Oklahoma Bank, plans for the new bank were made months before the official opening of the Unassigned Lands by three pioneer Texas bankers: T.M. Richardson and J.P. Boyle, who were to oversee the founding of the financial institution, and George T. Reynolds, a wealthy Texas banker and rancher who supplied the necessary capital.

Wanting to be the first bank established in Oklahoma City, Richardson planned to make the run on April 22 and stake a claim in the new city. To ensure that he would be ready for business as quickly as possible, he stopped in Texas on his way to Oklahoma for a safe, heavy oak desks, checks, and other material. Completing his trip to Oklahoma by train, he arrived on the border of the Unassigned Lands shortly before the run. His equipment soon followed.

After staking his claim, Richardson accepted The Oklahoma Bank's first deposit from E.E. Elterman on April 22. Elterman's bank drafts promptly were stored in the safe, temporarily housed in a makeshift tent. However, the following day a crude temporary building was completed using lumber that Richardson had shipped north from Dallas. Shortly afterward, Richardson approached John R. Tanner about the possibility of purchasing Tanner's two nearby lots. Tanner agreed, and once Richardson completed the transaction, he quickly completed a permanent 2,500-square-foot building to house the bank's operations.

quired 21 other financial institutions that were folded into First National. This expansion necessitated additional space.

In 1929, during the height of the Oklahoma City oil boom, work on First National's new home began. Occupying a one-half square block in downtown Oklahoma City, the structure became symbolic of the state's oil industry and its impact on Oklahoma's economic growth. A $5-million showplace, the new bank building, which opened in 1930, has remained a distinctive part of the Oklahoma City skyline for nearly 60 years; whenever people think of downtown Oklahoma City, they think of the First National Bank building.

During this early period Oklahoma

City's First National Bank began to take on the character of Charles A. Vose, Sr., who was to become the prime motivator of the institution for nearly 65 years. Vose first joined the bank in 1921, and by 1930 he and his family had gained control of the institution. Under his direction, First National, which by the 1930s had grown into one of the largest banks in the Midwest, weathered the Great Depression and continued its policy of aggressive acquisition. By the mid-1950s it was the largest financial institution in the state.

While at its controls, Vose insisted that First National Bank assume a lead-

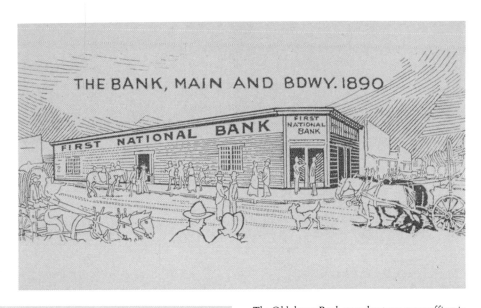

THE BANK, MAIN AND BDWY. 1890

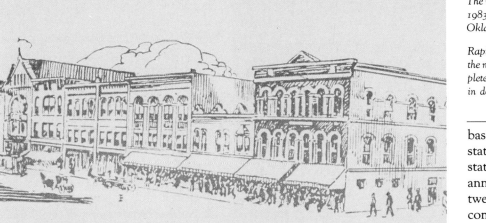

THE BANK, MAIN AND ROBINSON, 1905

The Oklahoma Bank moved to permanent offices in 1983 and was renamed The First National Bank of Oklahoma City.

Rapid expansion necessitated additional space, and the new three-story First National building was completed at its present location on Main and Robinson in downtown Oklahoma City.

ership role as a corporate citizen. In so doing, he continually stimulated the growth of Oklahoma's economy. During World War II it was First National that underwrote the purchase of property adjacent to the Municipal Airport to be utilized by the Army Air Corps as a supply depot. This purchase not only contributed greatly to the nation's war effort, but also helped the facility evolve into Tinker Air Force Base, the state's largest employer. The economic ramifications of Tinker Field to the central Oklahoma economy is staggering, with some economists claiming that one-quarter of all economic activity in the region is either directly or indirectly tied to the facility.

In addition to its pivotal role in Oklahoma's main industries of energy

and agriculture, First National's presence was evident in all sections of the state's economy. Working closely with the state's leaders, First National's management team underwrote much of Oklahoma's economic expansion during the oil boom years of the first two decades of the twentieth century and the later booms of the 1950s and 1970s. In addition, the bank's stature and resources helped in Oklahoma City's emergence as a medical center of national renown, particularly in the areas of cardiac care, burn research, and diseases of the muscoskeletal system.

While First National Bank of Oklahoma City was growing into one of the region's most successful financial institutions, First Interstate Bancorp was duplicating that growth on a nationwide

basis. A modern version of the multi-state banking organization, First Interstate Bancorp was conceived by A.P. Giannini during the early decades of the twentieth century. Utilizing a winning combination of charisma and business acumen, Giannini built a strong base of shareholders and customers among the thousands of immigrants who poured into the San Francisco Bay Area. Giannini's idea of a network of banks was so successful that it made significant gains with respect to many of the established institutions.

In 1927, to protect their markets, certain of these established institutions lobbied Congress to restrict the operations of federally licensed banks to one state; the lobbying effort succeeded. Giannini's response was to utilize his organizational talents to form Transamerica Corporation in 1928 to serve as a nationwide holding company for financial institutions.

Adopting a policy of aggressive acquisition in 1930, Transamerica took its first step in the creation of a nationwide network by purchasing an Oregon-based bank. Three years later the corporation acquired a group of Nevada

Nearly 60 years after its completion at Main and Robinson, the home of First Interstate Bank of Oklahoma remains a distinctive Oklahoma City landmark.

owned 25 financial institutions and had expanded its operating territory into 11 states by 1956. Once again the federal government intervened to stymie Transamerica's growth. As a result of the federal Bank Holding Company Act in 1956, Belgrano split Transamerica into two parts—Firstamerica, which handled banking, and Transamerica, which retained the nonbanking interests.

Firstamerica Corporation began operations on July 1, 1958. Three years later, on April 3, 1961, another corporate change resulted in the bank holding company adopting the name Western Bancorporation. By the close of the 1960s the corporation held assets in excess of $10 billion. During the following decades growth and expansion continued throughout the West. By the 1980s Western Bancorporation had become one of the nation's 10 largest bank holding companies.

On June 1, 1981, the holding company changed its name to First Interstate Bancorp. By then it controlled 21 banks in 11 states with 900 offices servicing 450 communities. Under the corporate arrangement each individual bank maintained local autonomy. The entire system, however, was tied to a network of banking services that transcended state boundaries.

The new name facilitated the creation of innovative concepts in financial services, such as the introduction of the nation's first bank franchise system on March 1, 1982. Under the program, franchised banks used the First Interstate name, advertising, signs, common products, and computer services, while retaining local ownership and management. In 1982 First Interstate Bancorp took the lead in the formation of a nationwide network of automated teller machines that allowed customers anywhere in the United States to make cash withdrawals.

As First Interstate Bancorp was assimilating the tremendous growth of the 1970s and 1980s, Oklahoma's economy came under vigorous assault, across the board. Oil selling for more than $30 per barrel plunged to $11 per barrel or less, and natural gas that once brought up to nine dollars a thousand

financial institutions. Other out-of-state purchases followed, with acquisitions in Washington in 1936, Arizona in 1937, and more Nevada banks in 1941.

The federal government again interceded in the growth of Transamerica in 1948, when the Federal Reserve System ruled that the acquisition of numerous out-of-state banks constituted a potential monopoly and could stifle competition. Although Giannini appealed the decision, Transamerica's expansion stopped while the case slowly wound its way through the courts. Finally, in July 1953, the United States Court of Appeals reversed the Federal Reserve ruling. Unfortunately, Giannini did not live to see victory; he died during the appeal process.

Frank N. Belgrano, Jr., succeeded Giannini as head of Transamerica in May 1953 and continued his predecessor's policy of aggressive expansion. Under Belgrano's direction, Transamerica

cubic feet dropped to $2 or less per thousand cubic feet. The precipitous drop in energy prices was accompanied by a rapid deterioration of both agriculture and real estate markets. This wholesale economic downturn had a tremendous impact on many of First National's customers, whose borrowing capacity during the boom years far exceeded their ability to repay their debts once the markets declined. Due to widespread loan default and decreasing collateral values, the capital base of First National Bank was depleted. When First National's management was unable to stem the economic tide, it was closed by the Federal Deposit Insurance Corporation on July 14, 1986. At that time it was the second-largest bank in America ever to be declared insolvent.

The following day First Interstate Bank of Oklahoma, N.A., opened as the state's third-largest financial institution with $1.4 billion in assets thereby establishing Oklahoma's first interstate banking institution. As a part of First Interstate Bancorp, which at that time boasted assets in excess of $49 billion, First Interstate Bank of Oklahoma brought financial resources of a magnitude never before available to Oklahomans. As one of the largest domestic lenders in commercial business, the First Interstate network serves an area covering some 57 percent of the United States, as well as encompassing international banking locations in the Asia-Pacific area, Europe, the Middle East, Latin America, and North America.

First Interstate Bank's relationship with First Interstate Bancorp provided its customers with numerous increases in available services, while at the same time maintaining its hometown identity. As a part of the First Interstate franchise system, customers could visit any of First Interstate Bancorp's affiliated and franchised banks in 19 states, from Hawaii to Washington D.C. and from North Dakota to Louisiana, and receive the same services, such as check cashing and credit card services, they would receive in Oklahoma City. In addition, by leveraging off the resources of a $60-billion institution and by drawing on those resources, First Interstate provides quality services second to no other financial institution.

As a part of its corporate commitment to expand its service to Oklahomans, First Interstate Bank purchased Norman Bank of Commerce and the Expressway Bank of Oklahoma City. In addition, a branch office of First Interstate was opened in the Waterford development in north Oklahoma City in July 1988.

By the beginning of First Interstate's second century of service to Oklahomans, the bank had regained its prominence among the state's financial institutions. Its relationship with First Interstate Bancorp brought a renewed commitment to the state and a sharp increase in its resources. First Interstate Bank of Oklahoma is one of the strongest financial institutions in the Southwest.

The First Interstate Bank of Oklahoma's main office lobby is a unique example of architectural design.

CROWE & DUNLEVY

Composed of 84 attorneys, 17 paraprofessional legal assistants, and an 87-person support staff, Crowe & Dunlevy provides the highest-quality legal services to its clients.

Crowe & Dunlevy was founded five years before statehood in 1902 and has enjoyed steady and consistent growth. The firm is composed of 84 attorneys, 17 paraprofessional legal assistants, and an 87-person support staff.

Crowe & Dunlevy is organized as a professional corporation and is engaged in almost all areas of the practice of law. Although considered an institution in terms of its historical presence and commitment to the Oklahoma City community, Crowe & Dunlevy represents a strong mix of youth and experience. The average age of firm members is 44, while the average age of all attorneys is 37.

The firm is committed to a philosophy of providing the highest-quality legal services to its clients efficiently and at reasonable cost. The firm strives to maintain state-of-the-art library, administrative, and other services conducive to the realization of this objective. The Crowe & Dunlevy library is recognized as one of the most extensive libraries in the southwest region. Presently, the library numbers more than 18,000 volumes in 10 satellite libraries, making it the largest private law library in the state of Oklahoma. In addition, recent developments in data-retrieval technology have greatly increased research speed capabilities through the use of electronic data bases, covering such diverse areas as business and marketing, biological and medical information, scientific and engineering data, and energy and natural resources.

The firm is engaged in all aspects of the general practice of law, including matters relating to corporations and other business organizations, securities, taxation, real estate, oil and gas, health care, commercial transactions, banking, bankruptcy and creditors' rights, probate, estate planning, antitrust, labor relations and employment law, administrative agencies, insurance, aircraft titles, municipal bonds, and the trial of civil and criminal cases in all courts.

In order to manage this diversity of practice and for purposes of administration, Crowe & Dunlevy is organized into three basic departments: Litigation, Business/Corporate, and Oil and Gas. Each department is subdivided into practice areas of concentration. Due to the wide range of experience, the firm is able to respond to clients with its ability to assemble a legal team with knowledge and expertise in a particular field. This philosophy of specialization encourages timely solutions to client needs in a practical problem-solving environment.

The firm's Litigation Department constitutes approximately one-half of the total legal staff. The firm is staffed to handle virtually any type of litigation, including antitakeover, banking, securities, commercial and contract, bankruptcy and creditors' rights, product defense, natural resource, workers' compensation and employment discrimination, nuclear energy and toxic substances, tort, antitrust, foreclosure, and constitutional law matters.

Various attorneys in the firm specialize in labor-related matters, including union elections and decertifications, labor disputes, contract negotiations, employment discrimination, and wage and hour laws.

The diverse range of expertise of the attorneys involved in general business and corporate matters allows the firm to service the needs of organizations ranging from small businesses to major publicly held corporations. Experience ranging from incorporation, public and private offerings of securities, mergers and acquisitions of business units, partnership organizations and transactions, labor matters, general taxation, commercial law, loan restructuring, and other matters are available within this practice area.

The firm has a strong background in the design of pension and profit-sharing plans, as well as complex tax litigation. Crowe & Dunlevy represents clients before the Internal Revenue Service and the Oklahoma Tax Commission in connection with taxpayer audits and the administrative consideration of proposed tax deficiencies. In addition, its attorneys handle both civil and criminal tax cases.

Historically, Crowe & Dunlevy has enjoyed an extensive practice on behalf of banks and other financial institutions. The firm currently represents numerous banks located both within and outside the state of Oklahoma. Attorneys in the firm have considerable experience in the formation and opposition to formation of both state and national banks, the establishment of one-bank and multibank holding companies, mergers and acquisitions, commercial laws applicable to financial institutions, compliance with federal and state regulatory requirements, the organization of savings and loan associations, and negotiating and otherwise dealing with the regulatory authorities, including negotiating memoranda of understanding, formal agreements, cease and desist orders, capital forbearance and open-bank assistance applications and similar documents, and the acquisition of distressed financial institutions pursuant to purchase and assumption agreements.

Crowe & Dunlevy's real estate and finance practice section is prepared to handle all aspects of real estate transactions. Services include counseling clients on business transactions, including the recommended legal structure of long-term commercial real estate transactions. Crowe & Dunlevy presently provides services to banks, savings and loan associations, and other institutional lenders in connection with major real estate lending and equity transactions.

Health care law is one of the most recently recognized specialties in the practice of law. For a number of years, the firm has been active in the representation of hospitals, physicians, clinics, and other corporations or forms of business entities that provide services to patients or engage in activities ancillary to the delivery of medical or dental services. The firm is experienced in the formation, organization, and operation of such entities as MeSH organizations, HMOs, PPOs, PPAs, IPAs, and all types of joint ventures, including hospital-physician building partnerships, ambulatory surgical centers, CT imaging centers, fertility centers, catheterization laboratories, MR imaging centers, home health care, physical fitness and rehabilitation centers, primary care clinics, and group purchasing activities.

In addition, the Health Care Law Section contains lawyers experienced in legal matters peculiar to health care, such as certificates of need, Medicare/ Medicaid, patients' rights, medical staff issues, risk management, inurement issues, nonprofit/for-profit relationships, and fraud and abuse.

Since Oklahoma is a major center for energy-related industries, the firm's Oil and Gas Department, in conjunction with other practice groups, has developed the necessary expertise to serve the special needs of the energy industry. The members of the firm's Oil and Gas Department have extensive experience in oil and gas matters, including litigation, title matters, corporation commission work, energy financing, property acquisition and contracts, and operating agreements. The firm can assemble experienced teams to respond to clients' needs in complex oil and gas matters and the application of government legislation, regulation, and administrative orders. The department also has experience in other environmental areas including water resources law and its regulation.

The firm is engaged in all aspects of general law and is organized into three basic departments— Litigation, Business/Corporate, and Oil and Gas. This philosophy of specialization allows the firm to respond to client needs efficiently and constructively.

LINN & HELMS

A long-established Oklahoma City-based law firm with an excellent reputation dealing in major cases on a national scale, Linn & Helms was founded by James Paul Linn and J.D. Helms in 1970. At that time, however, the founding partners already had accumulated more than three decades of courtroom experience and had previously worked together in Spearman, Texas.

Linn, who received his LL.B. from The University of Texas School of Law in 1950, first served as a prosecutor and then opened a private law practice in Spearman. Within a few years he built a successful general-purpose legal practice that went far beyond the realm of being just another local attorney. Through his travels and out-of-state contacts, he represented clients nationwide.

Such a firm fit well with the plans of another young graduate of The University of Texas Law School, J.D. Helms, and in 1957 the two combined their talents to form Linn & Helms. Although the firm remained in Spearman until 1969, its reputation as "attorneys' attorneys," with the ability to represent a client on a nationwide basis was well-established.

Wishing to relocate in a larger metropolitan area, Linn & Helms moved to Oklahoma City in 1969, and in Sep-

The Oklahoma City-based law firm of Linn & Helms has a long-established reputation for legal expertise practiced on a national level.

tember of the following year founded the Oklahoma City-based Linn & Helms law firm. Built on a philosophy of "Whatever was the client's business was the firm's business, wherever that business might be," Linn & Helms for four years steadily expanded its client base by utilizing Linn's unique trial talents and Helms' unsurpassed support skill. The successful evolution of the firm brought about a need for expansion, and in 1974 the first moves in a carefully planned policy of growth and diversification were made.

By 1975 the state's economic boom accelerated the expansion and necessitated additional legal expertise to provide the firm's clients with the best-possible service. Linn & Helm's reputation for success attracted a number of bright young attorneys foreseeing unlimited opportunities and possibilities of advancement. By the mid-1980s Linn & Helms offered the services of 12 partners—Linn, Jack L. "Drew" Neville, Jr., Bernard J. Rothbaum, Jr., William P. Warden, Raymond E. Tompkins, James D. Thomas, David E. Pepper, Ronald L. Ripley, Libby Hougland Banks, Michael S. Richie, Russell A. Cook, and Stephen R. Johnson; three of counsel members—Helms, Von Russell Creel, and Jack T. Conn; and nine associates—Susie Pritchett, Mark A. Donaldson, Terry A. Lensgraf, Brinda K. White, Michele O'Neill, John D. Singleton, Mark L. Weintrub, Conner L. Helms, and Tim Haley.

While numerous Oklahomans and Oklahoma-based companies utilize the firm's legal services, Linn & Helms consciously expanded its legal talents so that its members were educated and licensed to practice law anywhere their clients might need help. This resulted in a wide range of out-of-state clients, which were attracted by Linn & Helms' reputation of success in the nation's courtrooms. As Linn explained, "We are successful as a law firm because we are successful in the courtroom."

In addition, Linn & Helms successfully endeavored to remain in the forefront of changing legal theory. Helms says, "As the law changed, so did the firm." This progressive attitude allows

The Linn & Helms boardroom.

Linn & Helms to offer its clients the best and most up-to-date legal services available based on current law.

To do this, Linn & Helms utilizes the entire spectrum of its members' specialized legal talents; yet the firm has not attempted to restrict members to a single field of law. This not only aids the clients but also allows individual attorneys to expand their legal expertise through working with other members of the firm. This specialization, in conjunction with general legal expertise, allows Linn & Helms to offer a team approach to a myriad of nationwide clients. As Linn points out, the job of an attorney is to reduce a complex situation to the simplest-possible explanation that can persuasively be presented to a jury. By bringing specific people together to handle specific situations,

Two views of the Linn & Helms lobby area.

Linn & Helms developed a technique of combining the firm's legal talent for the mutual benefit of individual attorneys and clients. As Linn & Helms' successful courtroom reputation grew, so did the firm's nationwide clientele.

Linn & Helms' litigation practice includes general civil and criminal cases at both the trial and appellate levels in state and federal courts nationwide. In civil litigation, the firm's experience encompasses virtually every area—including contract, oil and gas, commercial, securities, antitrust, bankruptcy, personal injury, civil rights and discrimination, tax, tender offers and corpo-

rate takeovers, class action, and other complex matters. The firm's criminal defense practice primarily consists of legal counsel for white-collar crimes in federal court. In addition, the firm provides legal representation before state and federal regulatory agencies.

Linn & Helms' unique personality is one of the main factors in its success. According to Helms, "Individuality is the key to winning in the courtroom, and the firm encourages individuality." Legal arguments are strengthened by an honest and frank appraisal of all aspects of a client's case. Dissenting legal arguments are encouraged from the

staff, so that every possibility is investigated before a case goes to court. This ensures the best-possible representation for the firm's clients.

During its growth Linn & Helms maintained its philosophy of corporate citizenship through community service, not only in the area of free legal services but also as to individual community involvement—such as the Linn-Helms Law Library at Oklahoma City University and J.D. Helms' service on the State Board of Regents for Higher Education. Pro bono cases are undertaken regularly to assist those lacking adequate financial resources to ensure due process. In no instance is the potential unpopularity of such legal actions taken into consideration in accepting these cases. The members of the firm proudly proclaim that "the doors of Linn & Helms are always open to those who cannot pay."

In addition, the firm has produced two judges dedicated to public service, William R. Burkett and Richard Countness, and individual special legal service to such civic projects as the National Cowboy Hall of Fame and Western Heritage Center, and the U.S. Marshals Foundation.

MANAGEMENT SERVICES CORPORATION (MSC)
LEAR SIEGLER HOLDING CORPORATION

Committed to the Total Capability— Single Support Concept, Management Services Corporation (MSC) has been providing management and technical support services to government and industry on a worldwide basis since 1961. These services cover the entire spectrum of logistic and management support, ranging from the development and building of a single prototype to the development of a total logistic support system.

The success of the organization is directly related to its flexibility to tailor its unique capabilities to fit the requirements of the individual customer and vary from aircraft, ground vehicle, and water vessel modification and maintenance to facility management, base operations, and support services. Many agencies of the Department of Defense, as well as NASA, FAA, domestic aircraft and systems manufacturers, and foreign governments utilize MSC's talents.

With 2,000 experienced and qualified people working on three continents—North America, Europe, and Asia—MSC fills a vital segment in the technical and contract services industry by offering superior management based on quality service. This combination of outstanding corporate management and qualified personnel ensures that Management Services Corporation's clients receive the quality service they expect.

Located at 3100 North Interstate 35 in Oklahoma City, MSC, by offering administrative support from its headquarters, relieves on-site project managers of time-consuming duties and allows them to concentrate on direct mission-oriented management tasks. In all its work, Management Services Corporation adheres to a policy of sensitivity to the needs of individual customers and responds immediately and objectively to any anticipated future requirements. The use of fully trained and qualified personnel eliminates the need for extensive backup support from internal resources on project sites. This, coupled with the cross-utilization of highly qualified people, stringent quality control, and rapid response, allows MSC to use few people to ensure that a job is done right the first time, thereby increasing efficiency, improving performance, and cutting cost for its clients.

To provide quality service for its customers, MSC utilizes experienced contract field teams, with broad experience in providing support services. Relying on advanced methods of production and quality control, the corporation field teams oversee all contract administration, quality assurance, purchasing, production, material control, accounting, payroll, engineering, staffing, manning, and reporting functions necessary for trouble-free operations. For projects beyond the capabilities of field teams, Management Services utilizes a field services concept to contract for the operation of transient aircraft maintenance services at various USAF bases, plus the operation of motor pool maintenance, aircraft maintenance programs, cargo handling, and railway services for the U.S. Army.

Technical programs designed to operate and maintain simulators, provide engineering and technical support to research and development laboratories, and offer training, audiovisual support, communications, precision measurement equipment laboratories, and computer services are another aspect of Management Services Corporation. A large part of MSC's work force is involved on a continuous basis with the modification or major rework and systems installations in manned airborne weapon systems.

Management Services Corporation's only business is service, and under the direction of its president, Charles T. Scott, the firm has become an integral part of the nation's defense and aircraft industry. Its unique concept of total capability, which encompasses all skills necessary to accomplish all or any combination of logistics and technical support and maintenance facilities management programs, has made MSC one of the most respected and reliable management corporations on a global basis.

NICHOLS HILLS BANK AND TRUST COMPANY

Today Nichols Hills Bank and Trust Company stands at the threshold of the dream of G.A. Nichols. It was Nichols' vision in 1929 to develop this 2,780-acre Nichols Hills community like no other to be seen in the entire state of Oklahoma. A similar vision was shared by the bank's founding board of directors—men such as G.T. Blankenship, a former member of the Oklahoma House of Representatives, and attorney general of Oklahoma, and Richard A. Coyle, whose grandfather was the same G.A. Nichols who developed this area nearly 60 years ago.

Nichols Hills Bank was founded at its present location in 1975 at 6410 North Avondale Drive, adjacent to 63rd and North Western Avenue. It is an independent, state-chartered, commercial bank with assets that intially totaled $1.3 million, serving its customers with 13 employees.

A unique combination of board members, along with management personnel, combined their talents to ensure that Nichols Hills Bank realized growth and profitability each year since its inception. The bank has continually expanded its services while maintaining a safe, secure, personal, and cordial atmosphere for customers. Somewhat unique to banks of its size, Nichols Hills Bank's president and chief executive officer, Kenneth L. Lawton, Jr., has strategically located his office in the institution's main lobby. Lawton not only observes the day-to-day operation, but frequently leaves his office to greet customers.

Local ownership and leadership have committed the bank to serve the community, not only by providing a strong financial base, but with civic involvement as well. The Red Bud Classic is a prime example. Nichols Hills Bank was one of the founding sponsors of this marathon event, helping bring it to national acclaim with more than 4,726 participants in 1987 during this two-mile and 10-kilometer competition.

With service a paramount factor in Nichols Hills Bank's successful growth, it expanded its original full-service financial facility, offering its customers the complete range of banking

services—including checking, savings, certificates of deposit, wire transfers, collections, money orders, cashiers' checks, notary services, loans, and investments—by adding a complete trust operation in 1985. At that time the bank was renamed Nichols Hills Bank and Trust Company.

As the bank grew through the decades of the 1970s and 1980s, expansion became necessary; in 1980 work was started on an addition to the original structure. The six-story Nichols Hills Bank Tower was opened in 1982. Its design and decor blends with the natural elegance of the surrounding community.

By 1988 Nichols Hills Bank and Trust Company's assets totaled more than $90 million. It now serves approx-

The lobby of the Nichols Hill Bank and Trust Company.

imately 8,000 customers with a total of 60 employees.

During this impressive growth Nichols Hills Bank and Trust Company has remained an active member of the community it serves with its local ownership and leadership . The following is a statement by G.T. Blankenship, chairman of Nichols Hills Bank and Trust Company and Nichols Hills Bankcorporation, Inc.: "Our goals are simply to please our customers with the best, most pleasant of services, to loan money at reasonable rates, and to provide a safe and secure place to keep your money."

LIBERTY NATIONAL BANK AND TRUST COMPANY

The lead bank of the state's largest and strongest bank holding company, Liberty National Bank and Trust Company was founded on September 3, 1918, by a group of Oklahoma City financial and civic leaders, headed by L.T. Sammons.

In the ensuing years Liberty initiated a policy of active acquisition, which made it a leader among Oklahoma's financial institutions that offered a broad range of banking and financial services to meet the diverse needs of its individual and corporate customers. Within three years of its founding, the institution acquired Oklahoma City's Guaranty State Bank, and in 1925 another Oklahoma City-based bank, the Oklahoma National Bank, was purchased. In the following 3.5 decades Liberty became an important part of the state's economy and financed billions of dollars of growth and development throughout Oklahoma.

Another acquisition was made in 1960, when Liberty merged with the Bank of Mid-America, and in July 1984 Liberty joined with Tulsa's First National Bank and Trust Company to form Banks of America, Inc.—the state's largest financial institution. Additional acquisitions took place in 1986, when Liberty acquired certain assets and the insured deposits of the First National Bank and Trust Company of Norman and the Citizens National Bank and Trust Company of Oklahoma City, which gave Liberty three locations in Oklahoma City and two locations in Norman.

Liberty originally was housed in a converted barbershop in the Lee Building at the intersection of Main Street and Robinson Avenue; however, it quickly outgrew this facility, and during its first half-century the bank occupied a series of sites in downtown Oklahoma City. Fifty years after its founding Liberty announced the construction of the 36-floor Liberty Tower, the city's tallest and largest building and the first major structure completed in the revitalization of downtown Oklahoma City. Ten years later, in 1978, work was begun on the Mid-America Tower, which together with the Liberty Tower forms Mid-America Plaza, one of the Southwest's major financial centers and a showplace of downtown Oklahoma City.

One of the keys to Liberty's continued success has been innovation—as the banking industry changed, Liberty added new services to meet the new demands. In 1966 it was the first Oklahoma bank to introduce the credit card and by 1977 had become the state's largest credit card issuer. In 1973 Liberty initiated its highly acclaimed and award-winning Let's Talk Business program designed to educate Oklahomans in the role of banks in the state's economy, and three years later it installed the first on-line ChecOKard automatic teller machines in the state, which provided instantaneous responses to customer inquiries.

Throughout its history Liberty's management has stressed that the bank is an integral part of the community that it serves. As a part of this policy, the institution and its employees are active participants in a myriad of community projects that support the arts, education, and numerous other charitable and civic activities. In addition, Liberty was the first Oklahoma bank to provide Braille bank statements and automatic teller machines for visually handicapped customers, as well as specialized equipment to allow hearing-impaired customers to transact banking business.

Liberty's senior management team of Raymond H. Hefner, Jr., chairman of Liberty Bank; William M. Bell, president and chief executive officer; and W. Kenneth Bonds, vice-chairman, combine more than three-quarters of a century of banking experience and plan to ensure that Liberty National Bank and Trust Company remains Oklahoma's premier "home-owned, home-grown, home-focused, and home-managed" financial institution.

Liberty National Bank and Trust Company is housed in the 36-floor Liberty Tower, the city's tallest and largest building and the first major structure completed in the revitalization of downtown Oklahoma City. Photo by David Fitzgerald

THE TRUST COMPANY OF OKLAHOMA

Growing out of an idea by the co-founders of the firm, C. Randolph "Randy" Everest, who serves as chairman of the board, and Paul H. Mindeman, who is its president, The Trust Company of Oklahoma was organized by 11 Oklahoma City-area banks to offer an independent, quality trust service that could not be otherwise provided by the organizing banks. In addition, this new independent trust company would not compete with referring banks for commercial banking clients.

Bringing five decades of experience in the trust industry with them, Everest and Mindeman quickly raised one million dollars in capital from the participating banks, and, after securing a trust charter from the Oklahoma State Banking Department, The Trust Company of Oklahoma began operations in January 1981. At that time it was the only trust company in the nation organized and owned by a consortium of community banks.

In its first year of operation The Trust Company focused on placing stock with other Oklahoma financial institutions to raise additional capital and broaden its potential customer base. To encourage investment, voting stock was offered to the banks so they could share ownership. The effort was a success, and within a year 41 state and national banks, holding 65 percent of the stock, were participants in the venture. The remaining 35 percent of the stock was held by the management team, and was used as an inducement for corporate stability, which provided long-term continuity between management

and customers. This continuity allows The Trust Company of Oklahoma to consistently give its customers the highest-quality service possible on an individual basis.

The policy of active expansion continued, and in January 1986 American Trustcorp (ATC) was formed as a holding company and acquired all the stock of The Trust Company of Oklahoma. This move allowed the extension of operations into neighboring states, and that same year ATC purchased The Southland Trust Company of Dallas, Texas, which it renamed The Trust Company of Texas. Today The Trust Company of Oklahoma is managing $600 million for its customers—45 percent in employee pension and other benefit plans, with the remainder in personal trusts and agencies. Ninety-nine percent of its customers are Oklahomans.

To serve its statewide operations, The Trust Company maintains offices in Oklahoma City, Tulsa, and Muskogee, staffed with 60 financial specialists, with its top 10 people having more than two centuries of experience in the trust industry. The firm has three chartered financial analysts on its staff. They provide expert investment advice for living trusts, trusts established under wills, investment management under agency agreements, and employee benefit plans. The Trust Company does not accept deposits, nor does it make loans.

The founders of The Trust Company of Oklahoma are (from left): Carl L. Shortt, Jr., executive vice-president; C. Randolph Everest, chairman and chief executive officer; and Paul H. Mindeman, president.

The Trust Company of Oklahoma has but one goal—to pursue the best interest of its clients on an individual basis to assure maximum attention and peak return.

Its sole activity is to provide high-quality trust and investment management services and to serve its clients as trustee, personal representative, conservator, guardian, escrow agent, oil and gas agent, real estate agent, or custodian.

The independence of action provided by The Trust Company allows it to act with each client's interest as the paramount concern. As Everest is quick to point out, "An independent trust company has but one goal—to pursue the best interest of its clients . . ." Neither individual nor corporate funds are pooled, but are managed on a separate basis to assure maximum attention and peak return. Only stocks listed on the New York Stock Exchange or "A"-quality or higher rated bonds are purchased.

The prudent management of its clients' assets combined with quality of service are the keys to The Trust Company's success. The firm's investment specialists tailor each client's investment portfolio to best suit individual needs, while the highly experienced administrative officers provide truly personalized client attention. This specialization, blended with a unique level of attention to individual portfolios, has allowed The Trust Company of Oklahoma to outperform 78 percent of the nation's investment management companies in its first seven years of operation.

HTB, INC.

A national leader in the architectural-engineering-planning profession, HTB, Inc., originally was formed in Oklahoma City in 1942 to plan and design Army Air Corps bases as a part of the nation's war effort. HTB quickly expanded beyond its initial imperative and successfully completed work for numerous schools, hospitals, highways, and municipal projects in America, as well as overseas. Such projects as Oklahoma City's historic Number One Fire Station, United Founders Tower, Northwest Classen High School, the Oklahoma Department of Transportation headquarters, and renovation of the old Perrine-Cravens Building into Robinson Renaissance; the lobby of First Interstate Bank in Oklahoma City; Tulsa's St. Francis Hospital and Reading & Bates corporate headquarters; Saudi Arabia's Ministry of Defense and Aviation Building; the National Press Building in Washington, D.C.; the San Jose, California, airport; and the Port of Catooa in Tulsa thrust HTB into the forefront of the engineering and design industry.

For 45 years HTB has applied an individualized client-oriented approach to each project. This practice, coupled with rigid control standards for budget and time constraints, has allowed HTB to build an enviable reputation for on-time and on-budget completion of projects. HTB continually has been recognized for its award-winning designs and innovative solutions to client needs.

Artist's rendering of HTB's planned expansion of Oklahoma City's Will Rogers World Airport.

Much of the firm's present business comes from repeat clients, many of whom have relied on HTB's prize-winning professional services for decades.

HTB's pioneering effort in the nation's aviation industry is reflected in the founder's vision of preparing for tomorrow's aviation needs today. This commitment is illustrated clearly in the firm's master plans for Oklahoma City's three municipal airports, which as early as the 1960s included a contemporary air terminal that linked the community to international transportation routes. Today HTB is working to prepare Will Rogers World Airport—the

hub of the Sooner State—for the twenty-first century.

HTB has played a major role in the growth and development of the Federal Aviation Administration's Mike Monroney Aeronautical Center since the 1950s, when the firm was instrumental in helping to obtain the necessary federal legislation for revenue bond financing and produced the center's original design. Since that time HTB has continued to help plan, expand, and provide maintenance design for the world's "Air University."

The massive task of renovating and reconditioning Tinker Air Force Base's 3001 Building after a disastrous fire reflects the capabilities of HTB's large professional staff. The firm prepared the construction documents, an accumulation of 26.9 miles of paper, for the reconstruction of more than 750,000 square feet, including 17 acres of roof area, of the jet engine repair plant in a notable manner. Completion of this work normally would have required two years; HTB accomplished the task in only 10 months.

An abiding commitment to the continued growth of Oklahoma has made HTB synonymous with the term "community involvement." Rex Ball, the corporation's chief executive offi-

The renovated Maywood Church, on the left, and new structure on the right, will be the headquarters of HTB, Inc., a national leader in the architectural-engineering-planning profession and will form the core of the Harrison-Walnut Redevelopment Area.

cer, insists that the firm's talents and resources be cultivated and applied toward the good of the community as a whole. As a result, HTB exhibits a special sensitivity to projects that form the fabric of the community. This interest in the vitality of Oklahoma City and the belief in its ability to overcome any obstacle is reflected in the firm's active participation in civic, educational, and social programs as well as support of the fine arts. In the spring of 1988 the firm was honored community-wide as the Corporate Humanitarian of the Year by KOCO Channel 5 for its outstanding efforts on behalf of the community.

HTB has continuously been involved as a leader in projects that enhance and foster the quality of life and economic growth in Oklahoma. Projects such as the renovation of old Central High School into One Bell Central in Oklahoma City represent landmark historic preservation efforts. The firm's One Bell Central design displayed an excellence through preservation of original remnants of Oklahoma City's first high school in the interior design of the new office building. The former main entry became a memorabilia museum for Central High School alumni. These extra efforts to bond the old and the new resulted in One Bell Central receiving Oklahoma City's first annual Mayor's Award of Civic Achievements. The project received an Honor Award from the Oklahoma City Sec-

tion of the American Institute of Architects and one of only two national Honor Awards from the American Society of Interior Designers.

Another local HTB project that exemplifies the firm's commitment to the future of Oklahoma City is the selection of Stiles Circle, in the Harrison-Walnut Redevelopment Area, as the site for the corporation's new headquarters. The firm's decision to renovate the historic Maywood Church and develop connecting and adjacent office buildings will serve as an impetus for others to follow. When completed, this redevelopment area will contribute significantly to the downtown central business district and the Health Sciences area, while providing great promise for the future of Oklahoma City and the central city's economic growth.

In any community, schools are the key to opening the doors of opportunity for young people and fulfilling the American promise, and HTB has been there from its beginning to assist. One example is the Eugene Field Elementary School. When space needs and deterioration necessitated the replacement of the 70-year-old structure, HTB met the challenge with both Oklahoma City and its students in mind.

Although the original building

Interior view of HTB's award-winning renovation of Central High School into One Bell Central. A landmark historic preservation effort, One Bell Central received nationwide acclaim.

could not be saved, HTB recognized the historic value of the structure by incorporating elements of the former school into the new design. Large columns and a decorative concrete band were removed from the original school and applied to the new so that the sentimentality of the old lived on. Located on the original site, the new inner-city school complied with all curriculum requirements and expanded space needs by placing the playground on the roof. The surrounding residential neighborhood is respected with school entries that resemble small homes and lend visual compatibility. Entrances, windows, and other features are scaled down to a child's field of vision.

In recognition of HTB's commitment to Oklahoma City's quality of life and its design excellence in individual projects, the corporation was selected as the first Outstanding Oklahoma Firm of the Year by the American Institute of Architects in 1987, the inaugural year of this award.

HTB's work at Eugene Field Elementary School preserved the historical value of the old school by incorporating elements of it into the new design. To save space, the playground was located on the roof.

THE BENHAM GROUP

From the recesses of the computer's memory comes the image of a small lake. A touch of the architect's fingers to the keyboard and that lake becomes the foreground in a photograph displayed on the terminal screen. Too big? The lake becomes a pond. A rocky shoreline is "painted" in, using some of the computer's 16 million available colors to tint the scene. Trees, again from the computer's memory, are called up and sized to fit the scene. A highway overpass is "painted" in the background.

The architect leans back in his chair to admire what he has produced: a computer-generated "photograph" of some future kid's lake with a new Lake Hefner Parkway in the near distance—both superimposed on a photograph of the existing landscape.

Up and down the lake road, stopping at landmarks and intersections, architects and engineers with The Benham Group had snapped scenes using a camera with film discs to photograph the proposed route of the Lake Hefner Parkway. They fed that film from disc to television receiver to computer and ultimately to color slide to answer the common question posed by residents living along the proposed route: "What will a six-lane highway look like from my backyard?"

The system that answered the question for neighborhood representatives is one of four types of Computer Aided Design Systems (CADS) that can give clients of The Benham Group astounding sneak previews of their projects. For example, three-dimensional modeling with special lighting capabilities allows a developer to "see" all sides of

his planned office building in morning, afternoon, and evening light as the structure rotates on the screen. In addition, computer-generated motion paths move the on-screen pictures to let another client "drive" through a proposed business complex, then "walk around" inside the buildings to see how his flat floor plans will look in three-dimension. Other sophisticated systems plot highway routes and store on computer the color-coded routes of electrical and other utility services for giant airports, military bases, and industrial plants.

Such space-age engineering technology was not even dreamed of in the early years of the twentieth century,

Pictured here is one of the state-of-the-art computer-aided design systems utilized by The Benham Group to provide clients with realistic three-dimensional images of their projects.

when The Benham Group got its start. Although the tools of the trade have changed dramatically in the eight decades since the firm's founding, the dedication to service practiced by The Benham Group and its professional staff remains the same.

Oklahoma City was a feisty, frontier town when a young engineering graduate of New York's Columbia University heeded the advice of Horace Greeley to "go west." Webster Lance Benham arrived in Oklahoma City the same year Oklahoma became a state, in 1907. He found a community bursting at its seams and desperately in need of streets, water mains, sewer systems, bridges, and power stations to keep up with its explosive growth. It was the right place for a young man with dreams of helping to build a civilization on the prairie.

Going to work with a vigor that matched the young state's enthusiasm, Benham was employed as an assistant city engineer in charge of paving and sewers and as an instructor of civil engineering at Epworth University, the forerunner of Oklahoma City University. In addition, he was a partner in an

One Benham Place—corporate headquarters of The Benham Group, a nationally recognized engineering, architecture, design, and planning firm.

independent engineering firm before founding Benham Engineering Company in 1909. Benham designed some of the city's early streets and water and sewer lines. Dams and reservoirs, office buildings, and parks for an expanding city and a vibrant young state came from Benham Engineering's drafting tables.

Meeting wartime needs, Benham was officer in charge of construction of Camp Funston at Fort Riley, Kansas, in 1917-1918, the job a forerunner to his designing and directing the establishment of Camp Polk and Camp Livingston in Louisiana in the early years of World War II.

As the years passed projects designed by Benham Engineering Company and its successor, The Benham Group, became milestones in transforming a patch of America's Great Plains into what central Oklahoma's Unassigned Lands are today.

These outstanding architectural and engineering milestones in central Oklahoma include:

1909-1910 Oklahoma City Stockyards plan and utilities
1914 Oklahoma State Fair grandstand
1922 Oklahoma City Waterworks
1940 Engine Test Building, Tinker Air Force Base
1948 Major expansion of Oklahoma City wastewater-treatment plants
1963-1964 Booster stations to bring water from Lake Atoka, in southeastern Oklahoma, to Oklahoma City
1967 Interstate 40/Crosstown Expressway
1969-1972 Draper Water Treatment Plant

Growing with central Oklahoma, The Benham Group's engineers designed many of the region's public works projects. Among them was the North Canadian Wastewater Treatment Plant, which, when completed in 1981, helped ensure a clean, safe environment. In 1988 The Benham Group was selected to expand the plant from 60 to 80 million gallons per day of advanced treatment.

1972-1975 Mercy Health Center and HCA Presbyterian Hospital
1978-1979 General Motors Plant (during construction)
1981 North Canadian Wastewater Treatment Plant
1987 The University of Oklahoma Energy Center and Hitachi Computer Products Plant, Norman
1988 Interstate 40/Interstate 35/ Interstate 235 interchange

The firm that Webster Lance Benham founded in 1909 with himself as its only employee is now in the top one percent of architectural and engineering firms in the nation, with approximately 500 employees in seven states.

Webster Lance Benham died in 1952, and his son, David B. Benham, assumed direction of the company. The younger Benham, a 1941 engineering graduate of the United States Naval Academy and a naval officer during World War II, had joined the firm in 1946. During the 1950s the company added architecture to the growing list of engineering services offered. Once established, the architectural program began making its mark, winning national recognition for many major projects in the following three decades.

As the corporation continued its growth during the 1960s, satellite offices were established in other states to provide coast-to-coast services for clients. By 1988 The Benham Group maintained division offices in Oklahoma City and Tulsa, Oklahoma; St. Louis, Missouri; San Antonio and Dallas, Texas; Phoenix, Arizona; Washington, D.C.; Las Vegas, Nevada; and Sacramento, California.

The firm's staff—largely graduated from the University of Oklahoma and Oklahoma State University—serves a broad range of government and private clients, including such corporate giants as Ford Motor Company, Anheuser-Busch, and General Motors Corporation.

Designed by The Benham Group, the Wall Street Journal's printing plant in Oklahoma City relies on satellite communications to publish the latest economic news from throughout the world.

CONTINENTAL FEDERAL SAVINGS & LOAN ASSOCIATION

A History of Integrity

Buildings of brick and stone and marble simply house the men and women who work in them. But sometimes these men and women are part of organizations of enduring character, institutions of great service contributing to the welfare of a whole community from one generation to another. For such an institution, its building becomes a symbol, a landmark, cherished by thousands of people.

In this chronicle is presented the history of Oklahoma's pioneer savings and loan, an institution that has mirrored the growth of this state for more than 90 years.

"... organized when Oklahoma City was less than 10 years old, this association has grown up in intimate relation with our state . . ."
The Daily Oklahoman
August 1927

Continental Federal is Oklahoma's oldest savings and loan association. The date of the charter reads December 6, 1898. That was the official beginning —as Oklahoma City Building and Loan Association. The reasons behind its founding go back to the Run of 1889, and the founding of the State of Oklahoma. Many of the association's founders made that run. Most served as leaders in the community. All of them kept faith in Oklahoma during its first lean years when it struggled to survive. The founding of the Oklahoma City Building and Loan Association was an expression of their belief that the worst was behind—and their desire to help Oklahoma grow and prosper.

An Oklahoma City street scene circa 1929.

Oklahoma City Building and Loan opened its first office in 1898. Pictured here (from left) are Jess Dunn, A.L. Welsh, J.M. Owen, and John Threadgill.

A New Territory

"Use doth breed a habit in a man. We are creatures of habit, and it is almost as easy to acquire the habit of saving as the habit of spending. We strive to breed in people the habit of thrift."
J.H. Hess, General Agent
Oklahoma City Building and
Loan Association
First Annual Statement, January 1, 1900

The early 1890s were precarious years for Oklahoma City: crop failures, the financial panic of 1893, a population drop from 9,000 in 1890 to less than 5,000 in 1894. But Oklahoma City was blessed with a group of aggressive citizens who never lost faith in its future.

The "upswing of 1898" found expansion taking place in homebuilding—and a need for easier home financing. That led to the establishment of the city's first cooperative home loan organization, Oklahoma City Building and Loan, the fourth such organization to be established in the growing Oklahoma Territory.

When Oklahoma City Building and Loan opened its doors, it offered a twofold program: savings accounts drawing interest and mortgages for homebuilding. In these early days, the association's basic goals were the same as they are to-day: to provide a safe investment for savers and to lend money to help our customers build for the future.

The Dustbowl and the Depression

"35 years of safety, earnings, sound management. The Oklahoma City Building and Loan Association is now international in scope; as many of our investors have drifted to almost every state in the union, and to foreign lands."
J.M. Owen, President
Oklahoma City Building and
Loan Association
December 31, 1930

The early 1930s put financial institutions in Oklahoma to exacting tests. First came the Wall Street crash of 1929 and the Great Depression, followed by the Dust Bowl, the worst drought in a century of recorded weather.

But the Oklahoma City Building and Loan Association survived to become one of the first home loan associations in Oklahoma to be eligible for a federal charter. On November 9, 1934, it became Oklahoma City Federal Savings and Loan Association.

The Postwar Years

"In looking forward to years of peace, we hope for a return to private initiative and action. Your association is prepared to do its part. As long as there is no ceiling on free enterprise, America will remain great. All of us must see to it that it is ever so."
J.M. Owen, President
Oklahoma City Federal Savings and Loan
Association
December 31, 1945

ANDREWS DAVIS LEGG BIXLER MILSTEN & MURRAH

500 West Main, *a pen-and-ink drawing with watercolor by Greg Burns.*

When tax lawyer L. Karlton Mosteller selected Oklahoma City as the location for a new practice in 1939, some of his colleagues may have thought it a strange and bold choice. Writer John Steinbeck's depiction of Oklahoma as a world of dust and poverty overshadowed the business opportunities that were just beginning to emerge in the areas of oil, gas, and agriculture. Mosteller saw opportunity and believed in Oklahoma and in his own ability to build a successful tax practice. He was right on both counts. Oklahoma City flourished, and Mosteller's practice grew to become one of Oklahoma City's largest full-service law firms.

Fifty years later Andrews Davis Legg Bixler Milsten & Murrah remains strongly committed to Oklahoma City—to its past and to its future. The firm's offices are located in the 500 West Main office building, which originally was constructed in 1929 as a downtown department store. The six-story structure, totally renovated in 1982, is a symbol of the firm's participation and belief in keeping Oklahoma City's downtown alive and vital.

Today Andrews Davis is a general civil practice firm of more than 55 attorneys, with a comparable number of support personnel. The firm represents its local, national, and international clients in the areas of tax, trusts and es-tates, banking, commercial and public finance law, litigation and negotiation, business and corporate law, securities regulation, mergers and acquisitions, real estate, natural resources, communications, health care, bankruptcy, labor and employment, and aircraft finance.

Andrews Davis is helping to shape the future of Oklahoma through its participation in innovative development of the law. Several of its lawyers were instrumental in drafting the Oklahoma General Corporation Act of 1986, which gave the state a completely new corporation law. Many of the standard contracts used in the Oklahoma real estate industry were developed by Andrews Davis attorneys. The firm has been in the forefront of the development of communications law in the Oklahoma courts. Members of the firm also have authored legal treatises and are frequent lecturers and contributors to legal periodicals.

Andrews Davis' pride in Oklahoma is reflected in the number of civic organizations that its members and associates participate in and support. These range from arts and humanities groups such as Ballet Oklahoma, Oklahoma City Chamber Orchestra, National Cowboy Hall of Fame and Western Heritage Center, Oklahoma Museum of Art, and Oklahoma Art Center to social service organizations such as Red Cross, the Genesis Project, A Chance to Change, and Oklahoma City Food Bank. Other members assist groups that promote education, youth enrichment, sports, and leadership, such as Leadership Oklahoma City. In addition to individual member involvement, Andrews Davis has sponsored civic and education activities.

As the decade of the 1980s ends, Andrews Davis continues to see opportunity and believes in Oklahoma. Although the state's economic foundations have been shaken in recent years by a downcycle that has shattered traditional concepts, the firm is confident that new opportunities will emerge. Karl Mosteller saw the opportunities in Oklahoma City 50 years ago; Andrews Davis remains committed to that legacy today.

FOUNDERS BANK & TRUST COMPANY

9520 North May Avenue.

Celebrating its silver anniversary at the same time as the Centennial of the Run of 1889, Founders Bank & Trust Company was initially organized as Founders National Bank in 1964 by a group of northwest Oklahoma City civic and business leaders optimistic about the continued growth and development of that portion of Oklahoma City. Originally located at 5613 North May Avenue—at the intersection of May Avenue and the Northwest Expressway—Founders Bank was initially capitalized at one million dollars. A strong customer base was quickly developed by offering personalized banking services to nearby households, local commercial accounts, and the local medical community.

Founders Bank has enjoyed a quarter-century of success, growth, and expansion. The key to this success has been the stability of its corporate management and its aggressive and innovative, yet financially secure, banking practices. Founders' capital expanded from one million dollars in 1964 to more than $25 million 25 years later. Throughout its history Founders has had only two chief executive officers: Edward W. Miller, who oversaw its operations for more than two decades, and Wayne D. Stone, who, with more

than 15 years of prior banking experience, was named chairman, president, and chief executive officer in 1985.

Under their direction, Founders became the first bank in northwest Oklahoma City to install automatic teller machines and also the first to provide a detached drive-in facility for the convenience of its customers. In addition, in 1985 Founders became the first bank in the state to recognize opportunities in new Oklahoma banking laws and, as a result, merged with Commerce Bank (formerly The Village Bank). This added a second location at 9520 North May at the intersection of May Avenue and Britton Road. Another major banking innovation introduced by Founders was The Oklahoma Card (a Visa/ MasterCard program). Accepted worldwide, The Oklahoma Card is available to Founders' customers at no annual fee and at lower than market-rate interest.

In 1970 Founders Bank added a Trust Department so that its customers would have complete banking services. Reflecting the expansion, the institution's name was changed to Founders Bank & Trust Company. To handle its

trust customers more effectively, Founders was the first Oklahoma bank to introduce the innovative Funds Management Trust concept. While individuals and businesses traditionally have kept all their liquid funds on deposit at one financial institution, this often exposed the funds to the risk of exceeding the FDIC or FSLIC insured limits. To eliminate this concern, Founders' Funds Management Trust coordinates the placement of funds in various fully insured financial institutions while also providing a high rate of return. Such a program allows Founders' customers to take advantage of the bank's professional investment advice while at the same time enjoying increased safety, convenience, and income.

Founders also introduced a Corporate Automated Sweep account. Founders' financial cash managers analyze a firm's appropriate account balance level, then all funds in excess of that level automatically are transferred to a trust account for investment. This allows Founders' customers to better utilize funds and increases profitability. Through such banking innovations Founders' Trust Department had grown to more than $80 million in managed assets in 1989.

These types of products and service innovations, as well as its attitude toward the community, are indicative of Founders Bank & Trust Company's commitment to its customers. Because of this commitment, Founders is the largest bank in its primary market and the third-largest bank in Oklahoma City.

5613 North May Avenue.

CITY BANK & TRUST

City Bank & Trust traces its Oklahoma City legacy to March 1903, four years before statehood, when the Farmers State Bank—which later changed its name to City National Bank—was established at the intersection of Robinson and Grand avenues, where the Myriad Gardens are today.

On February 11, 1911, Dan W. Hogan, Sr., regarded as the "father" of the state banking industry, was elected president and director of the institution, and for a half-century City National was known as The Hogan Bank. The driving force behind City National's growth into a thriving commercial bank in the following decades, he saw the institution through the excitement of the Roaring Twenties and the upheaval of the Great Depression.

During this time Oklahoma City prospered and the downtown area boomed as building projects kept pace with the economic growth. One of the most famous Oklahoma City landmarks constructed at this time was the Ramsey Tower, one of two skyscrapers dominating the downtown skyline, located at the intersection of Park Avenue and Robinson Avenue. Built by the Starrett Brothers Corporation of New York, who also constructed the Empire State Building, it was completed in 1931, and four decades later, in 1971, became the home of City National Bank & Trust.

Under Hogan's direction City National Bank by the close of World War II was the third-largest banking institution in Oklahoma City, with much of its business involved in the state's agri-culture economy, the oil and gas industry, and commercial business ventures. Each succeeding decade accelerated the tempo of change and progress at City National.

On June 21, 1985, a group of investors led by William O. Johnstone, a native Oklahoman, purchased the institution and renamed it City Bank & Trust. With the acquisition came a commitment to build for the long-term future. Using downtown Oklahoma City as its base, but attracting customers from throughout the metropolitan area, the bank continued a policy of active growth.

In 1986 C-Teq and C-Cheq, tandem check-processing and financial data services companies, were formed as subsidiaries to perform transaction-processing services for more than 30 financial institutions statewide. That same year City Bank & Trust's holding company, City Bankshares, Inc., acquired Wilshire Bank and renamed it City Bank Wilshire. It is located at Northwest Expressway and MacArthur Boulevard, with a branch at Northwest 122nd Street and MacArthur. Focusing on retail bank services, the facility expanded the services of City Bank & Trust and provided its customers with the convenience of multiple locations.

Believing that a bank should be an active participant in the community it serves, management has stressed a firm

City Place, home of City Bank & Trust, on the corner of Park Avenue and Robinson.

commitment to civic and business projects. City Bank & Trust's officers actively participate in numerous programs, including the Arts Council of Oklahoma City, the Oklahoma City Chamber of Commerce, Forward Oklahoma, the Oklahoma Museum of Art, Red Earth, downtown Oklahoma City's first Opening Night, the National Cowboy Hall of Fame, Downtown Now, Leadership Alumni, the Oklahoma City Economic Development Foundation, and a host of other civic, professional, and business organizations.

During Oklahoma's semi-centennial Hogan pointed out that "changes come and changes go, but fundamental laws remain the same. Banking is the safe lending of money. It has always been our policy to invest our funds with the city to promote trade and commerce throughout the state . . . We believe that it is the banker's duty to take an active part in promoting the general welfare of his city and his state. To further these principles and these policies, we today . . . solemnly rededicate our pledge of service." A locally owned and managed, strong financial institution, City Bank & Trust continues to stress the same policy of community and customer service.

The interior redesign of City Bank's downtown facility was completed in March 1987. Pictured here is the second-floor entrance to the commercial lending area.

Chapter Twelve

Quality of Life

Medical and educational institutions contribute to the quality of life of Oklahoma City area residents.

Photo by Shelly R. Harrison

OKLAHOMA CITY COMMUNITY COLLEGE

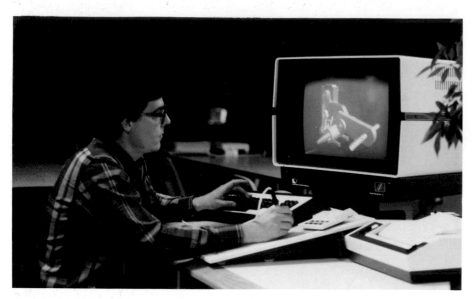

Students at Oklahoma City Community College learn not only the "know-how" but also the "know why" to provide them with the skills and knowledge to succeed in today's rapidly changing world.

Built on a philosophy that it takes well-trained minds, hard work, and determination to achieve excellence and even harder work, greater determination, and further training to maintain it, Oklahoma City Community College opened its doors on September 25, 1972, when 1,046 students began classes in a recently completed 60,000-square-foot building. Today OKCCC serves more than 22,000 students annually, 95 percent of whom are from the Oklahoma City area, in a modern, 500,000-square-foot educational environment. Such tremendous growth has made OKCCC the state's seventh-largest institution of higher education, with the sixth-largest enrollment of undergraduate students.

Planning for the school began in the late 1960s, when higher education began to feel the impact of the post-World War II baby boom. With the invaluable support of south Oklahoma City's business community and citizens, who overwhelmingly passed the necessary tax levies to support the school, a 143-acre campus was acquired at Southwest 74th Street and May Avenue, near I-240 and I-44, in 1971. In fewer than two decades OKCCC grew to become Oklahoma's third-largest community college, producing more than 500 graduates annually.

From its inception, Oklahoma City Community College has led the way among the nation's educational institutions with such innovations as individually paced classes, an open-space concept, and classes beginning seven times each academic year. OKCCC's wide range of students can choose from 58 associate degree programs or 32 certificate programs ranging from traditional education courses to instruction in industrial manufacturing technologies, business, management, health, and high technology, which may lead to an associate degree, an entry-level career position, or college credit toward a four-year degree.

Programs designed for entry-level careers provide not only the technical "know-how" but also the "know why" to provide the student with the skills and knowledge to succeed in today's rapidly changing world. Likewise, OKCCC's success in preparing students to continue their educations is reflected in its students' high academic standings at four-year schools.

Oklahoma City Community College is an integral part of the community it serves, providing a myriad of continuing education classes ranging from arts and crafts to real estate and language for all age groups. In addition, through a series of 30 advisory committees, OKCCC maintains close ties with local businesses, professional leaders, and industries to tailor the school's educational programs to produce graduates capable of filling the needs of the local economy.

Oklahoma City Community College's Alpha Center offers customized, ongoing programs designed to meet the specific training and educational needs of area businesses, organizations, and industries.

With a $13-million annual budget, Oklahoma City Community College and its 500 full- and part-time employees are an important aspect of central Oklahoma's economy. From its founding through 1987 OKCCC poured more than $107.6 million into the local economy. Oklahoma City Community College's total economic impact to date is estimated at a half-billion dollars.

Sitting on a 143-acre campus, Oklahoma City Community College provides educational opportunities for more than 22,000 students annually.

DEACONESS HOSPITAL

Deaconess Hospital is one of Oklahoma City's outstanding medical centers, possessing a large, multispecialty medical staff, advanced equipment, and pioneering new avenues of medicine throughout its 47-year history.

The hospital was originally built to expand medical services to unwed mothers by the Deaconess Maternity Home, which still serves many who seek support each year.

Deaconess has long been recognized as a leader in the medical community, providing the metropolitan area with its first intensive care unit, outpatient surgery center, and remote telephonic reading of EKGs.

In addition, the world's first fully functioning substitute bladder operation was successfully performed at Deaconess. And, in 1986, the same surgical procedure made five-year-old Kyle Putman the youngest person to ever receive this type of substitute bladder.

The Oklahoma Lithotripsy Center at Deaconess is the first, and only, facility of its kind serving central, southern, and western Oklahoma, and north Texas. Lithotripsy, the pulverizing of kidney stones by high-pressure shock waves, is effective for nearly 90 percent of the patients who would have pre-

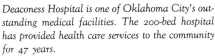

Deaconess Hospital is one of Oklahoma City's outstanding medical facilities. The 200-bed hospital has provided health care services to the community for 47 years.

viously had kidney stone surgery recommended.

Kidney stone surgery usually requires one week of hospitalization and a six-week recovery period. With lithotripsy, hospitalization is often eliminated, and patients return to normal activities in approximately one week.

Other advanced high-technology procedures performed at Deaconess include laser urinary stone treatment, open-heart surgery, angioplasty, digital subtraction angiography (the region's most modern system), and laser procedures. Mammography, MRI and CAT scans, computerized ultrasound with Doppler, and diagnostic nuclear medicine testing are also available.

Deaconess enjoys its reputation as "the place to have a baby in Oklahoma City." Family participation is encour-

aged during the birth experience. A neonatal intensive care unit with a full-time neonatologist adds crucial support.

The Senior Diagnostic Center of Oklahoma, a combined service of Deaconess and Willow View hospitals, is Oklahoma's first facility exclusively treating senior adults' emotional and physical health problems. As many as 85 percent of those with illnesses, such as depression, anxiety, or grief disorders, return to the mainstream of life and enjoy renewed health and enthusiasm.

A spirit of Christian concern and love is paramount at Deaconess Hospital. Many hospitals were established as compassionate ministries to the sick. In most cases, such church affiliations have become meaningless; in some cases, former denominational hospitals have become for-profit businesses. Not so at Deaconess. Its commitment to ministry and sincere caring is rooted in its ties to The Free Methodist Church of North America.

This unique combination of old-fashioned caring, a top-quality medical staff, advanced services, and space-age technology assures Deaconess Hospital an important role in Oklahomans' health care in the next century.

A patient is lowered into a tub of water in preparation for the nonsurgical, kidney stone treatment—lithotripsy. The Oklahoma Lithotripsy Center at Deaconess is the only facility offering lithotripsy to Oklahomans in the central, southern, and western regions of the state.

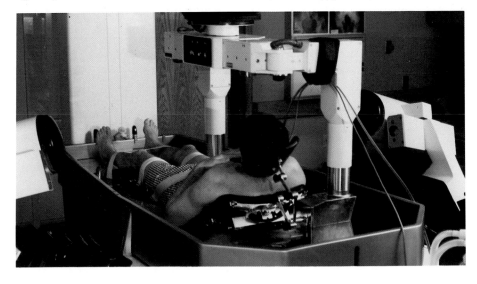

HILLCREST HEALTH CENTER

A decade and a half before the Run of 1889, Dr. Andrew Still first expounded the philosophy and science of osteopathic medicine. Believing that "disease is the effect of a change in the parts of the physical body," Still stressed that in treating disease, the body be considered as a whole and that its own set of self-regulating and self-healing checks and balances be used in the treatment regimen. Today's osteopathic physicians are trained in a technique termed manipulative therapy, which integrates modern medical, surgical, obstetrical, gynecological, pediatric, and geriatric care with manipulative management of the musculoskeletal or host component, a direct application of the approach advocated by Dr. Still more than 100 years ago.

Hillcrest Health Center, located at the intersection of South Pennsylvania Avenue and Southwest 59th Street in Oklahoma City, is a 186-bed primary care not-for-profit health care facility offering patients a full regimen of medical and surgical acute care services, including obstetrics and pediatrics. In addition, the health center provides a 60-bed behavioral medicine center in which adult and adolescent chemical dependency treatment is provided along with mental health services, outpatient counseling, and a crisis intervention service. The health center also operates a 12-bed transitional living facility for adolescents at a facility located 25 miles

Hillcrest Health Center, a 186-bed acute care facility, is located in southwest Oklahoma City just four miles due east of Will Rogers World Airport within the fastest-growing section of Oklahoma City.

south of Oklahoma City. A 14-bed skilled nursing facility, the only hospital-based facility in Oklahoma City, assures continuity of care for geriatric and other patients as does the health center's Home Health Agency. The emergency room is comprehensive-rated and is staffed by emergency medicine residency trained physicians.

Although the dream of establishing an osteopathic hospital in south Oklahoma City began in 1947, it was not until 1955 that the dream became a reality and a group of 12 dedicated osteopathic physicians and surgeons combined their enthusiasm, money, talents, and skills to form Hillcrest Osteopathic Hospital. The 12-bed hospital was filled to capacity shortly after opening.

In 1957, 24 patient beds, six bassinets, a new operating room, a larger laboratory, and an X-ray department were added. Three years later another expansion added 30 beds, and in 1962, under the federally funded Hill-Burton Program, two floors were added to increase Hillcrest's capacity to 106 beds. In 1974 a new three-story wing containing an additional 42 beds was completed, and in 1983 another building program finished the third floor of the main building into a 39-bed medical/surgical care unit; provided expanded space for physical therapy, pulmonary medicine, respiratory therapy, and medical education; and added a one-day surgery facility. In 1985 a 38-bed behavioral medicine center was constructed.

The strength of Hillcrest is community involvement combined with an environment of personalized patient care services, the scope of which speaks to the goal and intent of addressing a patient's total health care needs. The health center is firmly committed to support of the primary/family care physician as evidenced by creation of Good Neighbor Clinics, a network of independent family practice offices for which the health center provides marketing and other support services. The South Oklahoma City Physician Referral Service provides a quick and easy way for residents to make connection with a primary care physician or specialist if indicated. Good Neighbor Care is a spe-

As a teaching facility, Hillcrest Health Center maintains an active Pediatric Unit as part of its overall acute care regimen of services.

cial program organized to develop a network of occupational health care services for area businesses. The Sick and Safe Day Care Program provides working parents with professional medical treatment for sick children. In June of each year the health center sponsors the Corporate Fitness Challenge, a fun-filled medley of competitive events in which area businesses are invited to participate.

Education of young physicians is a major part of the health center's mission. One of 102 osteopathic teaching hospitals in the United States, the first class of interns started in 1962. Today Hillcrest is the only medical facility in south Oklahoma City providing an intern training program for general family practice physicians. Specialty training in internal medicine, general surgery, orthopedic surgery, and other areas of subspecialty medicine is also available.

Currently under way is a major expansion program that will make available new surgical, outpatient surgery, emergency room, labor and delivery, food-service and behavioral medicine facilities, along with expanded facilities for ancillary departments. Hillcrest Health Center is preparing for the last decade of the twentieth century in a way that will better perpetuate the philosophy and beliefs of Dr. Still—care and treatment of the whole patient.

SOUTHERN NAZARENE UNIVERSITY

Founded in 1899, Southern Nazarene University is Oklahoma City's oldest independent, four-year, liberal arts institution, serving the educational sector since before statehood. Located in Bethany, a community in northwest Oklahoma City, Southern Nazarene represents the mergers of six independent institutions from Kansas, Arkansas, and Texas, who joined the Bethany campus between 1909 and 1940, based on a common philosophy and standards of academic excellence espoused by the Church of the Nazarene. Through its eight decades of operations, SNU has grown steadily under the direction of men such as Drs. A.K. Bracken, S.S. White, S.T. Ludwig, Oscar J. Finch, Roy H. Cantrell, Stephen W. Nease, and John A. Knight. Under the current administration of Dr. Ponder Gilliland, SNU is on the threshold of becoming one of the nation's finest independent institutions based on the Wesleyan theological persuasion.

Originally known as Bethany-Peniel College, the institution's governing board changed its name to Bethany Nazarene College in 1956, and in March 1986 the board again voted to change its name.

Southern Nazarene University has earned a national reputation—not only for its academic programs in business, the sciences, fine arts, and education, but also for high moral standards and

Southern Nazarene University's leaders have directed operations from Bresee Hall for nearly nine decades.

value development—exemplified by its motto: Character, Culture, Christ. Today's student body of 1,300 undergraduate and graduate students is from 38 states and 28 foreign countries. SNU offers fully accredited bachelor's and master's degree programs in more than 70 major fields of study, including the preprofessional programs in engineering, law, and medicine.

Although classified as a liberal arts institution, SNU has distinguished itself as a reputable center for the sciences: home of the state's only undergraduate laser research program, an NLN-accredited nursing degree program, and a premed program that has recorded an 85-percent success rate in its students entering their desired school upon graduation. SNU's School of Education operates under the prestigious NCATE accreditation, and the Bresee College of Professional and Social Sciences rivals many of the region's top academic centers.

The university has received such awards as the Small Business Administration's Case of the Year and the national title of the Casbel Multinational Business Computer Game, sponsored by the College of Business of Georgia Tech. SNU also places much emphasis on the value of Christian education and the fine arts through such programs as the Staley Distinguished Lecture Series and the Rothwell Theological Lecture Series.

Herrick Auditorium has hosted some of the nation's top musicians. The men's basketball program has won two NCCAA national titles and one NAIA national title. The men's soccer program has won seven consecutive NAIA District 9 titles and made two appearances in the NAIA national tournament. The women's 1986-1987 volleyball team competed in the NAIA national tournament.

Graduates of Southern Nazarene University, such as Dr. John Peters, the

Right: More than 19,000 graduates have participated in the Spring Ivy Ring Ceremony, with nearly 45 percent of SNU's graduates taking a first job in the greater Oklahoma City region.

Professor Marilyn Rosfeld performs on SNU's 9.5-foot Bösendorfer Imperial Concert Grand piano, the only one found in a public facility in the state. The School of Music also utilizes a three-rank free-standing Schlicker mechanical pipe organ and a 7.5-foot French-double harpsichord.

founder of World Neighbors, Inc.; Ronald Mercer, corporate vice-president of Xerox; Robert Hale, the principal baritone for the New York City and Frankfurt operas; Ambassador Kenneth Tillet, Belize's permanent representative to the United Nations, and many others, are improving the quality of life both in Oklahoma and around the world by combining a strong educational background with Christian values and work ethic. Southern Nazarene University joins a progressive Oklahoma City in meeting the challenges of the next century.

UNIVERSITY OF OKLAHOMA HEALTH SCIENCES CENTER

Three years after statehood in 1907, the University of Oklahoma established a four-year medical school in Oklahoma City. Within a decade it also established a nursing school and two teaching hospitals on its small campus located west of Kelley Avenue on Northeast 13th Street.

The campus continued to develop modestly until 1968, when the state's voters passed a major bond issue called HERO—Health and Education for a Richer Oklahoma. This largely financed the capital expansion of the campus to meet the state's health care needs through a comprehensive array of health professional education, training, and research programs. Four years later the state legislature created a clinical branch of the College of Medicine in Tulsa, the OU Tulsa Medical College.

Today the university's Oklahoma City campus, the OU Health Sciences Center, consists of 12 buildings containing more than one million square feet, with a replacement value of $148 million.

Approximately 3,000 students are enrolled in seven colleges, including medicine, dentistry, nursing, pharmacy, public health, allied health, and graduate studies. During the time since its founding many Health Science Center graduates have made major contributions in their fields, including Dr. Edward Brandt, former assistant secretary for health and scientific affairs of the Department of Health and Human Services; internationally famous Dr. Kenneth Cooper, a pioneer of the aerobics movement; and Dr. Everett Rhoades, the director of the United States Indian Health Service. In addition, Dr. Virginia Stark-Vancs, a 1987 graduate of the College of Medicine, was selected in 1985 as one of the initial group of Howard Hughes Research Scholars at the National Institutes of Health.

Approximately 680 full-time faculty members function in a variety of settings at the HSC and within nearby affiliated agencies that comprise the Oklahoma Health Center. This widespread involvement means that the

The University of Oklahoma's Health Sciences Center is the hub of the 200-acre Oklahoma Health Center.

HSC forms the hub of a 200-acre confederation of health-related public and private organizations with an annual payroll in excess of $250 million and capital assets exceeding one billion dollars. Despite Oklahoma's economic downturn in recent years, the quality of HSC faculty and programs has never been better, according to Dr. Clayton Rich, provost and vice-president for health sciences.

Drs. Brad Slease and Robert Epstein perform complex, high-risk bone marrow transplants for patients who otherwise would die from intractable cancers. While the procedures performed in the bone marrow transplantation unit at Oklahoma Memorial Hospital are experimental, they provide end-stage leukemia victims with a chance to survive.

Cardiovascular surgeons Ronald

Elkins and Paul Stelzer performed some 250 open-heart operations on children in 1986. In addition, one of Elkins' innovations, which uses human heart grafts from a tissue bank rather than the traditional synthetic variety, promises to prolong the life of heart valve grafts in children and adults by up to five times.

In the College of Dentistry are two specialists who combine science and art to improve appearance and function of facial deformities. Oral surgeon Dr. Robert Markowitz repairs deformed or damaged jaws, while Dr. Joe Cain skillfully reproduces parts of the face, head, or mouth for cancer, birth defect, and accident victims.

Dr. Mary Ann McCaffree heads the 33-bed neonatal intensive care unit, which is comparable to any in the nation, at Oklahoma Children's Memorial Hospital, one of OU's affiliated teaching hospitals.

In the College of Allied Health, Dr. Joseph Barry is conducting research into inherited learning disabilities to improve early identification and treatment.

In the College of Medicine, Dr. Phil McHale has introduced into the curriculum a computer-assisted medical instruction that utilizes written programs for computer-driven simulations of such basic processes as how a rising blood level of carbon dioxide affects the body .

Dr. Elisa Lee of the College of Public Health is studying which of Oklahoma's diabetic Indians are most likely to suffer severe diabetic complications such as heart disease and blindness.

In separate investigations, Dr. Joseph Feretti and Dr. Patrick McKee, both of the College of Medicine, are applying genetic engineering techniques to develop better, safer drugs for the quick dissolution of lethal blood clots.

In addition, College of Pharmacy dean Victor Yanchick has established an organization to expand research opportunities and attract new industry to the state. In 1987 Yanchick's University Research Organization contracted with a New Mexico pharmaceutical company to test new compounds in-

tended to improve diagnostic imaging.

Such outstanding faculty and programs have enabled the HSC in recent years to continue to attract record amounts of private support, says provost Rich, who has presided over the HSC campus since 1980.

Oklahoma City's Presbyterian Health Foundation has awarded $4.3 million to advance medical education and biomedical research at the HSC campus since 1985. The W.K. Warren Medical Research Center in Tulsa, through the Saint Francis Hospital Medical Research Institute, has invested roughly $2 million annually since 1985 at the HSC to establish and enhance the funding of basic science and clinical research programs in medicine.

To establish what may be the nation's only full-time chair in gerontological nursing, the Parry Foundation of Houston, Texas, provided a million-

dollar endowment. After a national search, Dr. Mary Adams was selected to be the first recipient of the chair in the OU College of Nursing.

And in 1985, 1986, and 1987, approximately $250,000 has been raised through College of Medicine Research Fund dinners and private donations by the college's alumni, according to the college's dean, Dr. Donald Kassebaum. However, of more importance, Kassebaum points out, is that the dinners have brought together representatives of the state's premier health training and research campus with Oklahoma's leadership in civic affairs, business, and government.

One of the dozens of clinical and basic science research projects at the Health Sciences Center involves the early detection of cancer cells through this computer-assisted microscope.

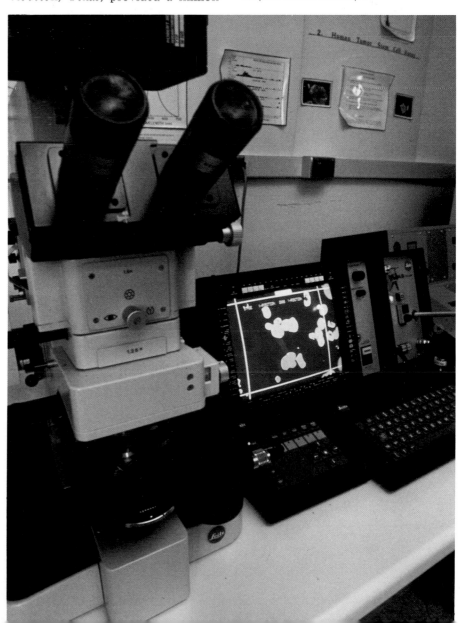

CENTRAL STATE UNIVERSITY

The early morning sun is just beginning to light the gray Oklahoma dawn when the first students start filling the Central State University parking lots at 6:30 a.m. Early risers, they will take a computer science course taught by veteran teacher Vernon Ribera, who says he would give the class at 5:30 a.m. if anyone wanted to enroll.

These students will be on their way to work in another hour. Many are employed in the office towers in downtown Oklahoma City, just a few minutes drive on the Broadway Extension. Others will head south on I-35 toward Tinker Field or out west to the industrial park on I-40. A few are full-time employees of the university who will work until 5 p.m. and then attend an evening class or two. The lights burn in Central State University classrooms until well after 10 p.m.

Located on a 200-acre campus in Edmond, Oklahoma, Central State University has all the charm and personal attention of a smaller school, yet the programs, facilities, and scheduling of a busy, urban university. Its location in a medium-size city makes it perfect for the some 2,000 resident students who

Old North Tower, made of sandstone quarried locally, was constructed in the early 1890s.

want a traditional environment. Yet for the more than 12,000 commuters from the five-county metropolitan area, it offers easy access at any time of day or night.

Soon to celebrate the 100th anniversary of its founding, December 24, 1890, Central State University had its beginnings as a normal school, an insti-

tution primarily dedicated to educating teachers. While the College of Education still continues to be the cornerstone of the university, the College of Business Administration now has the largest graduating classes and has more than 800 M.B.A. candidates enrolled in its many programs. Accounting is a major area in the College of Business, and

Drawing classes are often held outdoors on pleasant days, common during spring and fall months.

a new program has been added in actuarial science.

The College of Liberal Arts continues traditional studies in many disciplines, and is well known for its programs in political science, criminal justice, Southwest studies, creative writing, and music. The university's Jazz Ensemble and Civilized Tribe dixieland bands are known worldwide, particularly in Europe where jazz buffs abound.

The Central State University debaters are ranked in the top 10 in the nation, and the growing department of oral communication continues to produce top-rated television and radio students.

In the College of Mathematics and Science, computer science students have long been accorded recognition by the major industries in Oklahoma City and the state. To accommodate the demand from big business, CSU computer services for its students are unsurpassed. All software and equipment are

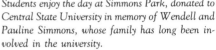

Students enjoy the day at Simmons Park, donated to Central State University in memory of Wendell and Pauline Simmons, whose family has long been involved in the university.

on the cutting edge of the industry, and students now can access the mainframe from their dormitory rooms. Microcomputer labs can be found in most buildings on campus, making access to computers only a few steps away.

Professional programs in the college include nursing, premedicine, predentistry, and preengineering. The quality of its chemistry and biological studies have long been recognized in the field of medicine.

When the summer session rolls around, the campus is deluged with educators working on a master's degree in administration, counseling, or one of the many specialized degrees in the College of Education. During summer

school the average student is a 27-year-old female working on an M.A. in education.

She may spend most of her summer afternoon in the Max Chambers Library, where more than 700,000 volumes are accessed through the most modern computerized on-line catalog. Hours may be spent in the microfilm reading rooms, where students use an extensive microfilm collection of periodicals and government documents.

Because of its strong programs in education and coaching, athletics play an important role in campus life. CSU teams have been ranked nationally in the past decade in football, wrestling, women's tennis, golf, track, and softball. Regional attention has been focused on baseball and both men's and women's basketball.

Central State University is classified by the Oklahoma State Regents for Higher Education as a regional university with the mission of meeting the educational needs of the citizens of the greater central Oklahoma metroplex. While research goes on in nearly every area, the primary function of the university is instruction of its students and community service through many programs, including the Bureau of Government Services, the South Central Safety Institute and Driving Range, the Special Pre-School, counseling and evaluation services for elementary students, KCSC classical radio station, and Channel 2 public service television.

Students learn plant anatomy in a botany class at Howell Hall.

MERCY HEALTH CENTER

A general acute-care health facility with a 432-bed capacity, Mercy Health Center, located on a 40-acre site at the intersection of Memorial Road and Meridian Avenue in far northwest Oklahoma City, is dedicated to personalized and family-centered care. A part of the Sisters of Mercy Health System, St. Louis, the nation's second-largest not-for-profit health care system, Mercy is one of 100 health care facilities located in 38 states operated by the Sisters and dedicated to "total patient care." More than 500 of the state's leading physicians form the core of Mercy's medical staff.

The Sisters of Mercy's involvement in Oklahoma started in 1884, five years prior to the Run of 1889, and during the following century they developed into a major force in the state's health care industry. What became Mercy Health Center first opened in 1917 as a 25-bed, three-story structure at the corner of 12th Street and Walker Avenue near downtown Oklahoma City. In the following years it was sold and expanded several times, until the facility was purchased by the St. Louis Province of the Sisters of Mercy and renamed Mercy Hospital-Oklahoma City General in 1947. By 1964 Mercy Hospital was a $5-million major health care facility.

In June 1970 land was acquired at the intersection of Memorial and Merid-

The Sisters of Mercy's involvement in Oklahoma started in 1884, and during the following century they became a major force in the state's health care industry. What is now known as the Mercy Health Center opened in 1917.

ian for the construction of a state-of-the-art health care complex. In addition to the 695,580-square-foot hospital, the complex also contains a 10-story Doctors Tower and the McAuley Medical Plaza. Opened as Mercy Health Center on August 17, 1974, the complex offers Oklahomans a variety of specialized health services, including the Women's Pavilion, one of the most comprehensive one-stop women's health programs in the state; a state-of-the-art maternity facility; the community's only level three newborn intensive care nursery associated with a private hospital; a Heart Center that contains the most highly sophisticated biplane angioscope (BICOR) available for the diag-

nosis of heart disease; a comprehensive Senior Health program; a Cancer Center containing one of the most sophisticated radiation departments in the nation; and a Pain Management Team to help patients deal with and control their pain.

Mercy Health Center has led the way in many medical advances. The hospital's Cardiovascular Diagnostic Center performed the state's first open-heart surgery in a private hospital in 1959, and the following year Mercy became the first private Oklahoma hospital to operate its own blood bank. It was Oklahoma's first hospital to perform coronary angioplasty, the first private hospital in the state to perform an intrauterine fetal transfusion, and the first hospital in the world to utilize a BICOR capable of providing two-dimensional views of the heart at the same time.

Mercy Health Center oversees an extensive program of health education and promotion designed to improve the health consciousness of the neighboring community. To provide the best-possible health care to all Oklahomans, Mercy's Outreach program links the facility's sophisticated technology to a network of cooperative hospitals in outlying communities. The Yukon Mercy Emergency Medical Service extends the hospital's services to that community, and its Physician Referral Service helps individuals locate a physician.

Mercy Health Center is a 432-bed acute-care facility located on a 40-acre site at the intersection of Memorial Road and Meridian Avenue. As a family-centered care facility, Mercy Health Center provides specialized health services for "total patient care."

OKLAHOMA CITY UNIVERSITY

Every great city needs a great university. Oklahoma City and Oklahoma City University have been partners since 1904 in providing strong academic opportunities, outstanding cultural events, professional and adult education, and championship athletic contests, all in a personalized, value-centered setting.

Oklahoma City University is an independent higher education institution related to the United Methodist Church. The commitments of both the church and the city to the university have made possible the academically strong student body and the financial support from private sources that it enjoys.

The Noble Center for Competitive Enterprise, completed in 1983, houses OCU's Meinders School of Business, the B.D. Eddie Business Research and Consulting Center, the Oklahoma Commerce and Industry Hall of Honor, and the mass communications department.

The university attracts students chiefly from the state of Oklahoma and the surrounding region; however, also represented in its enrollment are students from 40 states and 59 foreign countries.

At OCU, students study in six colleges and schools: the Petree College of Arts and Science, the Meinders School of Business, the Margaret E. Petree School of Music and Performing Arts, the Wimberly School of Religion and Church Vocations, the School of Nursing, and the School of Law. Each of these units has achieved recognition for the excellence of instruction and preparation available for students. For example, OCU music and performing arts

graduates have gained national and international acclaim following their development through such groups as the Surrey Singers, the American Spirit Dance Company, and the Oklahoma Opera and Musical Theater Company. Two of its students, Jayne Jayroe and Susan Powell, have been selected as Miss America. In addition, 12 of the past 18 Miss Oklahomas have been OCU students.

The university also has become widely recognized as an important educational institution in the Far East, with programs being operated in the Peoples Republic of China, Singapore, and Malaysia. In addition, OCU students are able to study in special programs offered in Hawaii, the Republic of China on Taiwan, Great Britain, and other European countries.

OCU's athletic program is nationally prominent in both men's and women's sports. The men's basketball team has received bids to 12 postseason tournaments, and 11 OCU basketball players have received All-American honors. The OCU women's softball team and the men's baseball team were both ranked number two in the nation in 1988. The women's basketball team won the national NAIA tournament in 1988. The men's tennis team was ranked number 11 nationally in 1988.

The Bishop W. Angie Smith Chapel, completed in 1968, is a vital center of campus activities. The chapel houses the offices of the dean of the Wimberly School of Religion and Church Vocations, the dean of the chapel, and the dean of students.

The Dulaney-Browne Library, completed in 1970, houses Oklahoma City University's library resources. At present there are 162,000 volumes, 146,000 government documents, and 650 periodical subscriptions providing information and research opportunities for faculty and students.

Continuing to gain strength and provide new services—since the selection of Dr. Jerald C. Walker as president in 1979—the university's endowment has more than tripled, and the overall enrollment has increased 34 percent. This growth strengthened an already strong academic reputation based on an individualized, personal approach to student needs—a reputation that will continue to grow and develop with the university.

Today Oklahoma City University maintains its 84-year tradition of excellence by responding to the educational needs of a wide variety of students, and through a strong partnership with the church and the community it serves.

BAPTIST MEDICAL CENTER OF OKLAHOMA, INC.

Baptist Memorial Hospital began serving the Oklahoma City community in 1959. By 1978 it had evolved into Baptist Medical Center of Oklahoma, capable of diversification and networking with new forms of business outside the traditional modes of inpatient care. This corporate structure laid the groundwork for the comprehensive system now known as the Oklahoma Healthcare Corporation, serving Oklahoma and the surrounding five-state region.

Originally founded as a nonsectarian, nonprofit organization of the Baptist General Convention of the State of Oklahoma, Baptist Memorial Hospital was Oklahoma City's first medical facility located outside the downtown area. Today Baptist Medical Center is a vital part of the city's expanding northwest quadrant, a regional health care facility known for its outstanding services and response to human need.

For decades the idea of a Baptist hospital had been in the forefront of future planning for Oklahoma's Baptist General Convention, and in 1946 Dr. Andrew Potter, executive secretary/treasurer of the organization, initiated the fund-raising drive that resulted in the construction of the medical institution on a 62-acre site in far northwest Oklahoma City.

Following Potter's death, the planning and fund raising continued under the leadership of Dr. T.B. Lacket, Dr.

Baptist Medical Center of Oklahoma has grown from its original 188 beds to 577 today. A $12.5-million construction project begun in the summer of 1988 will create more private rooms.

H.H. Hobbs, Dr. Auguie Henry, the Reverend Anson Justice, U.S. Senator Robert S. Kerr, Dr. M.E. Ramay, Bryce Twitty, Judge W.R. Wallace, R.A. Young, and former governor Raymond Gary. Mr. and Mrs. LeRoy Smith donated a portion of the land. In 1955 the first public fund drive for a hospital in Oklahoma raised one million dollars. The Baptist General Convention matched these gifts.

Constructed on Oklahoma City's highest geographical site, Baptist Memorial Hospital initially contained 188 patient beds, a maternity ward, laboratory, pediatrics unit, physical therapy area, diagnostic section, emergency room, and surgery unit. John Hendricks administered the facility until 1960, when he was succeeded by James L. Henry. That same year the institution received full accreditation by the Joint Commission on Accreditation of Hospitals; the Women's Auxiliary was formed; and ground breaking was held for a four-story Doctors' Medical Building, constructed by the Baptist Laymen's Corporation. Henry G. Bennett, Jr., M.D., was appointed to the medical staff for which he served as chief of staff until his death in December 1984.

Within three years of its opening,

Baptist Memorial Hospital was operating at 93-percent capacity. Senator Kerr headed a fund-raising effort to finance a $2-million Phase II building program in 1962 that increased the facility's bed count to 376 and added an intensive care unit, a coronary care unit, a radioisotope laboratory, and an additional six stories to the Doctors' Medical Building.

Before the close of the decade occupancy had once more passed the 90-percent level. With the beginning of Phase III in 1972 Baptist Memorial Hospital became Baptist Medical Center of Oklahoma—total patient beds increased to 563, and 40 percent of the original structure was renovated.

Baptist Medical Center opened Oklahoma's first adult burn center in 1975. Today the 32-bed Baptist Burn Center, with its own intensive care unit, remains the only acute care facility for adult burn patients in southern and western Oklahoma and is one of the three largest in the United States.

Baptist Medical Center concluded its affiliation with the Baptist General Convention in 1978 and became an independent, nonprofit corporation.

The Baptist Medical Plaza, adjacent to the hospital, houses the offices of the medical staff.

Three affiliate corporations were formed: ProHealth, a for-profit company offering management and shared services to other health care institutions; Baptist Medical Center of Oklahoma Foundation, a fund-raising organization to augment the provision of services and equipment normally financed through patient care revenue; and Medicol, a medical collection service.

In 1983 the Oklahoma Health Care Corporation was formed as a parent organization, and the Oklahoma Ambulatory Care Corporation, Oklahoma Health Care Realty Corporation, and Oklahoma Heart Center, Inc., were formed. The creation of this health care system provided home health care, ambulatory diagnostic and treatment centers, joint ventures with physicians, and preferred provider organizations. In addition, Baptist Medical Center's Cancer Center of the Southwest was established.

Costing $3.5 million, the James Paul Linn Tower was dedicated in 1983 and added three stories to the existing Special Care Tower. In May 1984 the Oklahoma Heart Center was dedicated. Under the direction of Nazih Zuhdi, M.D., transplant surgeon in chief, and Christiaan Barnard, M.D., Ph.D., and scientist in residence, the facility was designed to promote the advancement of medical science related to prevention, diagnosis, and rehabilitation from diseases of the heart and circulatory system.

The Cancer Center of the Southwest holds an active and progressive role in the prevention of cancer and the quality care of persons with the disease.

The Henry G. Bennett, Jr., Fertility Institute offers a full range of diagnostic and treatment modalities for the infertile couples.

The Cochlear Implant Clinic brings the hope of restored hearing to adults and children who have lost their hearing due to sensory nerve impairment.

PACER Fitness Center provides medically supervised, comprehensive fitness, nutrition, and rehabilitation programs for Oklahomans recovering from illness or simply interested in maintaining peak health.

The Third Age Life Center was developed especially to support, enhance, and fulfill the lives of older adults.

The Baptist Laser Institute was established in 1987 to explore and utilize medical laser applications involving virtually all medical specialties.

In 1984 Baptist Medical Center became a shareholder in the Voluntary Hospitals of America, Inc. This system encompasses more than 600 hospitals nationwide, managing the advantages of scale and pooled resources to reduce

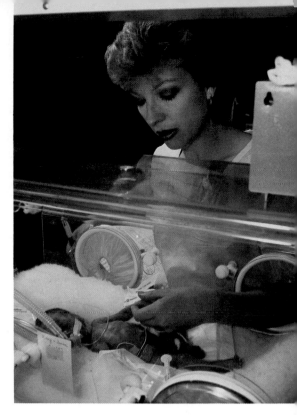

High-technology, high-touch neonatal intensive care benefits premature infants with every possible service.

costs, improve performance, and gain market share through capital pools, home health services, alternative delivery companies, referral networks, joint marketing programs, and other entrepreneurial endeavors.

In 1987 Baptist Medical Center saw the completion of the Raymond A. Young Conference Center and the 263-seat James L. Henry Auditorium. Three additional conference rooms, a full-service catering department, and a luxurious 13-room hotel enhance the medical center's ability to accommodate large groups and seminars.

The total number of beds at Baptist Medical Center is 577, and a new $12.5-million construction project is under way to create more private rooms.

Oklahoma Healthcare Corporation's resources now encompass more than 300,000 square feet of physician office space, numerous diagnostic and treatment facilities, a for-profit health services company, a physical fitness center, and a day care center—all located on an expanding campus covering approximately 40 acres.

For Oklahoma Healthcare Corporation and its primary affiliate, Baptist Medical Center of Oklahoma, Inc., providing a comprehensive system of outstanding health care will continue to advance the quality of life of those in Oklahoma City.

The Raymond A. Young Conference Center and the 263-seat James L. Henry Auditorium, along with additional conference rooms, catering, and a hotel, help to accommodate conferences and seminars.

BLUE CROSS AND BLUE SHIELD OF OKLAHOMA

Blue Cross and Blue Shield of Oklahoma has been providing health care benefits for Oklahomans for nearly a half-century. As the oldest and largest health care benefits provider in the state, Blue Cross and Blue Shield has a major office facility in Oklahoma City located at 3401 Northwest 63rd Street.

Blue Cross and Blue Shield of Oklahoma paid more than a quarter-billion dollars to its nearly 500,000 members within the state in 1986. That same year Blue Cross and Blue Shield processed more than a half-billion dollars in Medicare claims to 430,000 Oklahomans.

The growth of Blue Cross and Blue Shield began in 1940. Following a successful example of prepaid hospital insurance plans in several other states, community members in Oklahoma City and Tulsa formulated proposals to create a similar organization.

Opening its doors for business on April 1, 1940, Walter R. McBee was selected as Oklahoma's first Blue Cross Plan executive director. W.E. Hightower of Oklahoma City was named president of the board of trustees. Today the Plan maintains a 15-member board comprised of professionals from various career fields in Oklahoma. Operations continue to take place at Tulsa, Oklahoma City, and four area offices including Ada, Enid, Lawton, and Muskogee.

When the Blue Cross Plan began 48 years ago, the program was so successful that within the year 140 groups statewide had enrolled in the health benefits program. The initial cost was $18 annually for a semiprivate room membership, which included all dependents

and a one-dollar enrollment fee. This growth continues today in the rapidly changing health care industry.

To ensure cooperation with the Oklahoma State Hospital Association, Blue Cross required all member hospitals to be members of the association. Since most hospitals had enormous accounts receivable, the greater part of which they did not expect to recover, Blue Cross' offer of a guaranteed daily payment for patients was irresistible. To meet its stringent regulations, state hospitals were required to maintain adequate records and fulfill the Hospital Association requirements.

In 1941 N.D. Helland, who headed Oklahoma's Blue Cross and Blue

Blue Cross and Blue Shield of Oklahoma conducted Oklahoma City business operations in the three-story building at 1320 Classen Drive from the late 1960s until 1986.

Ralph S. Rhoades, president and chief executive officer.

Shield Plan for a quarter-century, became executive director. Within one year of Helland's reign, the number of Blue Cross participants had doubled. This rapid growth left no doubt as to the organization's financial success, and a number of services were added. The cost of outpatient care in accident cases; all drugs, medicines, and surgical dressings; as well as basic metabolism tests, electrocardiograms, oxygen and physiotherapy were added in 1943. Reciprocity of benefit agreements were made with surrounding states the following year.

In 1945 a medical/surgical benefit program, known as the Blue Shield Plan, was incorporated as a companion to the Blue Cross Plan. General anesthesia coverage was added, and the ward plan was discontinued in 1947. Benefits were expanded to cover X-ray costs in accident cases, obstetrical care limited to family contracts, and quarantinable and venereal diseases the following year.

In 1950 Blue Cross and Blue Shield increased its coverage to 90 days and added in-hospital medical costs. Payments to the osteopathic physicians were approved in 1952, and within the next year the organization's first non-

group enrollment was held. Two years later 225 surgical allowances were added. In 1956 coverage for nervous and mental conditions for 30 days in any year was added, as were microscopic tissue examinations. A $25 deductible contract was offered on an elective basis in 1958. One year later special plans were implemented for senior citizens and students.

A major change occurred in 1962, when a joint underwriting of major medical coverage was initiated by Blue Cross and Blue Shield. In 1966 the organization was named as the fiscal intermediary for the hospital portion of the Medicare program.

Another major addition to Blue Cross and Blue Shield came in 1966 when, under the corporate leadership of W. Ralph Bethel who served as chief executive officer from 1967 to 1977, a Medicare supplement called Plan 65 was introduced. Plan 65 proved to be so successful with more than 75,000 members, that in 1987 an expanded Plan 65 product was added with optional coverage for vision, dental, and hearing, as well as enhanced medical and hospital benefits. In 1974 Blue Cross and Blue Shield of Oklahoma added dental coverage to its growing number of products.

Escalating medical costs prompted Blue Cross and Blue Shield to develop cost-containment programs. When Ralph S. Rhoades, current president and chief executive officer, was appointed to the highest senior executive position in 1977, the firm implemented new cost-saving features. The

In December 1985 Blue Cross and Blue Shield of Oklahoma purchased a six-story building at 3401 Northwest 63rd. This building houses the firm's Oklahoma City operations.

The founder and first executive director, W.R. McBee (right), is shown with his successor, N.D. Helland, who served the Plan as executive director from 1941 to 1967.

company has become a leader in the movement to help control rising health care costs.

During 1987 Blue Cross and Blue Shield provided health care coverage for one out of every six Oklahomans and paid a total of $234.8 million in member benefits while processing another $554 million in Medicare Part A claims.

Although the Blue Cross and Blue Shield network is nationwide, each Plan is autonomous in its own state and develops separate market products. In Oklahoma, the firm offers a Triple Option health program in which members can select health care benefits to meet their needs. The Triple Option is comprised of traditional coverage—Healthshare Gold, or alternate health care systems including the preferred provider organization, Prudent Purchaser Option, or the health maintenance organization, BlueLincs HMO.

This allows Oklahomans to select insurance coverage and providers in the most cost-efficient manner by waiving deductibles and co-payments in certain situations; reducing premiums through preadmission certification, second surgical opinions, outpatient surgery and home health care; and providing a managed health care service through preventative care and reduced hospital stays. BlueLincs HMO, a Blue Cross and Blue Shield subsidiary formed under Rhoades' direction, provides managed health care services to more than 43,000 Oklahomans.

Another subsidiary developed under the current leader is Member Service Life, which provides a comprehensive benefit package of life insurance and disability income. Blue Cross and Blue Shield is a total health benefits provider operating under the name GHS Holding Company. The parent company also controls Member Service Administrators, a division that is the third-party administrator for self-insured

W.R. Bethel, president and chief executive officer from 1967 to 1977.

groups.

In the battle of rising health care costs, Blue Cross and Blue Shield of Oklahoma continues to do its part by contracting with acute care hospitals and physicians. Hospitals are members of the F.A.I.R.-Fixed Allowance Incentive Reimbursement program, and physicians join the Participating Network. Formulated to help stabilize health care costs by eliminating payment problems, improving claims processing, and providing fair, predictable payment for services, these programs have positioned Blue Cross and Blue Shield of Oklahoma on the competitive edge of tomorrow.

HCA PRESBYTERIAN HOSPITAL

Operated by Hospital Corporation of America (HCA), one of the world's largest health care providers, Oklahoma City's HCA Presbyterian Hospital offers its patients the most up-to-date health care facilities available at the lowest possible cost and in the most convenient manner.

Its staff of 1,800 and more than 175 volunteer auxiliary members are involved in providing Oklahomans with the entire spectrum of health care services—including endocrinology, urology, general medicine, general surgery, cardiovascular and thoracic surgery, microsurgery, neurosurgery, neurology, nuclear medicine, obstetrics/gynecology, oncology, orthopedics, pediatrics, plastic surgery, ophthalmology, otorhinolaryngology, special procedures, X-ray, gastroenterology, and pulmonary medicine.

The hospital's roots were planted in 1910, when Dr. Foster K. Camp and his wife, Janet, purchased St. Luke's Sanatarium in downtown Oklahoma City and renamed the facility Wesley Hospital. They expanded its services through a series of moves until it was located on the southwest corner of Northwest 12th Street and Harvey Avenue, where it remained for 63 years.

From its formation, Wesley Hospital was affiliated with the University of Oklahoma School of Medicine as a teaching hospital. It was the first pri-

vately owned hospital in the southwestern United States to receive accreditation for its affiliated teaching programs. In 1912 Wesley Training School for Nurses, which remained in service for more than four decades, was established.

When World War I ended, six local physicians returned to Oklahoma City and organized Oklahoma City Clinic, then purchased Wesley Hospital in October 1919. In 1961 ownership was transferred to the Wesley Hospital Foundation, which three years later affiliated with the Washita Presbytery of the United Presbyterian Church. Wesley Hospital became Presbyterian Medical Center of Oklahoma,

Inc., and then Presbyterian Hospital, Inc. In 1985 it was acquired by Hospital Corporation of America (HCA).

The concept of a comprehensive medical care and teaching complex—the Oklahoma Health Center—included Presbyterian. In 1972 construction began on a new Presbyterian Hospital—a $36-million private, acute-care facility. Opened to patients on December 1, 1974, it contained 407 beds, 31 nursery bassinets, 13 surgery suites, an intensive care unit, a coronary care unit, and complete laboratory services.

Within a year the staff doubled, a pulmonary functions laboratory and an electroencephalography laboratory were opened, and patient services and training programs were greatly expanded. In addition, an agreement was reached with the Oklahoma Medical Research Foundation that called for Presbyterian to provide housing for the foundation's inpatients. A sleep disorders center, one of only 25 accredited centers in the nation, was opened in 1976; three years later a genetics diagnostic center was opened to offer genetic diagnosis, counseling, and education. In 1982 a $6-million expansion added several specialized programs.

HCA Presbyterian Hospital's CancerCare Program is a comprehensive program of state-of-the-art treatment and diagnostic procedures that utilizes

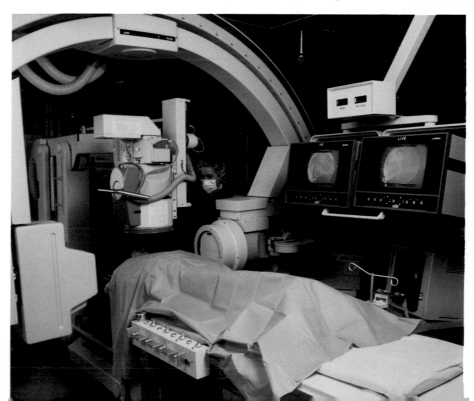

one of the state's largest group of board-certified physicians through the hospital with specialists in hematology, obstetrics and gynecology, surgery, pathology, and urology. Presbyterian works through its network of physicians to provide complete diagnosis, screening, and outpatient treatment modalities, as well as public educational programs and smoking cessation programs designed to emphasize and teach cancer prevention life-styles.

The hospital has just begun an outreach oncology program and a joint obstetrics/gynecology oncology statewide network program with the University of Oklahoma Health Sciences Center. The Oklahoma Cancer Information Service is the only service of its kind in Oklahoma endorsed by the National Cancer Institute; it provides free information on all topics related to cancer.

Presbyterian Hospital's Cardiac-Care program remains in the forefront in the fight against heart disease by performing new nonsurgical treatment techniques. However, if surgery is required, Presbyterian provides the most advanced facilities for heart bypass operations available. Blood conservation techniques used during surgery allow the collection and cleansing of the patient's own blood so that blood transfusions are not necessary. Also, long-term prevention measures, such as diet and exercise, are provided. Presbyterian provides cardiac care to 19 Oklahoma communities through Remote

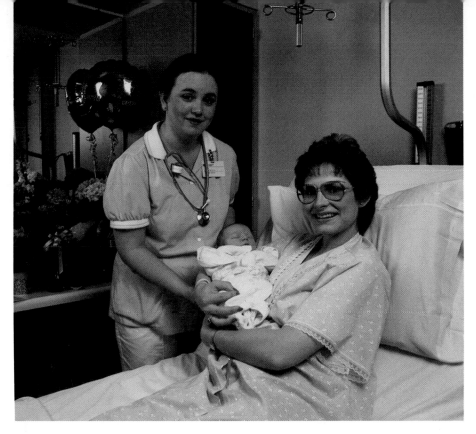

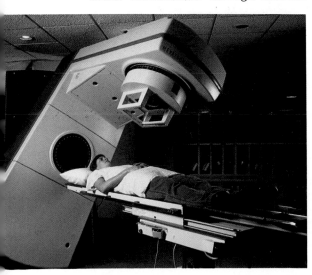

Cardiac Monitoring, which provides rural communities with sophisticated monitoring equipment and skilled personnel who are able to interpret and respond to a variety of cardiovascular abnormalities.

Presbyterian Hospital's Gastroenterology Clinical Research Unit has been a testing ground for medication breakthroughs in bowel treatment for 10 years. That's why doctors at the Mayo Clinic come to Presbyterian to see how digestive diseases are treated.

When it comes to BabyCare, Presbyterian has something to offer for the entire family. Classes are offered on what to do before having a baby, on the delivery, and on what to do after the baby has arrived. Refresher courses and sibling classes are also offered. A variety of birthing methods include a home-like birthing atmosphere or a traditional delivery room. Highly skilled physicians and nurses in the Neonatal Intensive Care Unit are equipped with the latest in state-of-the-art equipment and procedures.

The institution also maintains an extensive EyeCare program. A physician on staff that performs eye surgeries has recently become qualified to perform a pioneer surgery procedure, the corneal shaving procedure. Presbyterian is one of two hospitals in the country that can perform this type of surgery.

The hospital is the site of one of only three full-scale brain rehabilitation programs in the world. HCA Presbyterian Hospital also operates a chem-ical dependency treatment center established in 1981 that is based on strong family involvement. It utilizes both inpatient and outpatient treatment for adult and adolescent chemical dependency and co-dependency, as well as family and individual therapy. Co-dependency treatment corrects a set of learned behaviors—generally acquired when living with a chemical-dependent individual—whereby a person's self-esteem and identity are used in an attempt to control others despite adverse consequences.

HCA Oklahoma Center for Athletes (OCA) works with recreational, amateur, and professional athletes to reduce the risk of sports injuries through special conditioning. It also treats sports injuries through one of the country's leading teams of sports medicine specialists, which includes orthopedic surgeons, physical therapists, exercise physiologists, certified athletic trainers, and nutritionists.

In addition to its general and specialized health care programs, HCA Industrial Health Management Services offers a consulting team approach to provide, among other things, preplacement, annual or periodic, disability, and insurance examinations; on-the-job injury care; cost-containment evaluations; medical record documentation for government and legal requirements; research affecting industry; audiometric screening; toxicology; and health and safety education and training.

STATE FAIR OF OKLAHOMA

The State Fair of Oklahoma is the third-largest fair in the nation—annually attracting more than 1.7 million visitors. In 1989 the fair will celebrate the centennial of the opening of the Unassigned Lands.

Located on 435 acres at Northwest 10th Street and May Avenue, Fair Park contains 28 permanent buildings with 1.45 million square feet of exhibit space, of which 450,000 square feet is comfortably air-conditioned. Another 2 million square feet of outdoor exhibit space is available—featuring fountains, towering arches, 60,000 free parking spaces, and beautifully landscaped trees and flowers. The State Fair of Oklahoma is the largest shopping mall in the state during its annual 17-day run.

The Oklahoma State Fair traces its beginning to an agricultural exposition, banquet, and ball held for a delegation of visiting United States congressmen on September 17, 1889. Although the dust had barely settled from the Run of 1889, Oklahoma City's civic leaders were determined to display the natural bounty of the new land. Though the lateness of the growing season limited the displays of produce to native grasses and other natural products, a midday banquet was held at Round Grove—roughly four miles west of the present-day fairgrounds—and that evening an elegant ball was staged in the Bone and McKinnon Building in downtown Oklahoma City.

In 1893 leading Oklahoma City merchants organized the Oklahoma Territorial Fair and Exposition to promote and reflect Oklahoma's progress in agriculture, industry, commerce, education, and culture. In the following 15 years the exhibition either was presented as a street fair along Grand Avenue in downtown Oklahoma City or at Delmar Gardens, a 140-acre amusement park along the North Canadian River.

As the movement for statehood accelerated, a group of Oklahoma Citians met in January 1907 to create a State Fair Association, headed by C.G. Jones. Selling $100,000 worth of stock, the State Fair of Oklahoma Corporation was organized as a private, self-supporting, nonprofit organization. Much of its financing came from such civic-minded firms as the Oklahoma Publishing Company, the Oklahoma Natural Gas Company, and the Oklahoma Gas & Electric Company.

To provide a permanent home for the exhibition, a 160-acre site was selected on school land located at the intersection of 10th Street and Eastern Avenue. The first Oklahoma State Fair opened in September 1907 and attracted 75,000 people.

In 1908 Henry Overholser was named president of the fair board, and in 1914 the name was changed to the Oklahoma State Fair and Exposition. Two years later the facility boasted 60 permanent structures and assets of more than $387,000. As the fairgrounds became a year-round center of activities, city officials sold $300,000 worth of bonds in 1917 to finance improvements. The fair board deeded the property to Oklahoma City; however, it retained all existing assets. The city would operate the park for 11 months annually, and the State Fair would have exclusive use every September. This arrangement lasted until 1917, when the State Fair board resumed full control.

During the Great Depression and World War II, the Eastern Avenue site deteriorated; when the fair again boomed in the postwar era, many of the wooden buildings were in disrepair. In 1950 the State Fair board proposed a $4.75-million bond issue to finance a

Above: By 1987 the fair had grown and expanded to the point that it served 1.7 million patrons during its 17-day run. On a typical fair weekend, more than 200,000 visitors pass through the gates. Photo by Fred Marvel

Right: The State Fair of Oklahoma by 1964 had been at its present location at Northwest 10th and May for 10 years. The arrows to atom's space tower was the focal point of the fair.

new State Fair Park at 10th Street and May Avenue. The new park opened four years later, in September 1954. In 1957 another shared-responsibility agreement gave the city control of the fairgrounds for 10 months every year and established a one-month period,

In 1954 the State Fair of Oklahoma moved to its present location at Northwest 10th and May. The grounds were almost bare, with a few buildings, the grandstand, and almost no landscaping. That year the fair attracted 416,677 visitors.

In 1987 the 435 acres of State Fair Park are beautifully landscaped. The 28 permanent buildings are filled with interesting exhibits of general interest to our visitors. The annual 17-day event is the top entertainment attraction in Oklahoma during the autumn. Photo by Fred Marvel

prior to the annual fair, of joint control. The State Fair board retained exclusive control during September. In 1980 the State Fair assumed all operations of the fairgrounds.

Attendance soared—tripling from 450,000 in 1960 to 1.4 million in 1981. The fair reflected the state's economy shift from agricultural to industrial.

Between 1962 and 1971 the board spent $2.5 million improving Fair Park. By charter the State Fair Corporation was required to spend all funds generated in excess of the cost of the fair's operation on improvements, and another $15 million was spent on fairgrounds improvements. By 1986 the State Fair of Oklahoma was the largest 10-day fair in America. Beginning in 1987 the fair expanded its run to 17 days, and quickly became the third-largest fair in the nation.

Located conveniently at the intersection of I-44 and I-40, the State Fair offers easy access. Its patrons can visit one of America's largest midways, in addition to seven distinctly different exhibit buildings and spacious horse and livestock areas. The fair's Space Tower, built in 1968, rises 330 feet and offers its passengers a magnificent view as it rotates 360 degrees. The futuristic monorail whisks fairgoers along a 1.25-mile journey around the fairgrounds. The fair's 10,000-seat grandstand and the 12,000-seat arena annually host a myriad of events from races and rodeos to ice shows, circuses, and concerts.

Included among the State Fair's 28 permanent facilities are the 70,000-square-foot International Trade Center Building, which boasts an air-supported dome roof; the Made in Oklahoma Building, which is expressly intended for displaying Oklahoma's products and services; the Kitchens of America Building, which specializes in food-related items from producer to homemaker; the Hobbies Arts & Crafts Building, housing displays of embroidery, hand weaving, decorated eggs, the junior arts and crafts exhibit, pie-baking contest, and other hobby demonstrations; the Modern Living Building, containing 36,750 square feet of displays designed to make living easier and more enjoyable; the Gardens & Flowers Building, which presents visit-

ors with the best new products and ideas offered in home and garden improvements; the Travel & Transportation Building, displaying the latest advancements in automobiles and trucks; and Cottonwood Post, which plays host to cowboy dance contests, gunfights, country and western bands, and Native American dancing. The State Fair's Livestock Exhibit buildings consist of two horse barns; a livestock pavilion; a beef barn; a poultry building; a dairy cattle barn; a horse show barn; a swine, sheep, and goat barn; and a covered exercise arena—486,080 square feet of show space.

The State Fair employs more than 1,200 people during its annual run, and its exhibitors, concessionaires, and attractions employ another 10,000 individuals to make it one of the largest employers in the metropolitan area. The State Fair is the state's greatest vehicle for promoting and developing national and international trade. Beginning with 1921's Always Good—This Time Better—All Ways, the 1989 State Fair of Oklahoma will feature Fair of America—A Centennial Celebration—the climax of a seven-month celebration of the centennial of the fair and the 100th anniversary of the opening of the Unassigned Lands. In 1989 the fairgrounds will host many national and international events, including the national U.S. Olympic Festival.

Patrons

The following individuals, companies, and organizations have made a valuable commitment to the quality of this publication. Windsor Publications and the Oklahoma City Chamber of Commerce and the Oklahoma City Economic Development Foundation, Inc., gratefully acknowledge their participation in *Oklahoma City: A Centennial Portrait.*

Andrews Davis Legg Bixler Milsten & Murrah*
Baptist Medical Center of Oklahoma, Inc.*
The Benham Group*
Blue Cross and Blue Shield of Oklahoma*
Cain's Coffee Company*
Central State University*
City Bank & Trust*
Clear Channel Communications KTOK-1000 AM Radio KJ-103 FM Radio*
Continental Federal Savings & Loan Association*
Control Data Corporation Small Disk Division*
Crescent Market*
Crowe & Dunlevy*
Wm. E. Davis & Sons, Inc.*
Deaconess Hospital*
Devon Energy Corporation*
DonCo Carriers Inc.
First Interstate Bank of Oklahoma*
Fleming Companies, Inc.*
Founders Bank & Trust Company*
Great Plains Coca-Cola Bottling Company*
Gulfstream Aerospace Technologies Corporation of Oklahoma*

HCA Presbyterian Hospital*
Hillcrest Health Center*
HTB, Inc.*
The Journal Record Publishing Company*
Kerr-McGee Corporation*
KWTV-9*
Liberty National Bank and Trust Company*
Linn & Helms*
Lippert Bros., Inc.*
McAfee & Taft A Professional Corporation*
Management Services Corporation (MSC) Lear Siegler Holding Corporation*
Mercy Health Center*
Nichols Hills Bank and Trust Company*
Norick Brothers, Inc.*
Oklahoma Brick Corporation
Oklahoma City Community College*
Oklahoma City University*
Oklahoma Gas and Electric Company*
Oklahoma Natural Gas Company*
OXY USA Inc.*
Southern Nazarene University*
Southwestern Bell Telephone Company*
State Fair of Oklahoma*
The Trust Company of Oklahoma*
Unarco Commercial Products*
University of Oklahoma Health Sciences Center*
USPCI, Inc.*
Yordi Construction, Inc.*

*Partners in Progress of *Oklahoma City: A Centennial Portrait.* The histories of these companies and organizations appear in Chapter Eight, beginning on page 153.

Suggested Readings

Bernard, Richard M. "Oklahoma City: Booming Sooner." In *Sunbelt Cities: Politics and Growth Since World War II*. Austin: University of Texas Press, 1983.

Blackburn, Bob L. *Heart of the Promised Land: An Illustrated History of Oklahoma County*. Los Angeles: Windsor Publications, 1983.

Blackburn, Bob L.; Henderson, Arn; and Thurman, Melvena. *The Physical Legacy: Historic Buildings of Oklahoma County, 1889-1931*. Oklahoma City: Oklahoma County Historical Society, 1981.

Bunky. *The First Eight Months of Oklahoma City*. Oklahoma City: The McMaster Printing Company, 1890.

Chapman, Berlin B. *Oklahoma City, From Public Land to Private Property*. Oklahoma City: N.p., 1960.

Eastman, James N. "Location and Growth of Tinker Air Force Base and Oklahoma City Air Material Area." In *The Chronicles of Oklahoma*, vol. L, no. 3, 1972.

Faulk, Odie B. *Oklahoma: Land of the Fair God*. Los Angeles: Windsor Publications, 1986.

Harlow, Rex. *Oklahoma City's Younger Leaders*. Oklahoma City: The Harlow Publishing Company, 1931.

Hill, Gilbert. "History of the Oklahoma City Chamber of Commerce." A series of articles published in the *Oklahoma City Times*. Complete set available in the vertical files of the Metropolitan Branch of the Oklahoma County Library System.

Kerr, W.F. and Gainer, Ira. *The Story of Oklahoma City*. Chicago: S.J. Clarke Publishing Company.

Lockwood Greene Engineers, Inc. *Oklahoma City Business and Its Trade Territories: A Study and Plan for Expansion*. Oklahoma City: Industrial Department of the Oklahoma City Chamber of Commerce, 1931.

McRill, Albert. *And Satan Came Also: An Inside Story of a City's Social and Political History*. Oklahoma City: Semco Color Press, 1955.

Maver, George J. "Oklahoma City: In Transition to Maturity and Professionalization." In *Urban Politics in the Southwest*, edited by Leonard E. Goodall. Tempe: Institute of Public Administration, 1967.

Meredith, Howard L. and Shirk, George. "Oklahoma City: Growth and Reconstruction, 1889-1939." In *The Chronicles of Oklahoma*, vol. LV, no. 3, 1977.

Nelson, Mary Jo. *History in Mortar*. Oklahoma City: Oklahoma City Times, 1972.

Oklahoma City Chamber of Commerce. *Bigger Possibilities for Factories in the Great Southwest: Oklahoma City*. Oklahoma City: Oklahoma City Chamber of Commerce, 1932.

——— . *Production Sheet of Oklahoma City Chamber of Commerce and Projects for 1933*. Oklahoma City: Oklahoma City Chamber of Commerce, 1932.

Petty, A.E. "New Downtown: Oklahoma City's Goal for its 1989 Centennial." In *Journal of Housing*, vol. XXXIV, 1977.

Scott, Angelo C. *The Story of Oklahoma City*. Oklahoma City: Times-Journal Publishing Company, 1939.

Shirk, Lucyl. *Oklahoma City: Capital of Soonerland*. Oklahoma City: Oklahoma City Board of Education, 1957.

Smallwood, James. *Urban Builder: The Life and Times of Stanley Draper*. Norman: University of Oklahoma Press, 1977.

Smith, Larry. *Survey of Industrial Parks in Oklahoma City*. Oklahoma City: Oklahoma City Urban Renewal Authority, 1972.

Stewart, Ronald Laird. "The Influence of the Business Community in Oklahoma City Politics." Unpublished master's thesis, University of Oklahoma, Norman, 1967.

Stewart, Roy and Woods, Penn. *Born Grown: A History of Oklahoma City*. Oklahoma City: Fidelity Bank, 1976.

Index